dangerous peace-making

hurt; dangerous; injury; emergency

chance; opportunity; mechanism; loom

HELENA MEYER-KNAPP

PEACE-MAKER PRESS

危

PEACE-MAKER PRESS
OLYMPIA, WASHINGTON

Copyright © 2003 by Helena Meyer-Knapp

Published by Peace-maker Press
PMB 30, 1910 Fourth Avenue East, Olympia, WA 98506

Designed by Kathy Campbell
Printed by Gorham Printing, Rochester, Washington
Font—Minion

Library of Congress PCN 200396794
Meyer-Knapp, Helena
Dangerous peacemaking

Bibliography p.
ISBN 0-9740364-0-4

1. War—termination; 2. Peace;
3. Pacific settlement of international disputes; I. Title

NOTE ON STYLES AND SOURCES

JAPANESE

The two characters on the cover of this book together make the single word which, in Japanese, stands for crisis.

The first character indicates danger; the second combines opportunity with the sense that these are crucial moments.

Confusingly, to western ears both characters are said with the same syllabic sound: "ki."

Kiki—

Peace-making repeatedly demands contrasting ways of being: flexibility with commitment, memory with the willingness to forget, hope with critical realism, urgency with patience, practical thinking with strong principles.

NATIONAL IDENTITIES

Describing events in contested regions demands that a writer make choices about which names to use to identify people and places. In general, I have adopted the names in common usage in US academic and news writing. There are some important exceptions. I call the six counties in Ulster the "North of Ireland" and I call the region around the city of Jerusalem "Israel/Palestine." In making these choices, I recognize that I, too, have entered into contested territories. I chose to do so to bring into greater prominence the images that move Irish Republicans and Palestinians, whose political rights are too often hidden from view in the most common appellations: Northern Ireland and The Occupied Territories. Similarly, in the story about peace in South Africa, I have purposely capitalized the words White and Black when they refer to the parties engaged in making and unmaking the peace.

SOME KEY DATES

Each account of a specific attempt to end a war begins with a listing of dates. These do not constitute a linear description of events, each one responsible for the next on the list. Nor do they constitute a definitive listing of all the crucial moments affecting the peace. Rather, they are offered to enable the reader to contextualize the story that follows.

SPELLING
The prices on the back of this book are in British pounds as well as dollars but the spelling and punctuation conform to usage in the United States and therefore not to usage in Britain.

FOOTNOTES AND ENDNOTES
Footnote markers are scattered throughout the text. In the longer chapters they convey a small piece of extra information useful whilst reading. In the specific stories about peace-making they point to links and connections between the stories.

Endnote markers appear frequently in the longer chapters. The markers themselves are all the same in appearance, but they point in two different directions: to short citations referring to specific pages in the articles and books that helped frame a particular part of this text, (all of these are cited fully in the References) and to short discussions of additional concerns that flow from or lead into this work.

ILLUSTRATIONS
Photos and short blocks of text are at the edges of the pages throughout.

The visual images are my own, collected over the last 15 years in travels around the United States and overseas, as I was learning how to analyze and construct stories about communities engaged in peace-making. The List of Illustrations in the Resources section identifies each photo, explaining its geographical and historical context and its placement in the text.

The verbal images have been culled from the media. Journalists often create riveting portraits of far way places. I hope their writings will transport you, briefly, into these seven war zones, to catch a glimpse of the suffering and the urgent need for peace.

CORRECTIONS AND COMMENTS
I welcome reader comments about this book.

In the months since the first printing appeared, several have kindly pointed out typographical errors. For this new printing I have corrected every one I have discovered thus far, though there may be some hidden still from view.

During this same period the book has brought me into interesting conversations both with new contacts and with old friends. I appreciate all letters, e-mails, reviews and other invitations from readers.

I can be reached by e-mail at meyerknh@evergreen.edu
and by mail c/o Peace-Maker Press
        PMB 30, 1920 East Fourth Avenue
        Olympia, WA 98506

CONTENTS

危

Peace At Last?

Nobel Peace Prizes rarely go to women, let alone to housewives. And yet, on October 10, 1977, the Nobel Peace Prize Committee announced that it had decided to offer its 1976 Prize to two Irish housewives, Betty Williams and Mairead Corrigan. The two had mobilized a massive, grass-roots peace movement in the North of Ireland, and their prize arrived carrying with it high hopes that this activist campaign would soon pressure and persuade the sectarian Republican and Unionist militias to stop killing each other.* After all, the Irish people had already endured the violence, known locally as "the Troubles," for over seven years. Peace was clearly overdue.

Sadly, Williams and Corrigan did not end the war or stop the killing. They could not, and while the women's work revealed that hundreds of thousands of ordinary people longed for peace, the Nobel committee was misguided in counting on popular pressure to make the peace happen. The two women had indeed provided the impetus for both Protestants and Catholics to speak out for peace, and to support it when it came, many years later. But as individuals, the two women were the wrong people and they were in the wrong place, too far from the inner circles of political power, to bring about an end to the military action.

This book is about the complex interactions among people and power, geography and violence that bring about the ending of a war. It has been in the making for a while. In 1995, I spent a year at the Bunting Institute, now known as the Radcliffe Institute for Advanced study at Harvard. Earlier research on the Cold War had set me grappling with how that particular,

---

* The militias included the IRA (Irish Republican Army), one of several Catholic groups fighting to re-unify the North of Ireland with the Republic of Ireland (Eire). Their side of the struggle was known as "Republican." Their opponents, of which the best known was the Ulster Volunteer Force (UVF), were Protestants fighting to remain part of Britain. They were usually called "Unionists."

hostile, dangerous and sometimes violent conflict might end. In the early 1990s I found myself observing its actual end, learning in real time how two long-standing foes can bring a relationship out of the war zone. No sooner had they made peace, than the United States and USSR began an active collaboration against another enemy, Saddam Hussein. I connected topical issues to historical research, which revealed that even unchallenged final victories, in the American Civil War, World War II, and the collapse of South Vietnam, neither brought peace easily, nor brought it at the earliest possible moment. Clearly, peace-making was, to a remarkable degree, a matter of choice. Since that year at Harvard, the picture has gradually become clear— bringing the people who make the key choices into focus, highlighting the factors that precipitate their decisions and revealing the turbulent character of the peace-making process itself.

At the outset, nations and people who chose to begin a war often have little concern for the risks and chaos that will accompany its ending. Since their quarrel is just and their willingness to sacrifice steadfast, victory is assured. But victory cannot, by itself, bring a stop to the killing. No war can end until particular peace-makers decide that the time has come. Furthermore, "spoilers" in the combatant communities are often committed to continued war, making ending it much harder than anyone could have imagined. No matter how urgent the pleas from the wider world, peace has to wait until the leaders or their trusted confidants begin direct talks with enemy leaders, quite likely secret talks, in which they will make real agreements about weapons, land and power. Even then, ending a war for good is a chaotic and dangerous process.

The tangible power that ordinary people hold is to remain committed to peace and to be steady in precarious times once the peace process has begun. Just as important, while the fighting continues, popular movements do and must step up to the moral obligation to make visible the dreadful suffering which war brings. The Williams/Corrigan story is worth relating since it is a reminder of how often pleas for peace can be, themselves, both controversial and dangerous.*

---

*President Jimmy Carter affirmed this in his own speech on receiving the Peace Prize in 2002: "None has provided more vivid reminders of the dangers of peacemaking than two of my friends, Anwar Sadat and Yitzhak Rabin, who gave their lives for the cause of peace in the Middle East." Oslo, December 10, 2002.

Williams and Corrigan became Nobel laureates with little more than a year of activist experience behind them. Both had been driven into the public arena by the same event: the deaths of three of Corrigan's nieces and nephews, innocent bystanders to a confrontation between British troops and IRA paramilitaries. The disaster began with a single gunshot on August 10, 1976. Williams was nearby and arrived on the scene at once, but could only stand by helplessly as the Corrigan children were flung into the debris left by a car careening out of control, its driver shot. The children died, crushed by the car as it rode up onto the sidewalk. Corrigan raced home from a vacation to find her life's purpose changed forever. Just three weeks later, the two women attended, indeed found themselves at the head of the first of many rallies for peace, repudiating the violence on all sides, hoping for, calling out for and swelling a tide of energy for peace which they thought would be able to submerge the sectarian bombers and gunmen. Thousands of people attended that first rally; the estimates vary but numbers range from 27,000 to well over 60,000.[1] They began to dream their peace movement could reshape the whole culture of the conflict.

From the beginning the Corrigan/Williams endeavor was deeply controversial inside the war zone, bringing stinging accusations of disloyalty from active combatants on both sides. Protestant and Catholic militias continued to press for military victory, still judging violence to be the best means to maintain or to transform the status quo.[2] Indeed three months after the children were killed, the activists were themselves beaten up:

> Belfast, Northern Ireland, Oct. 10 (AP)—An angry mob punched, kicked and pulled the hair of the two top leaders of the women's peace movement here today, knocking one of them unconscious for a few minutes.
> Betty Williams and Mairead Corrigan were attacked after a hostile audience prevented them from addressing a meeting in a Roman Catholic section of Belfast. Outside the mob destroyed the two cars the women had arrived in.[3]

Undeterred by this and by other confrontations with the militias, and under the name "The Peace People," the two women crisscrossed their homeland, ventured into England and even traveled as far as Australia and New Zealand to spread the passion for an Irish peace.

Without qualm, Republican and Unionist militias on the ground repudiated the Nobel Peace Committee's optimism and enthusiasm for peace-making. At the awards ceremony itself, the combatants were out in public too:

> Oslo, Dec. 10 (Reuters)—Nobel Peace Prizes were presented today to two women who are campaigning to end bloodshed in Northern Ireland…
> Before the award ceremony, 50 demonstrators sympathetic to the Irish Republican Army, which is fighting British rule in Northern Ireland, chanted slogans such as "No to the Peace People" and "the fight continues."[4]

Meanwhile, indoors at the prize presentation, the Nobel committee applauded the momentum and the timing of the women's campaign. "One of the main reasons why the women proved successful in their campaign is that on both sides of the frontline a desperate yearning for peace has taken root.…But more than that, their courageous action cast a fresh light on the very essence of the grievous conflict that racked Northern Ireland. More clearly than ever before it appeared in its true light as a disease that ravaged a whole nation."

The speech went on to claim: "Betty Williams and Mairead Corrigan have shown us what ordinary people can do to promote the cause of peace. They have taught us that the peace for which we strive is something that has to be won within and throughout the individual human being. This is the message to which they have given renewed force through their activities."[5]

This is also the message that this book, rather sadly, calls into question. Anti-war activists regularly build popular support for, even passion for peace, but they cannot set either the timing or the terms that make it possible truly to stop the killing. In the fall of 1977 in Ireland, the will to fight on was still too strong, and no leader in London or Belfast, Dublin or Londonderry was willing to undertake the risky, demanding and complex business of making peace.

This book tells seven stories about the crucial moments in a war, during which peace-making begins to seem possible. Each story is replete with evidence that the changes which come during the ending weeks of a war are themselves fraught with danger and uncertainty. Each story of peace-making is different. In each a different impetus drives leaders to change direction.

Military raids and victims, disasters and interventions, mediators and bombers interact in unexpected or frustrating or courageous or horrifying ways to create that crisis from which peace-making can emerge. While they wait for the leaders to move, activists out in public act as reminders of the democratic social contract which so easily becomes secondary to the war effort.

Years, often decades, pass between the onset of massive popular calls for peace and the eventual renunciation of armed and violent strategies.[6] For more than 20 years, the Peace People, despite their Nobel Prize, failed to deflect the bombers and the bullets from their "necessary" and "just" purposes. There never was a real pause in the violence in the North of Ireland.

Within two months of the 1977 Nobel awards ceremony, a particularly large explosion left 12 people dead and 23 injured in a hotel in County Down. A year later, on a single day, one bomb killed 18 British soldiers on a bus while another killed Lord Mountbattan, a cousin of the Queen of England. Similar bombings soon began, in England: explosions at Kings Cross Station (the end of public garbage cans in the subway), threats against major London department stores (the onset of nightly security searches for small plastic bombs hidden in merchandise or on store shelves), mortars landing on the runways of Heathrow airport (a new kind of terror for tourists and business travelers) and bombs in the financial district of London (making it clear that no part of the British economy was safe). Even mere threats were very costly, as in 1997, when an IRA- sponsored hoax tied up traffic for hours on every single freeway in the English Midlands.

The largest bombings were covered on international news broadcasts, so outsiders had a sense that this was a war that flared up only intermittently. In the North of Ireland the realities of the danger surrounded people night and day, every day. They were in a war that was intensely personal and strongly rooted in their ordinary lives. The killings happened in pubs and in private homes; marked enemies and each side's own "traitors" came to understand that just sitting in their own living room watching television after dinner, they were still on the front line of battle.

Well over 3,000 people died, most of them one at a time over a 30 year time span. Thousands more were injured, victims of loyalty-testing, punishment beatings or brutal, personal assaults. Many of the casualties were simply unlucky bystanders, people drinking at the same pub or walking on the same street as the prime target. Troops in armored vehicles, snipers with guns and bullies in brass knuckles were out night after night. In cities like Belfast, the government built 20-foot high walls to impede the killing; like two peoples besieged, the city's residents lived in fortresses, each side barricaded inside their own protective and exclusive zone. Summer after summer, sectarian marches gave both Protestants and Catholics opportunities to renew their rallying cries for war.

The community remained at war, a tri-partite conflict waged among British troops and paramilitaries from both factions (Republican and Unionist). The Peace People, trying to change hearts and minds one at a time, had no means at their disposal to stop the killing and carnage.[6]

More than 20 years later, on October 17, 1998, the Nobel Peace Committee announced the 1998 Peace Prize. Once more, the prize went to two people who had made it their mission to bring peace to Northern Ireland. This time the prize and peace were closely connected.

In sharp contrast to 1977, the 1998 prize was widely expected. A carefully negotiated, long-term, military and political settlement for the North of Ireland, first announced on Good Friday at Easter 1998, had already been ratified by two popular referenda and elections to a newly constituted parliament. A massive bombing counterattack in Omagh in August '98 had been repudiated so forcefully even militias that had rejected the Easter settlement now committed themselves publicly to a cease-fire, seeming to recognize that the time for violence had passed.

The only suspense about the 1998 Nobel Prize lay in exactly which men among the key figures who had played a significant part in the Good Friday Agreement would be recognized. (This time the recipients were bound to be men; only one woman, Mo Mowlam, had been among the top leadership in the pivotal talks.) Would Gerry Adams, head of Sinn Féin, the political wing of the IRA, be on the podium so as to strengthen his power over the militant armed group? Would George Mitchell, an American statesman and tireless mediator of the negotiating sessions, be acknowledged? Would Tony Blair, British Prime Minister and strong advocate of regional devolution for Scotland and Wales, be seen to have paved the way for key new constitutional alignments in Ireland? Would Eire's (Ireland's) Taosaeich (Prime Minister) Ahern be recognized for softening Eire's constitutional claims to the northern counties?

In the end the prize went to John Hume, a Catholic, leader of the Social Democratic and Labor party in the North of Ireland, and David Trimble, a Protestant, leader of the Ulster Unionist party. Hume earned recognition because he had worked for nearly a decade in secret talks with Adams, playing a pivotal role in bringing the IRA into official talks. Trimble was almost the only Protestant leader ready seriously to work on developing power sharing political structures. Trimble's indirect links to the actual men who gave orders to Protestants for their part in the violence gave his peace focus political and operational credibility. Both John Hume and David Trimble were the leaders of their respective Parliamentary political parties in London as well. Neither had any credibility-damaging, official connections to terrorists.

Onlookers agreed that this was a conservative but sensible choice. These two, after all, would need to stay the course; they would be critical to the long term future in Northern Ireland. The Nobel Committee may have made a mistake that damaged the chances for an enduring peace in choosing Hume rather than acknowledging Adams, but at least their calculations about the odds for peace were correct.[7] Even in 1998 there were no guarantees, but the politicians and their armed forces had formally agreed to a cease-fire. They were offering a real chance for an enduring peace.

An enormous bomb that exploded in the city center of Omagh a few weeks before the prize announcement killed 29 and injured more than 350 people. It was the largest single attack in the province in more than 30 years. The bomb had been intended to destroy the peace agreements. Its result was the opposite. It cemented the peace. The leaders' public condemnation of the bombing was explicit. The day after the catastrophe, both repudiated any yearning for revenge:

> Gerry Adams said the bombing was "wrong—totally, absolutely wrong."
> He added, "I call upon whoever is responsible to admit responsibility and

cease these actions."

David Trimble called on all sides to avoid renewing the cycle of violence. "Above all, I call on any individual or group seeking retaliation to think again. Not only would it be wrong, it would be foolish,"[8]

In the city of Omagh itself, the shopkeepers and teachers, mothers and grandparents rallied by the thousands to appeal, through their silence, for a stable peace. The crowds were enormous, their solidarity unmistakable.

> Silence fell on grieving Omagh, where more than 20,000 Protestants and Catholics packed the town center yesterday to remember, through their sobs and tears, those killed in the Aug. 15 bombing.
>
> Hundreds of thousands more marked the slaughter—the worst in three decades of violence—with one minute's silence in town squares, churches, sports stadiums and shopping centers across Ireland....
>
> At the ceremony outside the courthouse in Omagh, leaders of the Catholic, Anglican, Methodist and Presbyterian churches in Ireland stood shoulder to shoulder. To one side, Gerry Adams and Martin McGuiness, reputed former IRA commanders...to the other, the Protestant and Catholic heads of Northern Ireland's newborn, cross-community government, David Trimble and Seamus Mallon.[9]

Even in traditionally Republican towns, the commitment to peace was obvious:

> After the Omagh bombing, residents of the town of Dundalk, which once harbored so many IRA safe houses, underground weapons networks and gunmen that the police called it El Paso...held a rally that attracted 15,000 people, half the town's population, to proclaim its abhorrence of the act and its determination to shed its old image.[10]

Millions of people had voted "yes" in the 1998 referendum on the peace accords, even though no one would give them a prize. The thousands who came out for peace after the Omagh bombing received recognition in the mass media only for a moment. The leaders who had signed the agreement and then rejected violence had finally joined, in public, with ordinary people holding fast for peace. Without all these kinds of support, peace would never have endured. Working together, it had a chance. The uncertainties continued, but August 15, 1998, was a crucial moment in peace-making in the North of Ireland. Three months later, the Nobel Committee offered its prize to Trimble and Hume, 21 long years after Oslo's first claim that peace was at hand.

Betty Williams and Mairead Corrigan never could have engineered a cease-fire in Ireland, let alone crafted an enduring political peace settlement. In making so bald a statement, I am both delineating and narrowing the scope of this book. This is a book about stopping killing by making an agreement that endures well enough to prevent a rapid return to militarized violence. This is not a book about pacifism, about inter-community dialogue, about compassionate concern, or about healing the wounds of war, all of which help to fully re-establish a viable peace. The Peace People in the North of Ireland, like many grass roots organizations, spent years laying the foundations for long term reconciliation between the peoples of the region.[11] Their educational work paid dividends in popular readiness to work constructively through the ambiguity, anxiety and physical damage of the time immediately following a cease-fire. Still, the work of crafting the political and military details, each one of which is essential to crafting an actual end to the killing, fell to others, to politicians whose commands controlled the violence and whose vision encompassed their personal futures as well as the future of the groups they represented.*

This book will set out in more detail the other conditions that brought a true peace within reach in Ireland in 1998. These include carefully designed rooms and settings for direct talks among the combatants and a willingness for sitting governments to negotiate as equals with men previously branded

---

*Lest these pages make it sound as though I do not admire such work, let me explain that I too am an activist, once serving as National Co-Chair of the Executive Committee of the Nuclear Weapons Freeze Campaign. That movement helped to make ending the Cold War conceivable. We also helped to diffuse some of the visceral anti-Soviet feeling in the United States, by building concern that the nuclear trauma threatened both sides equally. I am realist enough, however, to recognize that the movement alone could not have ended the Cold War. We needed Gorbachev to come to power in the USSR and we needed him to try to reshape the domestic politics of the USSR.

The 1989 opening of the Berlin Wall marked the big break. The cease-fire process in the Cold War began because Gorbachev refused to use Soviet troops to block East German popular uprisings, a military action well within Soviet tradition. Ending the Cold War made only slow progress while Reagan and then Bush hesitated to respond to Gorbachev's softening military stance. The subsequent collaboration, between the United States and USSR in the war against Iraq in 1990-91, sealed the new relationship.

as "terrorists." There were similar efforts in six other wars at more or less the same time: Bosnia, Israel/Palestine, South Africa, Chechnya, Rwanda and Iraq. Seen together, the stories make a picture of the complex realities of ending a war. Each entailed heavy risks even while it presented hopeful opportunities. Most often the crucial decisions were territorial and political.

The responsibility for peace-making belongs in a very few hands—those of the political leaders who ordered military violence in the first place. Instead of accepting responsibility for some failure on their own part to prevent or to end a war, the peace-oriented should lay that responsibility squarely at the feet of its rightful owners: the political leadership which sanctions the war in the first place.

Many of us want to do more. And we can, in the sense of easing the suffering, or trying to ease the suffering. Suggestions multiply in a war—support an embargo against South African apartheid, start writing to a family besieged by violence in Sarajeveo, advocate cuts in US funds that support the Israeli occupation, help monitor elections in a fragile postwar zone, send money for health care in Rwanda, set up a summer camp for teenagers from opposing sides to meet and talk—there is no shortage of campaigns to join. But the most important is actively to remind political and military leaders that working for peace will destroy neither the country nor their own political future. And once the first fragile stages of peace-making have begun the opportunities multiply.

Ordinary people, committed to peace, fully regain their power in the political process only as the war is ending, because only then does democratic politics begin to operate once more. But, if peace-making has begun, as the people in Omagh realized, the votes for peace will actually get counted and the bodies mobilized for peace will finally receive recognition.

ACKNOWLEDGEMENTS

This book has been part of my life's work and so, in some sense, every part of my own intellectual, personal and professional context deserves recognition. That would require a book in its own right, and I must be brief. Consider these words a small bow in the direction of some of the most important contributors.

I will begin where most authors end, with my husband Rob Knapp and our three children, Alex, Emily and Malcolm. I thank each of you for the critical readings you gave this text as it evolved and, more importantly, for the inspiration each of your lives provides for my ongoing work for peace. Rob, you are the bedrock on which this sometimes difficult endeavor could always rest. Thank you.

For their help in bringing *Dangerous Peace-Making* from manuscript to book form, I must acknowledge Kathy Campbell, Katrine Gorham and the entire staff of Gorham Printing. I cannot imagine an easier, more trustworthy, more enjoyable or faster way to "produce" a book. I also owe a good deal to my wonderful team of editors and proofreaders—Jo Curtz, Thad Curtz, Hal Spencer, Esmé Ryan, Susan Preciso and Rob Knapp—each of you has offered personal and professional support over a much longer term as well. The remaining errors in the manuscript are, of course, my own. There would have been so many more without your eagle eyes at work on my behalf.

Another group helped shepherd this particular manuscript through to completion. Known as the *Just Do It* writers, we began work at The Evergreen State College several years ago, a core group of members that has been together ever since. Many thanks to Susan Preciso, Nancy Allen, Linda Moon Stumpf, Joli Sandoz and Frederica Bowcutt.

The intellectual and activist ancestry for this book is to be found in a wide variety of places among people doing many different kinds of work. Sheila Forbes goes back to the very beginning, a companion since our undergraduate days at

Oxford. Elizabeth Kamarck Minnich has offered more than 15 years of a steady, attentive friendship and collegial relationship, and an early willingness to appreciate my need to understand peace-making via the rather painful study of war. Sally Ruddick was also there 15 years ago and to my great delight our paths have crossed again more recently. My mother-in-law, Faith Knapp, has been a steadfast model of citizenship and active engagement in public life. Supportive colleagues and friends of long standing include: Peter Scott, Mike Waddilove, Richard Danzig, Kai Lee, Rita Pougiales, David Smith, Joanna and Fran Macy, Fran Peavey, Carla Johnston, Glen Anderson, Carolyn Cooley, Eve Fagergren, Anna Fagergren, Marla Elliott, Si Kahn, Ben Shaine, Marci Thurston, Jane Jervis, Joe Meeker, Kim Maynard, Barbara Perkins, Anne Barstow, David Burrell, Tom Driver and the late Fontaine Belford. Others I have only come to know more recently, in particular Jeff Haus, Emily Decker, Gilles Malnaric, Larry Seaquist, Carla Seaquist and Simona Sharoni. Thanks to you all.

While the members of the "ancestors" group are widely scattered and their influences varied, another equally vital group came together for a single year at the Bunting Institute in the fall of 1994. Each of us became a sister to the others' work. The 38 fellows and the Institute's staff have stayed connected, thanks in part to one of Harvard's most primitive computer systems, which was nonetheless good enough to enable us to create the network which links us to this day. For their support at emotional, professional and intellectual levels, my joyful thanks go to Karen Wyche, Laura Harrington, Paula Gutlove, Kate Cloud, Sophie Cabot Black and Renny Harrigan. Florence Ladd deserves a special bow for her invitation to spend a whole year on a Bunting Fellowship—it was such a rich and stimulating environment. Sophie Bryan, my research assistant did invaluable work that year. She has a special place in this book.

Other professional groups generously supplied either funding or an audience or both. The Evergreen State College contributed sabbatical support, a Sponsored Research Grant and 19 years of stimulating opportunities for interdisciplinary teaching. The colleagues at Evergreen who have had an impact on this book are literally to numerous to mention. The Carnegie Council for Ethics and International Affairs, in conjunction with the National Endowment for the Humanities, provided funding for a six-week long research seminar on Globalization and Ethics. We spent our time in New York just before September 11, which will forever shape my understanding of the direct effects of war. The imaginative and companionable Fellows who attend the Society for Values in Higher Education each year, in particular the members of the enduring working group on Religion and Violence, have listened to several iterations of these ideas, offering helpful and constructive critique. So too have the members of the International Society for Political Psychology. And further away, but still important are faculty colleagues at the University of Hawai'i, Hilo and at Kobe Shodai, the Japanese university soon to become a part of Hyogo University. In both places, their warm hospitality combined with a chance for me to see the world from a quite different perspective, which contributed significantly to the final outcome of this work. I owe a good deal to each one of these entities.

Over the years, several local groups in my hometown, Olympia Washington, have provided support and encouragement. In the late 1970s I joined a dozen friends in a six-month-long study of global issues. The group stayed together for years and launched my work in national peace organizing on behalf of a Nuclear Weapons Freeze, which in turn prompted me to start thinking about how to bring long-running confrontations to an end. The Olympia Fellowship of Reconciliation has been a steady present for peace here for as long as I can remember. The Olympia Community Yoga Center has helped to keep my body limber and strong and my spirit centered in hard times. The Community for Interfaith Celebration is a true community, a place to celebrate the seasons of life, to study wisdom and compassion and to do so for the sake of the whole world. This is also the point to remember two particular people, Jessica Kelso and Rachel Corrie, young women who seemed destined to make a positive mark on the wider world. Both died much too young and yet, in their very different deaths, each one has shown the rest of us so much and made an enduring mark upon the wider world as well.

I have too many other friends to list them as individuals. I know I would leave someone critical out, and then always regret the mistake. So I will turn now to the family which gave me a place in this world and a hybrid ancestry that has endowed me with the endurance to finish a nine-year-long writing project. My parents: Roger and Paula Quirk, my sisters Jessica Rawson and Joanna Eley, my cousin Jenny Nutbeem and all of the children in the next generation: Francis, Henrietta, Sarah, Josephine, Patrick and Michael. You have provided me with complex, generous and close relationships, which I really appreciate no matter how limited our day-to-day contact.

I end with a special acknowledgement for my mother's father August Weber. He had the courage to stand publicly against the Nazis. He had the practical forethought to develop the means to keep his family secure, even in exile. He had the patience to endure his own last years in London, under-appreciated for his earlier courage. Each of these attributes is a model for constructive survival in dangerous times. I write these particular words the very same week that US President George Bush appears to be on the verge of yet another military assault, this time against Syria. When my sadness increases, I remember my grandfather. I am grateful that I seem to be acquiring his bushy eyebrows and I hope always to find his kind of courage to stand firm when the government seems wrong. I plan to take whatever risks are necessary, and still hope to live to a ripe old age to become a model for some other six-year-old making his or her way in the world.

—*Helena Meyer-Knapp*
April 2003
Olympia, Washington

INTRODUCTION

Peace-making: myth and reality

War stories are all too easy to find, their endings ready to be mythologized into glorious victories or tragic losses. In the last century alone, tens of millions died worldwide, and not a year passed when peace prevailed everywhere. As I waited at an airport just after Christmas 2002, yet another war permeated my surroundings. With an American invasion of Iraq seemingly imminent, the day's newspapers headlined sharply higher oil prices, impelled upward by war-driven fears about supply. The nearby television was showcasing "Warbirds," a documentary airing on CNN. The ad promised heroic stories of fighter pilots, judiciously intercut with footage of planes flying into the sunset and a voiceover lauding the awesome technology of the modern US Air Force. Newspapers and TV stories together encompassed the two key characteristics of war: that war is coercive, if often seemingly banal, in its demands for sacrifice, and that war is seductive in its intimations of heroism and glory. Once combat begins, these two—sacrifices that need to be compensated and avenged and heroism that insists on recognition—become big obstacles to making peace.

In the winter of 2002-03, as far as Americans were concerned, a war with Iraq was a prospect more than an actuality. For Iraqis, the war was already a reality with plenty of sacrifice and few opportunities for heroism, the consequence of 12 years of UN embargo, Saddam Hussein's militarism and UN coalition air forces patrolling and shelling both north and south. And now, new and devastating threats loomed, propagated by leaders on both sides who worked tirelessly to divide the world into "us" and "them." Amidst their year-end holiday festivities, Americans had been reminded repeatedly that Saddam Hussein was a monster with no compunction about using dreadful weapons, and that UN arms inspectors would prove him so.* To his own people, and to many in the Arab and Moslem worlds, the portrait Saddam displayed of himself was of a military hero and an adherent of the faith, ready to stand firm against the infidel, economic rapacity of the American Satan. Patriotism called both worlds to war. Honor would demand that they respond, and then each wartime death would have to be avenged. The entire war was made "right" by the justice of their respective causes.

War stories begin so simply, even though the actual fighting will all too quickly turn many lives into chaotic, complicated and horrifying experiences. The opposing sides spit out short, hostile epithets—"Cruel Huns," "Godless Communists," "Fascist Nazis," "Cockroach Tutsi," "Soviet Dupes," "Protestants" and "Catholics," "Zionists" and "Islamist Fundamentalists." Once combat begins, the epithets are no longer mere slogans. They identify real perpetrators who turned loved ones into real dead bodies, who destroyed real houses and shot down real planes, leaving a trail of damage all too easy to see. This is how vengeance joins patriotism and honor on the front lines, inspiring so many perfectly ordinary people to turn from peace-loving home owners to willing killers, at least at first. This is how leaders manage to justify the urgency of yet more war.

At the onset of a war, even peace-making is much too easily simplified by those who advocate fighting as well as by those who oppose it. The advocates say "our" side will triumph in "victory," which sounds as though starting a war is like beginning a football game. Warring forces will march onto the field, and at the end of the allotted time, a winner will be declared. Or else leaders promise that the enemy, unable to bear the cost, will have to accept "defeat." Thus, war seems like a competitive exercise or an investment, and the side with the most resources is bound to win. And for those who take a moral stand against the war in the first place, there is the conviction, almost

---

* In January 2003, the contrast between media coverage of the war in the United States and Canada was stark. The war made headline, front page and continuous coverage every day in the United States. For Canadians the story was never far away, but only occasionally did it rise to become the first item of business. The American media, like the media preparing for war in Serbia and Rwanda in the early 1990s, seemed to make combat both inevitable and reasonable. By the end of January, even the normally progressive *New Yorker* magazine was arguing that the only thing worse than war was leaving Saddam in power.

always dashed in practice, that a large enough crowd speaking out against the fighting will bring the combatants to their senses.

In fact, war bears little relationship to these ideals, neither to a football game, nor to a smooth exchange of cash for an equity stake in a corporation, nor to a well reasoned argument articulated by strong public pressure. Ending a war is a roiling, uneasy process. If metaphors from the everyday world apply, they are the metaphors from thunderstorms, volcanoes and chaos. War does not have, and never has had, the predictable and elegant mechanics of a Newtonian universe. Nor does war allow the measured dialogue and political debate which those who resist depend on to make their voices heard.

Instead, wars end in the midst of upheaval. Among the armed combatants, some remain determined to continue fighting. Desperate refugees wonder whether they will ever reclaim their lands. Political leaders are juggling the options to ensure their own long-term survival, even their recognition in the stories told to future generations. These and dozens of other factors intersect at crucial moments, opening an opportunity in which is embedded great danger as well as hope for better times. Suddenly, and often unexpectedly, a chance for peace makes itself visible. How long it will last and whether it will be pursued in good faith are almost always uncertain.

Clausewitz, the great military strategist, emphasized complexity and the interplay of chance and chaos in war more than 200 years ago.[1] His names for them were "fog" and "friction." Fog ensured that in the heat of battle, military information was impossible to analyze accurately.* Friction ensured that no matter how careful the design, military tactics and strategies could never be executed exactly as they were intended. The effects of an attack would always present the unexpected. Modern rhetoric about the ending of war, which refers to winners and losers or carrots and sticks, implies a rule-bound, logical universe that does not allow for the thick "fogs" and distorting "frictions," which are the reality in which peace-makers start to work. Among theorists who are Clausewitz's modern descendents, a significant number have turned to the scientists who visualized "chaos theory" for the language

---

* During the war against Iraq in the early 1990s, the US military learned first hand that increasing the amount of information does not help, since the time and capacity to process the information does not increase at the same rate.

that enables clear thinking about change and danger, fog and friction.[2]

Before developing an analysis based on chaos and complexity as a new model for understanding war's endings, we should explore fundamental flaws in the conventional models of war. We will look first at the game-based and economic metaphors for peace-making that predominate in America's strategic community, since both have become so widely used in ordinary media coverage of war as well.

Games, victory and peace-making

Competitive games, particularly football and chess, have long been favored as source metaphors among military strategists, journalists, commentators and official speech writers. These metaphors are vivid to the members of the inner circle developing policy, and they are equally important in building popular support for the policy options selected. Implicit in the game imagery is the assumption that there must be a connection between determining the winner in a war and determining the timing of the end of that war. Both chess and American football assign a special significance to the particular moments in which the winner becomes fixed. The winning and the ending go hand in hand. Strategist and public alike visualize the future ahead, and it looks manageable.

From chess comes the term "endgame," used to connote the dilemmas faced in the closing phases of a war.[3] In chess, endgames typically offer an ever smaller number of choices to the players. In a war, peacemakers rarely lose options; sometimes indeed the number of options at the end of a war abruptly increases. Furthermore, until the war is actually over, one cannot know precisely when it was that the final ending phase began. Only hindsight can tell for sure. Consider trying to discern the onset of the endgame in Ireland: was it with an abortive cease-fire in 1994? The day peace-talks began in 1996? When British Prime Minister Tony Blair was elected in 1997? The night before the final agreement in 1998? When the popular referendums passed a month later? In Omagh on the day of the bombing, or perhaps in 2002 when the peace-time government collapsed? As I write in 2003, all one can say is that the peace agreements in 1998 had a real chance of ending the war. Even now, it is impossible to say that the war is really over.

American football narrows the ending process still more by suggesting that the winner is the one who has more points when the "two minute" clock finally runs out. Players on a football field would collapse exhausted were the losers allowed to postpone defeat, trying repeatedly to reverse their fate with just one more drive for a touch down.* So a football game, like chess, has a prescribed battle-ground and a limit on the number of allowable players. Repeated forays back onto the field are not allowed. War has no such built-in limits, nor any measure of the kind of point spread that counts as winning. Losers like Saddam Hussein are free to go on trying even when the odds are overwhelmingly against them, regardless of the physical cost to their own side.

Furthermore, in war simply having the endurance to continue can sometimes reverse the outcome. Less than two years after the UN victory in the Iraq war, Saddam Hussein remained in power, while his principal opponent, President Bush, found himself, ignominiously, the first Republican President to lose an election for a second term in more than 50 years. Then again, 10 years later Iraq was bankrupt and the US economy was booming. The Iraq war was still not over and it remained impossible to tell who had more points. Among the wars in this book, in Rwanda and in South Africa victorious forces won overwhelmingly, their opponents utterly defeated, but neither war ended cleanly and clearly at the first possible opportunity. Wars are hard to end because ending them is a matter of choice, not a matter of rules, points or conventions.

In chess, the loser has no choice about conceding. There comes a time when he no longer has pieces to defend his king and the game is over. Checkmate. Furthermore, convention holds that a chess player is particularly skillful if he concedes the instant it becomes clear that all possible remaining sequences of moves will leave the king exposed to capture.[4] The US government, applying a related strategic notion, makes plans to execute every military engagement with such overwhelming force that the enemy ought to

---

* Of course, in American football, rules and coaching strategies do tend to turn the last "two minutes" of the game into plays that take as much as half an hour to execute. Even so, the amount of available time for any given game, with all the overtimes, remains finite and controlled by the rules and not by the energies and enthusiasms of the participants or their fans.

acknowledge defeat instantly, or at least the moment the scale of the US military might becomes clear. In other words, to US strategists in war, the loser ought to try actively to calculate the odds and stop fighting at the instant the indicators become clear. US-led coalitions tried this in two recent wars, Bosnia and Iraq, with no direct success on either occasion. Indeed, neither Milosevic nor Saddam Hussein considered that the NATO or UN forces had defeated them at all.[5] Such a strategy often does conserve US lives. American deaths, as a proportion of tonnage of weapons dropped, were minimal. The trouble is that most combatants do not think of war as chess, and they fight on till they get to or even get past what ought to be the bitter end.

In fact, many wars end only after a period of stalemate. No one earns the classic march to victory, and because there is no limit on "overtimes" and "extra innings," additional battles achieve nothing except more fighting and dying.[6] War has no fixed tally of participants; if some are injured, any number more can be made available by a bureaucratic military draft, or by coercive and terror-driven recruitment. The size and location of the field of combat can be as large as an empire or as small as the six counties in the North of Ireland. Above all, war has no specific amount of time allotted for the action.[7] Timing is the crux of the matter. Football has a clock. Chess has an endgame. War can go on for as long as the combatants have the will to fight.

Both chess and football are metaphors. Public debates about war are also replete with economic metaphors to illustrate these crucial moments at the end of a war. Among the most widely accepted in the United States is that our nation is bound to win because it always invests the most financially in the military. A related belief is that a gradual build-up of pressures, continuing until the costs outweigh the benefits, will inevitably bring peace.

Investments, costs and peace-making

The cases covered in this book offer no evidence of a relationship between comparatively larger investments in a war and any resultant ability to craft an enduring cease-fire. Israel built and maintained military forces more technically proficient than almost any in the world, and yet proved able neither to successfully settle affairs along the border with Lebanon, a mere 35 miles long, nor to end the rain of bombs exploding in the middle of Israeli territory. During the Intifada in the late 1980s, a young generation of Palestinians armed only with stones taught Israel it faced an enemy that need never "run out" of defenders or weapons.[8] Though the decision to negotiate with Arafat in the early 1990s was partly shaped by Palestinian successes in the Intifada, the actual negotiations did not begin until several years after that particular campaign had come to an end. Neither Israeli nor Palestinian military arsenals determined the date for the beginning of the Oslo talks. Russia's arsenal overwhelmed the Chechen forces, South Africa's the ANC's, Britain's that of the Unionists and the Republicans combined, and the US/UN forces were incommensurably larger than those of Saddam Hussein. In none of these cases could heavy military investment provide control, in part because combat strength and resilience do not result from the size of military forces alone.

The other economic image, cost-benefit analysis, sets up an additional fallacy about peace-making—that the accumulation of costs and of casualties, particularly of "innocent civilians," will spur an end to the fighting. Civilian suffering does make outsiders press harder for peace, but there is no evidence from these cases that civilian deaths, or indeed any particular number of deaths, inspires anyone with power to end the killing.

Researchers have long tried to prove a linkage between casualties and suffering reaching a certain percentage of the population or of the army and the decision to seek a cease-fire. Strategists too assume this logic.[9] The "amount" of damage each side perpetrates in different wars seems as though it ought to be quantifiable, if "amount" means the number of attacks/casualties. But comparisons are surprisingly hard to make. At one extreme, in Ireland, the Republican and Unionist militias needed no more than a few hundred "foot soldiers" to deliver bombs to targets hundreds of miles away and to carry out sniper attacks right there at home. Their final death toll numbered around 3,000. The suffering and sacrifice required in the North of Ireland was to live with everything from anxiety to terror, night and day, for 30 years, through the births and deaths of a whole generation. At the other extreme, in Rwanda, 800,000 or more died and many were killed by machete in face to face attacks. But this particular war lasted less than six months. Can either of these be said to be gradually accumulating pressures? At what point does either tip towards peace in an irrefutable cost-benefit analysis? Which is more destructive: constant threats of bombs and news of casualties that permeates all aspects of the lives of every citizen for 30 years, or a short, sharp catastrophe that leaves 800,000 dead almost overnight?

In one of the cases I studied in depth, Iraq, it could appear that deaths, albeit Iraqi military deaths, caused the cease-fire. But the situation was the reverse of what one might expect. It was the Americans, concerned about the havoc and carnage American pilots were spreading among retreating Iraqis, who chose to stop the pursuit. The Iraqi death toll was indeed horrendous, and though the dead were mostly soldiers, they were in desperate flight.[10] The ground war against Iraq ended the very same day.

But the Iraq war was not actually over. The longer war, the economic sanctions and "no-fly zone" war, did not end then nor for more than a decade. Thousands and thousands of deaths resulted from the embargo, even those of young children but American leaders simply blamed these losses on Saddam Hussein. Compassion awakened briefly in 1991, but it did not truly end the war.

I have not found mathematical arguments about war casualties and the cost-benefit analysis persuasive.[11] One cannot quantify how much grief weighs, nor whether the grief, which is bearable under the intense pressures of wartime, might perhaps become more intolerable once peace comes. If research into the consequences of injury in war proves anything, it suggests that suffering inspires the front-line combatants to continue to fight. Pain in civilian communities does not necessarily either lower morale or increase pressure to end the fighting.[12] Indeed, a focus on victims obscures from view the other factors that end war. Suffering matters most because it supplies leaders with a ready justification for stopping the killing when the time for peace-making finally arrives. Finally the leaders choose to accept, most often as a result of negotiations towards new possibilities, that the time has come for a settlement of political struggles and for the repair of the war zone.

Activists, protest and peace-making

The notion that suffering should impel leaders to move quickly to peace-making seems self-evident to peace activists. Indeed, the Nobel Committee in 1977 said just that—that Williams and Corrigan could bring the war in Ireland to an end by opening people's awareness to the pain and thus changing hearts and minds, one at a time. In the aftermath of the end of the war in Vietnam, many people had a good deal of faith in the power of activism. They too were operating with a version of the cost-benefit analysis, so dear to strategists, but in reverse. If they could simply bring a large enough mass of popular pressure to bear, then the political leadership would be impelled to stop the war. In reality, what activists usually achieve is to make visible the suffering that was too well hidden. In doing so they reawaken some level of political debate, but they cannot actually end the fighting. Indeed, usually those who are working for peace are reviled, the combatant leadership denigrating their courage, their loyalty and their wisdom.[13]

As the peace movement tells the Vietnam story to this day, only four years after a covert war falsely achieved public legitimization, in the 1964 Gulf of Tonkin Resolution, the ending of the war was in sight. President Lyndon Johnson was out of office, forced to abandon election to a second term by a movement powerful enough to end the whole thing. Vast demonstrations in 1968 were followed by yet more widespread protests in 1969 and 1970, by the killing of student protestors by the National Guard at Kent State and Jackson State Universities, and by a massive, activist campaign to get an avowed peace candidate elected President in 1972. These culminated in the virtually complete pullout of American troops from SE Asia by 1973. The peace movement could declare victory and go home to rest on its laurels, earned both for courage and success.

Even this bare-bones story has problems making a convincing link between aroused activists and leverage on the ending of the war. After all, the 1968 triumph over President Johnson occurred five full years before the official US troop pullout. More seriously, the story leaves out too many critical events, most seriously the war in Cambodia and Nixon's decision to burgle the Watergate. The real-life plot line was dramatically different by the time that the fighting finally stopped.

Firstly, the Vietnam War did not "end" when American men and women left the battleground. Even after 1973, US money kept on funding the combat to the tune of millions of dollars a month, while the death toll kept rising among the Vietnamese themselves, paid for by US taxpayers. In Vietnam, the fighting finally stopped in April 1975, and then only because the United States and Saigon governments abandoned their resistance to the Northern army's advance. Finally, American soldiers, embassy staff and their key Vietnamese allies fled, evacuating ignominiously in helicopters from the US Embassy roof.

A more powerful argument against the peace-movement's claim to the power to end a war lies in the behavior of Johnson's successor, Richard Nixon. Nixon won election by promising to end the fighting, but he expanded rather than ended the war. He sent US troops across the border into Cambodia in pursuit of the North Vietnamese, dragging Cambodians into a war so calamitous it came to be known to Americans by its movie name "The Killing Fields." The death rate was of genocidal proportions, though the people killing and being killed were all of the same national, ethnic and religious background. The peace-movement's victory over Johnson brought catastrophic losses for Cambodia, which endured these horrendous conditions until 1978.*

The event most directly linked in time to the war's ending in Vietnam was Richard Nixon's own resignation. He was brought down not by the protestors but by his own violations of America's ideals for government. Craving an absolute loyalty far sterner than regular, wartime patriotism, Nixon created "enemies" lists of Americans who dared raise doubts about the war,

---

* The suffering in Cambodia only finally began to ease, when Vietnam invaded in 1978, stemming the slaughter and occupying the country for several years. Thirty years later, though, the peace in Cambodia remained precarious and the scars from that ghastly war were still aching.

and then directed government offices to harass and harm them, one by one. Seeking revenge for the newspaper publication of "The Pentagon Papers," a critical analysis of the US war effort, Nixon ordered the burglary of a psychiatrist's office, the results to be used in the prosecution of the man who had leaked the papers, Daniel Ellsberg. But it was his second burglary, Watergate, that ended Richard Nixon's presidency.[14] Having come to see himself as entitled to the Presidency at whatever the cost, Nixon ordered his 1972 election campaign managers to burgle the national headquarters of the Democratic Party. In the process, he so violated American democracy that his impeachment became inevitable. Even the unity required by war was not adequate to protect him. In August 1974, just eight months before the fall of Saigon, Nixon left office, replaced by Gerald Ford. Ford's primary concern was to relegitimize the Presidency itself, and with much less personal investment in the war, he was able to let it end. Who knows whether a Nixon, untainted by Watergate and with Henry Kissinger at his side, could have watched the terrorized Americans evacuating from the Embassy roof without one last foray to prevent such an ignominious end to the war?

Am I saying that the peace-movement accomplished nothing? No. But their accomplishment was in the politics of wartime, not in its strategic outcomes. The peace movement rearranged the public debate about whether and when to fight, dragging the issues out of secret "war rooms" and gradually making it part of the business of Congress. In this they challenged the fundamental logic that separates government from democracy in wartime, even in  a democratic republic. Combat decisions are not normally made by democratic process. And yet, debate was not enough to end it. That took a complete change in America's leadership.

Peace at last

Peace is bound to come, because no war lasts forever. As part of its ending, combatants must craft an enduring cease-fire to mark the fact that killing and destroying property have been set aside, that struggles over land and power, rights and riches are henceforward to be settled by other means. Every war needs some kind of cease-fire agreement. Even the most overwhelming victories cannot actually end the killing unless the loser acknowledges the war is over.* This book describes the crucial moments that gave peace a real chance in seven recent, serious attempts to end wars: South Africa 1993, Israel/Palestine 1993 onwards, Rwanda 1994, Northern Ireland 1994/98, Bosnia 1995, Chechnya 1996/1999, and UN-US/Iraq 1991 and thereafter. Some of these wars really ended. In others, the peace-making turned out to be too dangerous and war began again. Long-term success or not, at these times and in these places there was, for a while, an opportunity to end a war. And that time, both dangerous and ripe with good prospects, is what this book is about.

Before going into more detail, I should define what I consider to be a war, and how I selected the seven cases.[15] It is war when organized and semi-organized groups are engaged in an armed and violent struggle for control of the political powers, the resources and the military authority of one or more particular pieces of territory. It is war if the combatants are following a coherent strategy, using organized or semi-organized military forces, though the weapons used need not be conventional. It is a war when the combatants have concluded that it is legitimate to kill, maim and injure to achieve their goals.[16]

Using this definition, I selected as stories for this book widely discussed wars and familiar events, even if most people cannot remember all the details. The wars in Rwanda, Bosnia, Ireland, Palestine, and South Africa made headline news worldwide, some for decades. Even Chechnya earned cover story status with *Time Magazine.* And, because they were covered so widely in the news, each war raised questions about whether outsiders could intervene usefully to bring it to an end. Many people now argue that with an international court for the prosecution of war crimes, the world community might be able to prevent the onset of wars. While I doubt the latter, in a global era each of us needs to understand war, peace-making and intervention.

---

* The ending dates of the European and Asian campaigns in World War II offer clear illustrations of this reality. The Allied victories had been assured for months (perhaps years), but the endings did not come until first the Germans, and then the Japanese, acknowledged their war was over.

They are so likely to be recurrent topics of concern for decades still to come.

Each war story I have crafted focuses attention on only a few of the pivotal factors that can make an enduring cease-fire possible. Northern Ireland points us towards alterations in a nation's constitutional context. For Ireland this included both Britain's devolution of power to Scotland and Wales, and the influence of British and Irish membership in the EU. The Irish situation also demonstrates that threats to peace can reverberate for years. Bosnia exemplifies the fact that a few quite small shifts in the military control of towns and villages can be pivotal in making or postponing peace. Land of more cosmic significance is obviously key in Israel/Palestine; the peace there has faltered because Jerusalem is among the most contested patches of land in the world. The 1993 Israeli/Palestinian cease-fire attempt also offers evidence that each combatant's most powerful political leaders have to be directly involved laying out the terms for political alignments, resource allocation and other settlements. The search for postwar justice in the South African case illuminates one way to repair the wounds of war, a repair that, in the long run, is central to whether or not peace is possible. Chechnya serves as a vivid reminder that very small armies can last out against much bigger ones, and that even a super-power sized army cannot claim victory until the loser is willing to admit defeat. Rwanda became an important case in part because it raised so many questions about the imperatives for outside intervention. In addition, Rwanda, although an astonishingly brutal war, offers a rare recent counter example to a classic but often mythic notion, that wars can end when the "enemy" captures their opponent's capital city.

These, then, were the reasons I selected the particular wars. Joining them together and making an organized picture of peace-making required examining three rather different aspects of each of the wars: (1) which values enabled people to continue to fight in the midst of dreadful suffering, thus "postponing" the search for cease-fire, sometimes for years, (2) which events and factors persuaded the key people to work to stop the violence, and (3) whether outsider interventions, particularly those aimed at achieving justice, affected the peace. In addition to the seven stories, these three themes are the core concerns of this book. Here let me summarize the argument.

Maintaining the resilience to fight for a long time rests on three moral

emotions, each of which has seductive and coercive powers, all of which rise up when a community goes to war. The first to awaken is
usually the sense of duty or honor, a dual notion
that confers both the obligation and the entitlement to fight and kill.[17] Avoiding humiliation
and responding when threatened arouse loyalty
and patriotism, ensuring that citizen and soldier
alike experience a protective love for homeland
and culture, intensified by deep, tangible com-

mitments to comrades in danger. Vengeance, the desire to repay the enemy
for the damage done, is the last of the moral emotions and by far the hardest to quell. In the urge for retributive justice to counter war's destruction
and death burns an energy for war that can endure for years. Each new death
reheats the passion for justice, and for some the end will always come too
soon.

These emotions are heightened by the fact that war entails high-risk living. Criteria for decisions that "make sense" in risky situations are based on
standards quite different than those that apply in tranquil times. Warrior
ethics and crisis ethics compound each other such that stress and danger
begin to seem reasonable and even inescapable. These ethics also silence the
voices of those who doubt the war's value. Government in war-time becomes
a "guardianship," to use Plato's term, and any opponents quickly learn how
hard it is to find a forum in which to truly debate the war's choices with those
in power. Thus, imagining any path back to peace begins to seem beyond the
ethical and social framework on which wartime survival depends.

Over the years, my work on war has been punctuated repeatedly by re-
curring threats and violence between Iraq and the UN/United States. This
war seemed to end with a cease-fire signed by the UN coalition and Iraq in
the Iraqi desert at Safwan Air Force Base on March 3, 1991. But a war can
only truly end when the loser has admitted defeat. Saddam Hussein never did
agree he had lost, and so the conflict continued. In the United States, it was
years before anyone admitted to still being at war with Iraq; thus no one was
trying to bring about cease-fire.

In each of the seven stories, particular people in particular places at particular times had to decide that the time had come to end the fighting. It was
never a straightforward process. In the time it took me to write *Dangerous
Peace-Making*, my hopes for an enduring peace in each of the wars waned
and then revived more than once. At first I considered trying to make a definitive statement about each war, to bring closure to the book. Having seen
so many countries and people struggle in and out of peaceful times, I decided
instead simply to urge readers to engage one more time with each story, to
find out where the peace rests when you read this book. These are important
stories, which governed millions of lives worldwide for decades. All of us owe
them mindful attention until these wars fade into the dust of history.

If the rise of patriotism and the crushing of democratic debate exemplify
war, and the specific details of peace-making vary from place to place, what,
if any, are the general patterns behind the first fragile phase of peace? To end
a war, the leaders must notice and respond to unexpected events, be ready to
give up for a while should the opportunity abruptly disappear, and understand that ending a war is generally a lengthy, turbulent experience. Events
are highly sensitive to tiny variations in conditions, and thus seemingly similar peace overtures can have very different results. One mediator helps. Another leaves empty handed. Single actions can create reactions that are much
bigger or much smaller than anyone expected; one bombing attack will pass
unrecognized and the next will produce outrage and a commitment to make
the peace permanent.[18] Many painful aspects of war remain even after a
cease-fire, including food shortages, damaged buildings, displaced people,
hostile people, and a shortage of jobs and fuel. Under such severe stresses,
peace-making can easily disintegrate into a renewal of the combat whether
by bad luck or bad will. The dangerous and fragile period of peace that extends between a cease-fire and an enduring peace can be very long, and often seems just as likely to reawaken the urge for war as it is to inspire the
courage to make the choices on which an enduring peace will rest. Final
outcomes are rarely certain until it becomes evident, after the fact, that peace
has somehow managed to endure.

In the midst of these uncertainties, outsiders bring yet more complexity
by their interventions. Military forces, humanitarian aid units, negotiators

and international justices sent to force an end to a war will find themselves working in morally ambiguous conditions. Although the short-term effects on lives saved and children rescued can often appear positive, long-term consequences are frequently quite confusing. The search for justice and reconciliation, for example, can help to heal the wounds of war, but done by the wrong people in the wrong places, trials and reconciliation commissions are just as likely to leave the wounds festering.

The longer I have worked on peace-making, the clearer it has become that the central attribute of a peace-maker is mercy—acting mercifully towards those who have done harm, and with the ability to call out a merciful response from those who have suffered. When mercy joins retribution and restoration in the repertoire of just acts, then peace really does have a chance.

Each of the four sections around which this book is structured takes up one of these topics. The next chapter, "Altered Hearts and Minds," deals with the ethics and political processes of wartime. Then come seven case studies, one for each war, which retell a part of the story about a serious attempt to end that war. Then there is a chapter that explores the complexity common to all of these stories, analyzing them in language that was developed by chaos theorists to characterize the behavior of turbulent organisms. The book ends with a chapter about justice and mercy, memory and peace.

ALTERED HEARTS AND MINDS

The ethics and politics of combat

When Napoleon asserted that "morale is to the physical as three is to one," he was not merely thinking of whether a soldier was optimistic or pessimistic at the moment of going into battle. He was referring to the moral component of fighting power— that deep inner motivation of a solider which makes him willing to sacrifice his life on behalf of a common cause.[1]

Peace, ethics and democracy

In the Introduction, I presented the conundrum: "How do people continue to fight on in the midst of dreadful suffering, postponing the search for cease-fire and peace, sometimes for years?" The answer lies in the deadly interaction of the moral component of fighting power with the coerciveness, secrecy and costly perversions even of democratic politics that pervade governments in war. Together, ethics and politics give war its inexorable momentum, its inescapable dominance over the cultural norms of a peace-time society. Combat ethics authorize killing and destruction in the name of justice, loyalty and resolve.* Governments, pressed by the exigencies of danger, silence doubt and debate about alternative strategies, while resorting to heirarchical command structures and even outright lies to achieve results.

> On this February day, as this nation stands at the brink of battle, every American on some level must be contemplating the horrors of war.
> Yet, this Chamber is, for the most part, silent—ominously, dreadfully silent. There is no debate, no discussion, no attempt to lay out for the

---

* These are the specific words that were used by George Bush to explain the US in its wars against Iraq and Al Quaeda after September 11, 2001. Thinking about their larger meaning occupies the first half of this chapter.

nation the pros and cons of this particular war. There is nothing.

    We stand passively mute in the United States Senate, paralyzed by our own uncertainty, seemingly stunned by the sheer turmoil of events.*

The United States Senate silenced? The all too real risks and uncertainties of war force senator and citizen alike into conduct quite outside their normal tolerances.

    The last 100 years repeatedly have subjected millions of people to hearts and minds altered beyond recognition by war. Almost no country has kept peace-time politics intact. Nor has any kept cruelty at bay completely. In Israel, for example, where domestic politics are traditionally fragmented and partisan, voters have spent years and years governed by "National Unity" administrations. These governments imposed the draft on Israeli young men and women while they ordered army tanks to demolish Palestinian homes, root up olive trees and mow down children on their way to school. Israeli Jews lived in terror of a suicide bomber whenever they rode the city bus or shopped in a supermarket. Americans, whose politics pivot on a balance of powers and regular opportunities for change, repeatedly elected Franklin Roosevelt to the presidency during World War II. And his military orders sent American bombers over Hamburg, Tokyo and Dresden and mandated the design of the atomic bomb, both moves aimed at incinerating homes and families in addition to demolishing strategic targets. On both sides of the Iron Curtain, Cold War administrations silenced debate for decades, while catastrophe threatened from their deployment of nuclear weapons. During the 1980s, the people of Argentina were terrorized by "disappearances" of teachers and doctors, students and mothers, each one wrenched from their home by government troops in the middle of the night, never to be seen again. Their only political "debate" was a weekly silent vigil by the mothers of

---

* From a speech given by Senator Robert Byrd in the US Senate on the same day as a key UN Security Council debate on the impending war with Iraq. Feb 12, 2003.

the disappeared in the central square of Buenos Aires. That governments and other groups resort to brutal strategies in war is without dispute. That it seems all too reasonable to do so without debate is also true.

After the attacks on September 11, 2001, Americans witnessed the speed with which war and democracy disconnect. The President declared "we are at war" that very afternoon, without either congressional advice or a consenting vote.* Within days, the United States Congress had endorsed spending $40 billion on combat and on reconstruction, pausing for only minimal discussion and resisted by a lone, dissenting Congresswoman voting "no." Strategic and tactical plans for the resultant war against the Taliban in Afghanistan were decided by the President and a small roomful of colleagues at Camp David, and funded, without challenge, by a Senate officially under the control of the opposition party.

When United States bombing began a few weeks later, the President stated explicitly that American citizens and other nations had only two choices: "You are either with us or against us." Protest, even doubt, were antithetical to patriotism. Then the Executive branch crafted a bill, The United States Patriot Act, which authorized bold restraints on freedom of association, on freedom of expression and on the right to privacy; Congress, allotting only one hour of committee hearings to the bill, approved it. The Act allowed the government to define mere associations among people as suspicious, with a direct loss of civil liberties for all, even

---

*This in direct violation of the US Constitution which declares that the right to declare war belongs to Congress. And yet I for one found it hard to disagree with him. After all, an attack, which destroys 20 percent of a nation's military headquarters, is surely a signal that the destroyers, at least, wish to start a war.

those not under suspicion. In a process alarmingly reminiscent of the McCarthy era during the Cold War, this assault on liberty was justified by conjuring up fear of attack from sinister, fanatical outsiders. America was at war.

Americans, believing themselves threatened by the Soviet Union and then by Iraq, surrendered liberties in return for a protective barrier erected and monitored by the government. War makes different demands in other cultures and other countries, but violence always requires that people surrender values they hold dear. The English shed their love for tolerance in World War I, as they physically tarred and feathered young men whose consciences prevented them going to the front. South Africans lost their birthright to citizenship under apartheid, because the government drove blacks and whites alike into exile for their refusal to support the regime. In Sarajevo, the people, who during the 1984 Olympic games had provided an admiring world with an exquisite portrait of multi-ethnic harmony had, by 1992, been impelled to espouse ethnic hatreds just to stay alive. Rwandan Hutu and Tutsi men and women who had intermarried were tortured into complicity in making evil choices, killing neighbors to earn the power to protect their own children, killing one child to save another.[2] Wars force on us practices we would never accept under other conditions. Those who protest will certainly suffer and many will die.[3]

And yet, for all its cruelties, war does more than take lives; it also adds depth to the lives of those who survive. Chris Hedges' book *War is a Force that Gives us Meaning* was aptly named.[4] Hedges is a journalist who did most of his work on the front lines. "War makes the world understandable; a black and white tableau of them and us. It suspends thought, especially critical thought. All bow before the supreme ef-

fort. We are one. Most of us willingly accept war as long as we can fold it into a belief system that paints human suffering as necessary for a higher good, for human beings seek not only happiness but meaning."[5] While Hedges knew, better than most, that huge numbers of those who experience the war in person will actually suffer dreadfully from its confusions and destructiveness, there are also many who because of the war discover a new meaning in their own existence. Comradeship in the midst of danger, and the realization that life itself is deeply valuable can be physically thrilling, and the self-respect that grows as people surmount the challenge ensures that, for many, going to war is not only morally right but also psychically rewarding.

If we think imaginatively enough, we all know that the reality of war is at least as likely to consist of weeping and vomiting, terror and woeful letters home, as it is to create opportunities for heroic action. And yet: "the myth of war creates a new artificial reality. Moral precepts—ones we have spent a lifetime honoring—are jettisoned. We accept, if not condone, the maiming and killing of others as the regrettable cost of war. We operate under a new moral code."[6] In war, those who reject that new code become the target of intemperate accusations of disloyalty, subversiveness, and even treason.[7] In the United States, the fountainhead of due process, debate seems antithetical amidst the urgencies of combat and danger. It is antithetical also to the practical realities of the protective, guardian state.

The rest of this chapter explores both of these issues in more general terms—the values that undergird the will for continued combat, and the political structures of wartime governments. Both of these are made urgent by the real risks that war brings down upon us.

The "will" of the enemy

That success in war depends on being guided by a special ethical code has been explicit since ancient times. The Bible describes the actual men and women who received the Ten Commandments, including the injunction not to kill, transforming themselves into an army that considered itself entitled to lay waste the entire city of Jericho. "Then they utterly destroyed all in the city, both men and women, young and old, oxen, sheep and asses, with the edge of the sword."[8] Harboring no doubts about the justice of their claim to the land of Canaan, and having labeled Jericho's existing occupants the enemy, the wandering Jews were free to ignore the sixth commandment,

"Thou shalt not kill." They were at war.

Carl von Clausewitz might well have applauded their thoroughness. He begins his description of the "purpose and means of war" by explaining that war's aim is to disarm a country, claiming that success depends on three factors: destruction of the enemy's forces, invasion of their territory and breaking the "enemy's *will*"[italics in the original].[9] He goes on to say that unless the will is broken, neither territorial conquests nor military defeats will persuade the enemy to seek a peace. This is the essence of the argument here: while it remains strong, the moral energy driving a war blocks the desire for peace. Its impediments arise both from the moral seductiveness of combat and from its coerciveness.

Tracking down Clausewitz's definition of "will" is not for the faint-hearted. He leaps from topic to topic; references to "courage," "hostility to the enemy," and "morals" can be found in widely scattered parts of the book. Furthermore, he alternates among the words "moral," "emotion," and "intellect" to characterize key components of will. Following Clausewitz this chapter addresses emotion and intellect, "hearts" as well as "minds." In the midst of violence, the seduction and coercion of war penetrate through our fears and yearnings, and also through our conceptual understanding of practical choices ahead. Indeed, while Western cultures tend to locate ethical considerations in the mind, others locate moral stamina in the belly and in the heart. In Japan, for example, core values emanate from a "rich heart."[10]

War is seductive when it draws out of people astonishing courage, deep commitment, physical stamina, razor sharp thinking, agility and prowess—qualities of heart, mind and body many people can barely imagine, let alone experience in peace-time.[11] War is seductive when they discover in themselves a transformative capacity to love someone else, a love that is cemented in the midst of danger. War is seductive because it gives each fighter permission to act directly and immediately on his own behalf, to take into his own hands the punishment of an enemy who has done him wrong.

But war is also coercive. Among soldiers any failure of courage or loyalty, any weakness, any refusal to take revenge on the enemy is grounds for punishment, both psycho-social and legal. Sufferers of post war trauma include those who actually did fail, or accuse themselves of having failed, of having lost the courage to fight and the desire to survive, and also those whose yearning to avenge the loss of loved ones simply faded. The military is harsh towards those who attempt to escape the duties they are allocated. Combatants on the front line can really punish those soldiers regarded as weak links in the battle hardened survival system. Civilians too can be brutal. They will report the family in the apartment next door to authorities for any suspicious behavior. Children are isolated at school as punishment for their peaceloving parents. My grandfather, a politician working in opposition to Hitler after his election as Chancellor, sent his children away from Germany rather than risk their becoming hostages used by the Nazis to compel his compliance with the regime. Wartime actions like these come to seem congruent within the ethical system on which combat depends.

Three specific moral attributes take on critical importance in dangerous times. They are a sense of honor, patriotic love and vengefulness. The three interweave to make war legitimate. All three were mentioned repeatedly by combatants in the seven cases I studied. Each one has been salient in cultures as varied as ancient Greece and Troy at the time of *The Iliad*, Japan during the Shogunate and contemporary Bedouin culture in Jordan. [12,13] A modern British general, with considerable combat experience, recently described the British variant: "In a real war it is the moral component which tends to predominate and history is lined with examples of armies that were both physically and conceptually superior to their opponents, but that were nevertheless decisively defeated by forces which attached a greater importance to the moral component of fighting power. In the British Army, this component has generally consisted of a mixture of a belief in a cause, loyalty to one's comrades, persuasion and compulsion." [14] Honor and patriotism surface everywhere when a war begins, but revenge lasts longest. Revenge impels onward those who reject peace-making, long after their sense of honor has been battered by the cruel realities of war, long after nationalist loyalties and patriotism have shriveled.

Honor

> In the normal man it is an absolutely normal impulse to move away from danger. Yet within an army it is recognized by all that personal flight from danger, where it involves dereliction of duty, is the final act of cowardice and dishonor.…Personal honor is the one thing valued more than life itself by the majority of men.[15]

Armies maintain codes of honor to confer on men both the entitlement to fight and the obligation to do so. Honor traditions vary quite widely from culture to culture, some compelling suicide for the cause, others centering on the capture of enemies, others on protecting their own side, but all armies instill this sense of honor on each front-line soldier as an individual. It becomes an embodied experience, ingrained through physical training. Soldiers build muscular stamina, marksmanship and technical skill knowing as they do so that they have become obligated to use these skills, that they are never to flinch under fire. Officers learn to command, and learn that they must never show any hesitation once battle is joined. Indeed it is honor that impels a nation to take up arms in the first place. President George Bush, arguing in 2003 for the war against Iraq, used the more modern word "resolve," but the word serves as the expression of almost identical meanings: both honor's sense of entitlement and its obligation to act. "Resolve" indicates the promise that the United States had made to itself and to the world to respond with force when called on.

Honor is seductive because it confers status. A man with resolve is clearly a man of standing. In the military, status is represented by medals, gold stars and a reputation for bravery. Sometimes the honor includes a title, and even in the egalitarian United States, the title endures even after retirement from the field. A sense of honor presses in with constant reminders that the soldier, the President and even the ordinary citizen have promised, even sworn an oath, to live up to their obligations. On what are these obligations founded? A sense of ownership. The country "belongs" to the President. The soldier loves "his" country. "My country 'tis of thee, sweet land of liberty, of thee I sing," as America's love song to itself goes. Each person as an individual is to feel the pride of ownership, and see in himself the embodiment of the whole. The President, of course, most of all.

But honor becomes particularly insistent when it, itself, is in danger. It is most coercive because of its deeply disturbing opposites, humiliation, shame and insult. Avoiding these is integral to maintaining the sense of honor. [16] Preempting the threat of humiliation is central to starting a fight.[17] In recent pre-war debates there has been some indication that, among NATO members, the United States was more responsive to the honor tradition than other nations. Germans were all too aware that dueling and calls to honor were central to their dangerous militarism in the last century.[18] The Dutch army even allows its soldiers to become members of a labor union. By contrast, the United States remained highly reactive to suggestions that the failure to go to war represented not wisdom but humiliating weakness.

Honor applies coercive pressures in part because it calls for timely responses to insult or attack. Shakespeare's Hamlet is agonized by his knowledge that honor delayed is honor lost. American newspaper coverage of the war in Bosnia in 1995 frequently referred to the United States as a nation whose honor was at risk because President Clinton seemed so hesitant about whether and how to intervene in that war. America was craven, our valor more in doubt than Serbia's, despite that army's military cruelty and ethnic cleansing; even more than Bosnia's, despite its repeated military defeats; certainly more than Croatia's, despite its evident desire for an ethnically pure state.[19] These other countries at least were willing to fight for their lives and hopes. The United State's failure to act to save the "innocent victims" placed this country in violation of essential obligations attendant on being a "super power."

If failure to respond to brutal attacks on an ally jeopardizes the right to honor, the dimensions of honor have recently begun to change for many nations. The honor of most other nations is more at risk because, with their participation in the UN Security Council, NATO, the Organization of Afri-can States, etc., each nation has acquired some obligation and entitlement to intervene.* UN forces often find themselves in a particularly invidious posi-tion in this regard. Their "rules of engagement" restrict the soldiers' right to use force, which is the tool on which the professional fighting man most depends to preserve his honor, to avoid becoming the target of insults. In Bosnia, insult and dishonor were a UN soldier's constant companion:

> The international community should understand clearly that the Bosnian Serbs are not only waging war against the Bosnian Government in Bihac, Mr. Myint-U said. "They are targeting UNPROFOR, detaining its personnel, and denying others essential supplies. This is a deliberately designed, care-fully calculated insult against the United Nations.[20]"

Peace-oriented interventions in war zones have created a particularly challenging modern version of the warrior's honor.[21] Honor has become most complex, quite different from the time when the notion was first imag-ined and it meant no more than the knight's obligation to his local feudal liege lord.

By 2003, war between the United States and Iraq, justified by both lead-ers as an honorable war, lay in a murky middle ground between the modern, internationalist and the ancient, private visions of honor. Originally justified, in 1991, as an intervention on behalf of "innocent" Kuwait, the UN assault was sanctioned by international support of the broadest kind. By 2003, the war had become a much more focused conflict between George Bush, leader of a super-power nation that had failed to bring about an uncontested vic-tory, and Saddam Hussein, the man who had refused from the very begin-ning to admit defeat. Each man quite obviously rejected the other's right to impose on him a humiliating failure.

To those for whom World War II remains a vivid story, the word "ap-peasement" offers perhaps the strongest evidence that honor and peace-making are each other's opposites. In the 1930s, Hitler's annexation of the Rhineland, Czechoslovakia and Austria passed without any significant

---

* In an odd reversal of this principle, the United States and Britain spent the early weeks of 2003 argu-ing that the United Nations risked its own "credibility" – that the UN was on the verge of humiliation because it was delaying the onset of war and perhaps even "appeasing" Saddam Hussein.

protest from other governments. This silence served to repudiate their presumptive obligation to stand up against the expansionist forces of Fascism. Neville Chamberlain, on his famous return from the Munich Conference about Czechoslovakia, spoke of "peace for our time." The passivity of British and other government leaders has come to be derided under its Churchillian appellation, "appeasement," and the ensuing, horrifying war against Hitler is widely assumed to have been made much worse because these leaders tried for too long to avoid a fight. "Appeasement" and "peace campaigner" now most often convey a weak-kneed refusal to act courageously when called.

But honor and peace-making are not the only opposites in wartime. As we have already seen in relation to peace activism during Vietnam, patriotism and a yearning for peace are also commonly perceived as contradictory.

Patriotism

> "For war, you need symbols to mobilize people, and for us nothing is better than history," commented Vesna Pusic, a sociologist at Zagreb University in the Croatian capital. "It is very convenient."
>
> Historian Milorad Ekmecic, a Bosnian Serb intellectual who now lives in Belgrade, the Serbian and Yugoslav capital, put it more starkly: "The history of nationalism starts as a children's fairy tale and finishes with Frankenstein monsters. This war wasn't designed—it was unleashed."[22]

If honor spurs men into fighting, and precludes leaders from evading the fight, then the protective loyalties of patriotism among civilians and strong intimate soldier-to-soldier bonds are among the reasons that war's experiences and memories can remain positive despite the carnage. The links among war, patriotism and death become tolerable in part because of what Barbara Ehrenreich calls "our human habit of sacralizing violence."[23] The passions of patriotism become endowed with deep spiritual significance, as in the Japanese commitment to State Shinto in World War II, the American devotion to the flag or Black South Africans fighting while singing their banned anthem, "Nkosi Sikelel' iAfrica."[24] The British need the right abstract "cause."[25] During the Cold War, a communist threat provided a comprehensive "cause" for American armed action. In recent years, the United State's claim to a historic role in liberal political development has sent the country's attentions towards what it calls "defense of democracy," and the protection of "innocent civilians." Above all, Americans fight on behalf of the "national interest."

The foundations of patriotic loyalties seem often to be laid very early. History, retold again and again as folk story, sets out essential constructs in stories about heroes, military groups and victorious battles. George Washington, King Arthur, Robert the Bruce, Peter the Great, the US flag above the ramparts, the Knights of the Round Table, the Battle of Culloden and the Siege of Leningrad are never to be forgotten. The heroes and the heroic moments may not even appear in the same stories as each other, but their combined resonance will carry forward until needed. Schools and families instill the images in spelling contests, in moral epigrams and even in playground games. National holidays reinforce the themes and then, during elections, political campaigners are shameless in their appropriation of patriotic symbols. Popular culture is also involved. John Wayne strode towards us in American movies of the 1950s and 1960s, the epitome of the rugged individualism that US armies fight to defend. To this day, Japanese television runs hugely popular historical samurai dramas as daily series, year round.

To make patriotism urgent, Slobodan Milosevic projected emotional appeals that Serbs avenge their historic losses at the battle of Kosovo 600 years earlier. Rwandan government officials turned to radio to urge criminal cruelty on their Hutu fellow citizens. The justification offered for their actions? Racial distinctions first given meaning a mere 100 years earlier by Belgian colonizers. Israeli settlers and Palestinian suicide bombers mark their

loyalties to the Torah and the Koran in written statements and in videos distributed widely among their most ardent supporters. Americans are devoted to the flag and students in our public schools say the pledge of allegiance every single day. Those who doubt that patriotism is coercive need only remember the feelings generated in classrooms when children refuse to participate in this ritual act. For adults, rising to sing the national anthem has a similar effect. If one stays seated, censuring looks come from all nearby; failing to place one's hand over the heart raises eyebrows. For those who do participate, the joy of choral singing can often create a small opportunity for a physically rousing experience.

More than most, we in the United States develop and maintain patriotic reflexes through school sports, both among the spectators and for the players on the team. Sporting contests are useful preparation for war because their physical scope makes a richly symbolic allegory for combat. Games teach participants to see competition as a territorial contest—the football player is trying to invade and ultimately score by penetrating his opponent's end zone. The winner of a distance race is entitled to consider the track his own, at least for the duration of the victory lap. And sporting stories inculcate values so well because they repeat themselves week after week, year after year, in every local paper in the country. "I liked swimming against him because of the tension of the race," Baumgartel said. "You know he's so good. You know he's there. It's an honor to compete against him."[26] Teams teach the young to surrender individuality to the community. Even tainted by rampant commercialism, professional sports offer constant reminders of this as an ethical ideal: "To make sure the players begin the season with a common purpose—winning—they planned a meeting prior to the full squad workout. It's reassuring that players who are earning millions of dollars are realizing the need to be thinking about playing together as a team."[27]

Games instill loyalty and facilitate its practice in repeated, usually annual, iterations of athletic rivalries. Local fans are expected to remain ardent, regardless of whether the team is winning. Indeed, if the team loses, then the prospect of another series of matches next year dulls the pain. No loyalist will settle for last place in perpetuity. The system extends to the international arena, in events like football's World Cup and the Olympic Games, which pit national dreams and aspirations against each other. During the Cold War, comparisons of aggregate medal counts became a surrogate venue for the ideological and military contest between Warsaw Pact nations and the United States. During the 2002 Football World Cup, Japan and Korea cohosted and also went into head-to-head competition in a startlingly complex re-enactment of their unresolved hostilities, the legacy of World War II. Since such values have been taught to children across an entire community, the militaries of the world can then take young men into the services, and all that remains is to teach them to convert patriotism into personal action.

In training new soldiers, the military imperative is to transform general loyalties into strong, direct bonds and commitments among all the members of a combat unit. Army training includes quite mundane mechanisms and yet the results have both seductive and coercive consequences, once in battle. The seductive parts bond soldiers closely into intimate and strong units. Interestingly enough, a substantial part of that is achieved in what one would call "domestic" arts, as the men are drilled in tending their uniforms, their barracks and their weapons.[28] Even cleaning a gun can begin to seem domestic, not unlike polishing a pair of boots to a brilliant shine. Thus a group of young men living and eating together construct bonds that resemble those in a college fraternity. Then they learn to be effective in a group, struggling through significant, physical challenges using non-verbal, synchronized action. This merges the fraternity bonds with the loyalties of a football team. Then they undertake risky maneuvers again and again, with assurances from their leader that they can make it only if they understand that the success of one depends on the success of all. These are the very same instructions given to corporate executives sent on challenge-based, team-building exercises. Together, the military unit scales the obstacle course; together it sweeps the bunk-room; together it traverses strange territory in the pitch dark, and eight weeks or so after they sign away their civilian rights, its members reemerge back into the culture as soldiers.

Since time immemorial, military forces have used these kinds of training strategies to create bonded relationships among young people, often among people who were complete strangers to each other until fighting began. The abstractions in their love of country, which spurred them into joining up in the first place, become tangible on the front line in their love for each other.

> "Near the front it was impossible to ignore the fact that out there were men who would gladly kill you if and when they got the chance. As a consequence, an individual was dependent on others, on people who could not formerly have entered the periphery of his consciousness. For them in turn, he was of interest as a center of force, a wielder of weapons, a means of security and survival. This confraternity of danger and exposure is unequaled in forging links among people…that are utilitarian and narrow, but no less passionate because of their accidental and general character."[29]

Beyond these intimate connections, many soldiers also maintain their loyalty to leaders and the greater cause. Passionate faith and adherence to the group can be made to endure as a result of a cult of personality—as carefully crafted by Nelson Mandela and Winston Churchill as by Saddam Hussein, Slobodan Milosevic, Yassir Arafat and Ariel Sharon.

The coercive features of military training include coming to realize that those who disobey orders will surely face military justice. Soldiers, whether conscripts or volunteers, have surrendered their right to decide for themselves whether or not they should fight. An IRA sympathizer in the North of Ireland or an American private stationed in Saudi Arabia knows he must stay on active duty until orders release him from the war zone. The generals and commanders who have armed these soldiers have the right to punish, even to put death, anyone who disobeys orders to kill.

By the time the fighting begins, most citizens, too, believe that they have lost the right to opt out. Unity comes before the individual conscience, and those who refuse to support the war may well be forced to leave. The labels that identify civilian resistors resonate with the suffering that awaits those whose patriotism fails: "refugee," "draft dodger," "exile," "stateless person." In most cases, the cost to a resister is immense: the loss of home, work and family contact. They may hope to protect life, limb and perhaps, an intact moral identity, but even that is uncertain.[30] For the majority who stay committed, the passion to fight on will be sustained by the urge to punish the enemy, every last one of those who have wrought such harm and destruction.

Vengeance

Attackers repeatedly shot the two at close range and riddled their vehicle with bullets.

At a memorial service for the slain settlers in Jerusalem, some mourners interrupted a rabbi's prayer with "Why don't you talk about revenge?"

"An eye for an eye!" said Yaffa Cohen, red-faced from anger and the stifling heat. Afterward, thousands joined in a funeral procession back to Itzhar for the burials.[31]

As the news media show, almost obsessively, an untimely death demands vengeance. An attack by a suicide bomber in Israel/Palestine, the murder of

危

a South African policeman, the downing of an American helicopter in a Somali city, or an assault on a Chechen village instantly prompt an outcry. Vengeance is integral to the will to fight, becoming more and more heated with each enemy action.

In exploring honor and patriotism, I have argued that they are hard to resist because of a combination of seductive and coercive forces. Vengeance, too, is hard to resist—also coercive, also seductive, but powerful as well for another reason. Vengeance is visceral. Its clamorous cry is a reflex reaction, which bursts out when the devastating news first arrives. The desire for retribution is not particularly hard to explain. If your child is dead, or your gunner's mate riddled by a hail of bullets out of the dark, if you come home to find your village obliterated, or your hand is amputated, life is forever changed. The urge for justice rushes in, in a torrent. Victims yearn for punishment to restore their own wellbeing, in the hopes that it will repair the specific damage that has been done. Some damage is personal, but in a war even the most deeply grieving parent is likely, also, to want justice for the sake of the civic order as a whole. Hamlet was plagued by a double call to action, personal grief over the death of his father, and a civic order that depended on him to punish the usurper king, Claudius. Ultimately Hamlet succeeded, but only at the expense of his own life, and that of many others as well. Even ordinary citizens have an obligation to the civic order. That is why so many hurry off to volunteer for service whenever a war breaks out.

That is also why, when Churchill announced that he had "nothing to offer but blood, toil, tears and sweat," the people of England seemed undaunted. They worked for five long years to keep the civic order of the country intact, an order whose symbol was the nightly BBC broadcast announced by the chimes of Big Ben striking 9:00pm from the tower above the Houses of Parliament. And night after night, in the planes flying out to attack Germany once more, new widows sent off their right to revenge for their dead husbands. Franklin Roosevelt's words describing Pearl Harbor as a "day of infamy" are repeated at every commemorative event. "Th[at] attack inspired a thirst for revenge among Americans that the Japanese...had failed to anticipate."[32] Proof that the United States would not leave the attacks of September 2001 unavenged echoed in the repeated reminders that this was Pearl

Harbor all over again.*

The language and feeling of revenge were intense in each of the seven wars I studied. In the North of Ireland, as combat was ending, militia men spoke out against the peace:

> The majority of the people of the UK want nothing to do with us, because they think that all our fighting and arguing has been trivial…But what if they had to endure 25 years of what we've had to stand here, our loved ones taken away, bombed out of existence.[33]

And then the cease-fire in Ireland was broken by yet more deaths.

> In claiming responsibility for the attack at a nightclub in the Glengannon Hotel late Saturday, the Loyalist Volunteer Force vowed yesterday to step up its campaign to avenge the assassination of its leader, Billy Wright, by Irish Republican inmates inside Northern Ireland's top-security prison.[34]

When United States assaults rained down on Iraq during the embargo years, the Iraqi government committed itself to respond in almost identical terms.

> Saddam Hussein vowed today to avenge Iraqis who died in the southern city of Basra, apparently victims of a stray American missile.
> "Your blood will not be shed in vain," he said in a message to the city's people. "Be patient, as victory is achieved through patience."[35]

Chechens fighting the Russians for control of their small republic dispelled despondency about their ultimate fate by focusing on the vengeance they would wreak before their forces fell to the Russians for the last time:

> "You Westerners always want to know how we will win this war," said Khamzat Aslambekov, deputy commander of the Chechen battle group that is spread out across the hills 40 miles southwest of Grozny. "There is no winning. We know that. If we are fighting, we are winning. If we are not, we have lost. The Russians can kill us all and destroy this land. Then they will win. But we will make it very painful for them."[36]

Ancient stories abound with examples of gods and mortals using

---

* The two events were said also to be similarly unprovoked attacks, which came quite out of the blue. In truth, neither can be described this way. America and Japan had been trading threats and ultimata for months prior to the December 7 raid. The US government had even exchanged fire with Al Quaeda, responding to the attacks on the American embassies with cruise missile attacks on bin Laden's alleged support bases in Afghanistan and the Sudan.

vengeance as the means to repair a damaged civic order, *thémis* to the Greeks. Since it is no longer really permissible, in the context of Western legal traditions overtly to be seeking vengeance, after the September attacks on the United States the President repeatedly assured the nation and the world that America was interested only in "justice" and not in revenge.[37] Still, whether it is called justice or revenge, the urge to react to an attack with an equivalent response seems almost impossible to deflect, a reliable justification for continued combat. Revenge will block the search for peace, even after honor and patriotism have begun to lose their luster, tainted by the horror and carnage. That very horror and carnage simply re-enflame the yearning for vengeance, as yet another bomb falls, and still more people are killed.

This yearning for a sense of justice must be tamed and refocused to bring about the true end of a war. It is one of the critical nodes around which peace-making revolves. Nelson Mandela and his compatriots in South Africa stand out, among the leaders of the seven wars in this book, for the extent of their consideration of justice as part of peace. While most combatants ending war release their prisoners, South Africans managed much more. They transformed the yearning for justice from a wind whipping the flames of war into a search for memories and stories that could anchor the commitment to peace. And South Africa stands out, also, as the one war in the seven that is truly over, the apartheid regime gone for good. Although the country is by no means tranquil, even after nine years of the new government, the old apartheid-centered war is no more. Revenge and justice go hand in hand in war. They are equally critical to peace.

Let me end these rather generalized descriptions of the attributes that foster resilience in war by rephrasing them as actions. People at war value courage over cowardice. They demand, and their survival depends on, a shared love of community, and on each soldier's loyalty to his military unit. Very quickly, sometimes within hours, ordinary people long for violent responses because they need to avenge their pain, to assuage the passionate desire to punish those who have done harm and to honor those who have lost their lives.[38] These values sustain the will to fight. They are implacable and they sharply constrict peace-time democratic virtues: dissent and debate, freedom of information and freedom of movement.

Guardianship and government

Citizens of a community under threat allow their "guardians" remarkable civil powers, even if some concede the powers hesitantly. While unity and patriotism provide the overarching ethical justification, successful war-time controls demand secrecy and censorship in place of free access to information, widespread surveillance and spying instead of privacy and freedom of association, and public lies about events and policies. Decisions in war follow hierarchical lines of command; economic costs and profits from military actions are simply ignored until after the war is over. These are the pivotal features of a guardian state. The citizens trade rights to their leadership in return for a promise that the dangerous enterprise on which they are embarking will not be needlessly dangerous, and that the cause that they pursue is just.

In Western political writing about the state, the notion of the guardian dates back to Plato, but this part of my analysis draws most heavily on more recent work, in particular Jane Jacobs' *Systems of Survival.* In that book, Jacob articulates that there exists a sharp contrast between the ethics of "commerce" and the ethics of "guardianship," which includes police work and war.[39] When a state or other political entity is performing its protective functions, it will base its decisions on guardianship principles—secrecy, power and reckless expenditure—each of which is in direct opposition to the standards necessary for trade. (1) Jacobs contrasts the willingness to lie for the sake of the cause, which is embedded in all military strategy, with the honesty essential for enduring contractual agreements. (2) She describes a strong system of command hierarchy and patronage, which would place an intolerably burdensome limitation on the individual initiative essential to commerce. (3) Perhaps most startling, Jacobs contends that loyalty becomes the key determinant in relationships rather than financial profit.

The United States Constitution provides a striking embodiment of these dual purposes of the state. The President is both "Chief Executive" who manages the peacetime government focused on commerce, and also "Commander in Chief," leader of the armed forces in time of war. Similarly, wartime changes everything about the way in which information is collected and disseminated. Propaganda is normal and although the Vietnam War created the impression that journalists routinely visit the front, Vietnam was the exception rather than the rule. Indeed, until the invention of satellite media connections, news from far away was always delayed and news of battles has long been censored. When a reporter like Chris Hedges ventures, unauthorized, into the battle zones, he does so at risk of life and limb. Most newsmen affiliate with officially sanctioned "media pools" to visit the front line troops, the modern system for ensuring war-time censorship. Since the United State's invasion of Grenada under Ronald Reagan, the American government has restricted all press movement in the vicinity of troops in action, trading access to a sanitized story in return for compliance with the official description of the war. [40] Like the citizens at home, the press trades its freedom in return for military protection and guaranteed access to at least one story a day.

The information that flows from war zones is controlled. So, too, is the amount of privacy to which citizens are entitled. Check-points and baggage searches, invasive background checks for employees, and the maintenance of security dossiers on the merest suspicion of disloyalty have long been a part of life in other war zones. [41] El Al, the Israeli airline, has refused to carry passengers whose profile it distrusts, compulsorily rebooking them on other airlines. The British police, searching for bombs, scan the underside of cars entering critical buildings with long-handled mirrors. Public office buildings simply deny entrance to the citizenry they supposedly serve. And where the right to privacy fails, censorship is nearby. Mail from the front is of course controlled, but there are other, less visible restrictions as well. In the aftermath of September 11, the United States Federal Government, in a massive retreat from the precedents set by the Freedom of Information Act, withdrew huge amounts of government agency material recently published on the World Wide Web. And none of this leaves its instigators with a sense of shame. After all, success in war depends on secrecy.

While systems of hierarchy and command also exist in peace-time, guardianship depends on more than a chain of authority. It depends on patronage as well. One reason the media barely raise a murmur of protest about restrictions on their access to stories is that they know that the guardians control information absolutely and will grant none to those who protest. Patronage will keep some young men who are otherwise eligible for combat away from the front lines. Patronage means that those who allocate civilian resources, whether housing or oil shipments or post-war reconstruction contracts, acquire enormous power. And these systems of patronage reward loyalty first. In a country at war, loyalty matters more than merit. Loyalty is also more critical than economic prudence.

Budgets for spying and "homeland security" increase dramatically in war, and official patterns of secrecy mean that no one will know how much. Military budgets are even more significant for what they tell us about the changed priorities of a guardian state. Despite the fears among cynics that leaders go to war to generate profits for military equipment corporations, much more striking is the economic reality that governments spend money for battle without any of the normal political debates about the long-term consequences and costs. While windfall profits accruing to military equipment corporations in wartime reap condemnation, no challenge is ever mounted that a war will threaten factories and transportation, or take money away from civilian education and health. Jane Jacobs is right. Guardian behaviors cannot be subjected to commercial considerations. A secret must stay a secret in war, no matter how much money a department or an individual could make by selling it.[42]

While I have been writing of the "guardian" state as though it were strictly a top-down entity, in war ordinary people participate as active and not merely submissive subjects. To a startling degree, individuals accept the constraints on their civilian rights, and when joining the military they discover themselves quite capable of doing concrete harm and injury to other people in ways they would consider abhorrent in peace. In wartime ordinary people kill total strangers.[43] Governments and voters spend vast amounts of their shared wealth, their tax revenues, on weapons and soldiers. They place at risk their factories, their houses and even their irreplaceable cultural treasures, because inflicting losses on others and withstanding them oneself make it possible to determine the outcome of the war. Guardianship serves not only to mobilize political institutions but also to build readiness to do and accept damage in the hearts and minds of ordinary people.

The pattern was similar in all seven cases. South Africa reveals how the web of war entangles one and all. On one side, young Black South Africans went off into the bush to learn to infiltrate White areas and leave car bombs behind to kill and maim. On the other side the television journalists reported stories fed to them by the police, knowingly making false accusations of terrorism against teenagers, some of whom were lured into protest groups by the police themselves. The policemen, in turn, were being rewarded by their seniors for reaching their quota of "kills." When the entire web fell apart after the collapse of the apartheid government, the Truth and Reconciliation Commission made visible for all to see the mutually reinforcing patterns of brutality and cruelty perpetrated by fathers and mothers, church-goers and teachers.[44] And much as one might wish otherwise, when a war looms, the first reaction among many young people, men in particular, is to join in, not to escape.

By the end of the last century, the internationalization of global interactions allowed idealists to begin to dream that human institutions might have become so "humane" that most peoples would no longer respond like the armies at Jericho. Multinational agencies including the United Nations have fostered collaboration over economic development and world health, and the International Criminal Court at The Hague now promises to punish those who violate what may perhaps be new social norms. Seen in this worldview, collective decision-making embodies the hope that the whole world shares a respect for human rights and for the settlement of disputes by peaceful means.

A similar vision of global harmony has begun to emanate from modern economic systems as well. The blueprint for the perfect form of contemporary global capitalism, in which there are no impediments in the relationships between producers and consumers, contains an assumption that worldwide there is a shared sense of value and work. Many corporations in fact have a huge interest in preventing war, because combat is so profoundly disruptive to world trading and financial patterns. The WTO and the economic facets of the European Union depend on a shared ethical framework, based on trust in the common acceptance of market rules, property rights and a widely accepted series of methods for resolving conflicts.[45]

And yet, despite both global political idealism and the commercial imperatives, the evidence remains inescapable that nation states exist to protect their people, and most have preserved their will to fight. War was still so common in the 1990s that more than 5 million people died worldwide.[46] Neither international organizations nor international trade had managed to assert persuasively that war was aberrant behavior. Indeed, power over when and how to go to war remained one of the most obvious attributes of a sovereign government. Furthermore, dissident communities still regularly depended on violence to achieve the political readjustments they sought. The authority to decide to go to war rests in a very small group of people in every guardian state; it is they who demand that we take these risks, while the leaders themselves remain at the top of the hierarchy, protected from danger. Risk itself shapes both the ethics and government of a war-torn community.

Risk and war

Risk is an important reason why war's efforts cannot be calibrated according to cost-benefit criteria. Survival in war depends on wisdom, speed and luck. In war there is too little time for the lengthy process of building a public consensus and, as in most kinds of crisis, ordinary people turn to expert knowledge for reactions fast enough to prevent a bad situation getting worse. And everyone depends on the right kind of luck. But risk does not fade when peace-making begins. Clausewitz was right. The outcome of war is at least one third chance. So is the outcome of peace-making.

Risk constrains two important features of wars and their endings. The first, which has ethical dimensions, I call triage. This assumes that in risky times, special criteria must be used to prioritize options. The second I call gambling, which encourages guardians to keep tight hold on their protective function. After all, with one more try, one last try, one can "win it all." Social theorists Mary Douglas, Aaron Wildavski and Alan Teger have been particularly helpful in allowing me to understand the choices in risky times.[47] But it is Clausewitz who, once again, shows so clearly their specific applications to war.

Triage—In crises ranging from famine to war, one finds widespread acceptance of prioritizing the protection of the leadership. If this lowers the priority placed on the lives and livelihoods of ordinary people, so be it. Indeed, the authorities, basing their actions on judgements analogous to medical prioritizing during an emergency, are themselves the ones who will decide what to sacrifice for the sake of the group. "A community [suffering famine] switches from its *regular* set of moral principles to its *regular* emergency set. The emergency is not an abrogation of all principles…On the contrary, the emergency system starts with a gradual narrowing and tightening of distributive principles…Protecting those in command and those already advantaged results in the skeletal institutions being preserved and channels of communication kept open…[T]he preordained victims meekly accept their fate."[48] [*Italics added*] Thus risk combines with the core ethics of war—honor, patriotism and revenge—to ensure that those most likely to suffer in a war will also, quite likely, easily accept their fate.

Americans spent 2003 in the midst of political and economic triage driven by war. State governments cut health benefits to poor patients in clinics, at the very same time the Federal government was requiring the states to divert large parts of their remaining funds to a smallpox vaccination program to mitigate a hypothetical bio-terrorist attack. Local school boards, like the one in Portland Oregon which cut 20 days from the schedule, were sacrificing the learning year for children while the military received much more money for training. A very stark example of such triage emerged from the compensation system designed to settle affairs with the victims of September 11. The plan was designed in the first instance to protect commercial airlines, since air travel is integral to almost every aspect of American life. Once they were safe, the plan metamorphosed into triage for the surviving relatives of the dead, who would receive payments proportionate to their prior income. Stock brokers were to get millions, janitors, a few thousand. The survivors of another catastrophic bombing, that of the Federal Building in Oklahoma City in 1995, would get nothing. After all, they were not victims of a war.[49]

Triage enables fighting to continue because those who lead the war are the least likely, personally, to suffer or die. Even in earlier times, when kings and commanders rode into battle with their men, they commanded from the rear, from a hill above the fray. With satellite communications, nowadays commanders can be hundreds of miles from the front. American political leaders have almost always been oceans away. From safety, confident of their right to decide, and in defiance of the uncertainties of war, US Presidents deployed forces worldwide in the Cold War for more than 40 years, kept troops in Korea for more than 50 years, drafted men for combat in SE Asia for more than 10 years, and kept fliers bombing Iraqi territory for 12  years. Although comments would surface occasionally, about whether a President had enough military experience himself to understand the risks to which he subjected front line troops, no one suggested, after George Washington's days, that the members of the political leadership who control when to make peace should endanger themselves at all. Safely ensconced in Washington DC, the private incentives to make peace were small. Indeed, if the war is failing, leaders who make peace too early risk their own political futures. George Bush the younger, watching his father's electoral defeat, learned directly the political costs of peace-making.

Gambling—Risk as gambling also impedes peace-making. No matter how well planned the strategy, no matter how efficient the logistics, all combat is a gamble whose real outcome is bound to differ from the plans on the drawing board. And social researchers have observed that gamblers, once they pass the stage where losses are greater than winnings, once their holdings have fallen even a small amount below the resources with which they began, will refuse to quit until their resources are close to exhausted.[50] Wars go on, even if defeat seems almost inevitable, until conditions have become remarkably desperate. The payoffs and risks of war contain so many uncertainties. A big, decisive turning point, a jackpot, never seems completely impossible.[51] While history textbooks are arranged to show that battles and wars unfold towards an inexorable outcome, wartime choices are considerably more ambiguous in day-to-day experience. Thus the notion that one more push for victory, one more battle, one more bombing run or one more naval engagement will turn the tide, is easy to believe. The Chechen "rebels" lost and regained the city of Grozny more than once. Palestinians mounted ever more dramatic bombings in the heart of Jerusalem despite tight border controls between Israel and the occupied territories. The February 1996 IRA bombing at Canary Wharf in London, a full 18 months after some in the Republican movement thought the time had come to seek a peace, was the biggest explosion in that war. And after Canary Wharf, the forces for violence once again controlled the agenda for over a year.

As Clausewitz puts it: "this noble capacity, to rise above the most menacing dangers, should also be considered a principle in itself, separate and active. Indeed, in what field of human activity is boldness more at home than war?...It is the very metal that gives edge and luster to the sword." Clausewitz lauds boldness over careful calculations about "space, time and magnitude of forces." He even understands that "in a commander, a bold act may be a blunder. Nevertheless, it is a laudable error." In the very next chapter he commends the refusal to accept defeat. "In a war more than anywhere else, things do not turn out as we expect...If a [commander] were to yield to the [countless] pressures, he would never complete an operation. *Perseverance* in the chosen course is the essential counterweight...Moreover, there is hardly a worthwhile enterprise in war whose execution does not call for infinite effort, trouble and privation" [*italics in the original*].[52]

In the gamble called war, suggestions that it is time to seek peace ring of premature defeatism more than a sensible cutting of losses. Above all, weakened leaders receiving settlement "offers" face the same choice that confronts the gambler down to his last few coins: quit with virtually nothing in one's pockets, nothing left to bargain with, or wager one more time in the hopes that this one will make the big payoff. And the payoff often comes. Leaders of the IRA, the African National Congress, Iraq, the Croatian Serbs, the Chechens and the Palestinians each know that they wagered yet another hope, against apparently overwhelming odds, and in doing so postponed, and in some cases altered the outcomes of their struggles.

Risk and peace-making

Strategizing and mobilizing to use violence to achieve a particular political outcome and seeing the government as a "guardian" represent facets of the ability to function in the special civic and ethical framework of war. Sadly we cannot call war an "abnormal" condition; it is merely an altered state of mind and heart and nation, made coercive by war's risks to life, land and community. When the decision to fight is justified as " no price is too high" the combatant community is obligated to sustain the resilience to fight on.[53]

A return to peace would almost certainly be easier, if peace-making itself were risk free. But it is not. Bringing former enemies together in the same room to find their agreements about the future allocation of powers and resources is hard enough. But the peace-making process takes place in the midst of the lingering pain of war—the pain of broken bodies and broken buildings; the pain of hunger and unemployment; the pain of anguished consciences, remembering their own brutal acts and the acts they failed to prevent. And peace-making itself is a highly risky process. Those who take it on face retribution from those who want more war. Those who fail to prevent more war risk their own political futures.

Last but not least, peace-making, like war, takes a very long time to complete. I spent eight years working on this project, during which I was witness to pivotal efforts on behalf of peace in each of the seven wars featured in this book. Sadly, I often saw concerted efforts in every one of the cases to cut off the peace-making process, to turn all sides back to war. With the exception of South Africa, none of the peace-making processes has ended, and even there people and institutions continue to be haunted by the memories and the pain of the apartheid regime. And yet, despite the long-term precariousness of their efforts, in each one of these stories of peace-making there were chances to end a war. Sometimes suddenly and sometimes only for a few crucial moments, leaders began taking meaningful steps towards peace, setting aside honor, patriotism, vengeance and fear in favor of trade, peace and trust.

In the stories that follow, the popular will for peace rarely makes an appearance. There will be a brief comment about a referendum in Ireland, and perhaps a few images of streets full of people in Jerusalem and in Omagh and in Belgrade, people brought together by their shared dismay at a particular threat of a return to war. My descriptions of the search for postwar justice in The Hague, in Rwanda and in South Africa will refer to the lives and fates of ordinary men and women, and the impact they can have on peace. But, for the most part the public's position will be hard to discern in this book.

The public will is also hard to discover in real life, at least in those first few moments when someone cracks open the door from war to peace. It was leaders who gave the orders for violence in the first place. They enforced the ethical and political climate that silenced the doubters. So, by the end of a long war, few ordinary people can believe that they have any say about whether and how the combat unfolds. They will have been living as spectators to their own fates, most of them anxiously awaiting those first crucial signs that the leaders have begun finally to walk towards peace.

In countries where citizens exercise a right to participate in politics, one of the surest strategies available if faced with the prospect of war is democracy's version of the pre-emptive strike—the vote. If the chance to vote has disappeared, as it often does when war actually looms, what remains is an openhearted mindfulness towards the suffering during the war, and an active participation in the peace-making process once the leaders allow it to begin.

In none of the seven peace-making stories to come will I describe every detail, every factor that might bring that war to an end. Instead, in each story you will encounter some of the pivotal people, you will follow them to their meeting places and watch them as they explore the ground on which to build hope for more tranquil times. Both opportunity and danger shadow their every move. Peace-making, like war, proceeds in the midst of crisis. But every war does end.

"Peace is Inevitable."

ALTERED STATES

Seven wars, seven peace journeys

The time has now come to explore peace-making as it evolved in seven quite different parts of the world. Though these places are widely spread geographically, their attempts at peace-making took place within the same span of years—1990-2000. These peace-making endeavors, as I describe them in the stories that follow, were focused on a number of critical issues:

Bosnia—The boundary lines, which would forcibly resettle into separate ethnic communities millions of people whose lives had once been intermingled geographically, emotionally and economically.

Israel/Palestine—Whether each of the two sides could bring themselves to accept coexistence in close proximity to the other on land over which each held a seemingly absolute and sacred claim.

South Africa—Management of the transition from an apartheid government based on racial oppression to a government enabling Black majority control, and healing wounds from centuries of colonization and decades of violence.

The North of Ireland—Discerning whether and on what terms to include groups with a history of violence that had long been excluded from political power in new governing institutions.

Chechnya—Peace-making between a major power and a very small, breakaway region, the pace and timing of negotiations and renewed violence largely set by one party's internal domestic power struggles.

Rwanda—Finding a way to end a war of genocidal proportions in which the winners were the victims of the genocide, leaving all parties facing huge questions about the relationship between justice and peace.

Iraq—A war that did not end despite official assumptions that it was over, thereby demonstrating the power of the weaker side to set terms for the future, and the importance of actively engaging with the enemy if one seeks to make peace.

At the time, each one of the peace-making efforts was much more complex than even the longer sketches to come can cover. The elements included in each story were necessary to enable peace to deepen but not sufficient to ensure it stabilized. More than 13 years have passed since the first efforts began in South Africa, and more than 10 years since the signing of the Oslo Accords for Israel and Palestine. Even the most recent official settlement, namely the Good Friday Agreement for the North of Ireland, is more than five years in the past. And, with the exception of the ending of the war between apartheid and the Black communities of South Africa, none of the wars has ended definitively.

One cannot even write a definitive statement about current levels of warfare in each of the different regions. As this manuscript goes to press, the most dangerous war is unquestionably underway in Iraq, where thousands of pounds of bombs are dropping every day while invading ground forces from several nations advance on Baghdad. Had the book gone to press two weeks earlier, Israel/Palestine would have received the label "most dangerous." At different times during their respective peace-making endeavors, each one of these regions was afflicted by disasters of dangerous proportions, and at others it was the recipient of skilled and eloquent actions and pleas for peace. The two sometimes happened within days of each other, as for example in Israel/Palestine, where the assassination of Yitzhak Rabin was followed by powerful public pleas for peace from his widow.

In each effort at peace-making there were moments when particular events resembled or connected to events in another part of the world. I have marked such links as they are mentioned and the chapter following these narratives lays out the patterns they share in common. Still, there was no one pattern that determined exactly how each one of these war stories would evolve. Chance was everywhere, in the making and unmaking of peace. Take each story as no more than one version of events as they actually happened, and merely one of thousands of versions of events that might have happened had danger and opportunity interacted slightly differently in these few crucial moments.* The key interactions, however, repeatedly involved the same people and the same issues: the leaders and their negotiations about power and resources, and about destruction, repair, refugees and justice. Every action included at least some degree of choice among the participants. Ending a war is, above all, a matter of choice.

---

* See the comments on the Note on Styles pages, which explain the selection of "some key dates", and the placement of footnotes in each of these stories.

bosnia

SOME KEY DATES   CEASE-FIRE DECEMBER 1995

1991 June 25 • Slovenia and Croatia declare independence from Yugoslavia. Germany and then the European Union recognize the independence. War breaks out.

1992 Feb. 29 • Bosnia / Herzegovina declares independence from Yugoslavia and their war begins.

April • Siege of Sarajevo starts.

June • UN peace-keeping troops arrive to protect Sarajevo airport to allow the transport of humanitarian supplies.

1993 • Bosnian voters overwhelmingly reject the peace plan proposed by UN mediators Cyrus Vance and David Owen.

1994 Feb. • Serb artillery attacks the Sarajevo marketplace. NATO issues ultimata, which lead to retaliatory bombing.

1995 Jan. • Cease-fire negotiated by President Jimmy Carter goes into effect.

May • Cease-fire breaks down.

July • Serbs capture Srebrenica.

Serbs capture Zepa.

UN War Crimes Tribunal indicts Bosnian Serb leaders Radovan Karadzic and Gen. Ratko Mladic for genocide and crimes against humanity.

Aug. • Croatians drive Serb forces and Serb residents out of Croatia.

NATO planes attack Serb forces.

Oct. 11 • Sixty-day cease-fire begins to allow for negotiations.

Nov. • Negotiators arrive in Dayton.

Nov. 21 • Accords announced.

Dec. 14 • In Paris, the Presidents of Bosnia, Serbia and Croatia sign Dayton Accords.

1996 Jan. • First prisoner exchanges.

Feb. 4 • Serbs withdraw their forces from Sarajevo.

1999 May • War Crimes Tribunal issues an indictment against Slobodan Milosevic.

THE WAR IN BOSNIA

Mediation and bombs, technology and peace

Wright Patterson Air Force Base is just outside Dayton, Ohio. With hangers, planes and dozens of anonymous buildings, it is a huge complex, and neither it, nor the city of Dayton, nor the surrounding countryside are ever likely to be ranked among America's most famous tourist or government attractions. Nonetheless, in November 1995, Wright Patterson was selected to serve as temporary guesthouse and negotiating center for the warring Presidents of Bosnia, Croatia and Serbia. They spent three weeks in Dayton talking, giving and taking, struggling to generate an enduring cease-fire so that peace could to begin to take hold in the Balkans, a region devastated by four years of war. When the talks were through, Dayton, like Versailles and Potsdam, even gave its name to the agreements made there, the Dayton Accords.*

Discerning the right setting in which to bring key leaders or their surrogates together to talk peace is one of dozens of fraught decisions that must be made before anyone can even begin to engage the substantive issues that end a war. In the 1960s, Americans and Vietnamese spent months in Paris arguing over the shape of the main negotiating table before they settled in for years of good food and fruitless "peace talks." Wright Patterson had none of the creature comforts of Paris; nor did it resonate with status comparable to the Presidential retreat at Camp David where Jimmy Carter ensconced the Israelis and Egyptians to make their peace.

Still, for Balkan leaders whose central struggles were over land, what Wright Patterson offered was equally valuable. It offered equipment and technology, primarily mapping systems and satellite data, which made laying

---

* The word "accord" has no particular meaning in international law, and is therefore a much safer term for a preliminary agreement than the word "treaty." It will come up again in other stories about attempts to make peace.

out possible frontier lines and territorial claims quick and easy. The National
Air Intelligence Center had the computers and wall-sized displays to demon-
strate the consequences of each decision they made about the smallest details
of the layout of towns, roads and river crossings. In addition, lest anyone
doubt America's seriousness, the same technology proved beyond doubt that
America's military could easily gather the necessary information, should the
United States decide to "force" the opposing sides into an agreement.

The full, official name of the Dayton Accords, The Balkan Proximity
Peace Talks Agreement, serves as a reminder that the war they were trying to
end had spread across a whole region, well beyond Bosnia proper. Confrontations between Croatia and Serbia over land in Croatia had contributed
critical tensions. The Serbs, fighting to unify all Serbs within a single territorial unit, attacked Croats; later the Croats retaliated, aiming to clear Croatian
villages of all Serb residents. The last major attacks before negotiations began
involved all three groups: Croatians, Serbs and Bosnians. The final settlements at Dayton crafted boundaries for Croatians and Serbians as well as for
Bosnians.

The negotiators arrived at Wright Patterson to begin their talks on November 1, 1995. They lived in a small quadrangle of red brick houses, meeting in formal negotiating sessions, and also more casually at the base officers'
club and in a local bar. The three Presidents of Croatia, Bosnia, and Yugoslavia mingled with American mediators and military men and a larger group
of diplomats from Russia, Germany, France and the United Kingdom. By the
time they were done, the governing powers, land and resources of Croatia
and Bosnia had been allocated anew, and plans were in place to separate the
warring armies. The ending of four years of killing and terror-driven forced
evacuations had begun.

When, in Dayton, the negotiators made decisions about land, about who
would get which piece and where, and where exactly the boundary lines
would be drawn, they were working from the realities of military deployments on the ground. Each side had already lost lands they coveted.
Bosnians, Croatians and Serbs came to the table well aware that in the talks
they could lose still more. The final allocations were complicated, because the
situation on the ground was complicated. Every mile mattered.

Inside Bosnia, the core of Bosnian government-held territory was triangle shaped with its base along the western border with Croatia. Serbs held
a wide strip of land on each of the other two sides of the Bosnian government triangle. Within this broad outline there remained truly contested areas: Sarajevo, Brcko, the corridor to Gorazde, Bihac and Eastern Slavonia.
Miles and miles of internal boundary lines required specification to locate,
precisely, the edges of the new country to be called The Federated States of
Bosnia. Croats feared they might not get Slavonia back. Bosnians feared that
long-standing military divisions on the ground in Sarajevo would be hardened into permanent frontiers, breaking their capital city in two. Serbs feared
that Brcko would be handed to the Bosnian government, severing the roads
and connections between the two wings of Serbian-held land inside the Federation. Despite such concerns, in Dayton each side had reason to believe it
was talking in considerably more positive military circumstances than had
been the case a year earlier, when all sides had agreed to an abortive cease-fire
in December 1994.

One of the challenging features of peace-making is to discern the difference between a real opportunity for peace, and a seemingly similar event
which will not bear fruit. There certainly were people who said, the moment
the 1994 agreement was announced, that it would not hold, that former
President Jimmy Carter had mediated a tactical, not a final agreement. But
the clearest indication that it would not hold was to be found on the ground.
The dispositions at the time of Carter's mission satisfied no one. The 1994
cease-fire turned out to be no more than a four month interruption in the
fighting. The winter break offered an opportunity to regroup, and a respite
from mountain combat during the cold winter months.

Croats in Croatia, Bosnian Croats and Bosnian government forces in
Bosnia and Serbs in Bosnia used the summer after Carter's cease-fire collapsed to grab an astonishing amount of land. While no American would
consider the parcels large, everyone on the ground could see their strategic
and their emotional significance. Government troops and Croats in Bosnia
recaptured land on the western frontier, driving up through Bihac and
threatening a key Serb-held city, Banja Luca. Croats forced the Serbs out of
the Krajina region of Croatia, but the Serbs kept important negotiating

powers by managing to hold on in the eastern-most province of Croatia, Eastern Slavonia. Meanwhile, Bosnian Serbs captured Zepa and Srebrenica, cities that had been designated UN controlled "safe havens." The Serbs were never likely to concede either of these two cities, long term, to governments other than their own. Meanwhile, Bosnian government forces were pushing northeast towards the apex of their own triangle, and they came close to cutting Serbian-held land in half. The tiny maps that appeared in American newspapers throughout the war were much too small to allow most outsiders to understand how much the final months of the war altered the territorial realities and aspirations of all sides.

The layout of forces on the land was not the only new military reality. Another feature was NATO's willingness, for the second time, to intervene directly on behalf of the Bosnian government to clear Serbs from some of their remaining strongholds. American mediator Richard Holbrooke arrived from America on August 15, allegedly to bring peace, and yet NATO's bombers began their attack on the Serbs besieging Sarajevo very soon afterwards. Once again, peace-making demonstrates its uncertainties. NATO's earlier bombing mission, in early 1994, had virtually no impact at all on the fighting. The bombers in 1995 helped lift the siege of Sarajevo, but then so did Holbrooke's negotiations, and so did the authority of the Russian military nearby.

Lastly and sadly, the ultimate dispositions of UN peace-keepers on the land force us to recognize that these particular outsiders were as unlikely as Jimmy Carter to bring enduring peace to the Balkan states. UN troops may have been called "peace-keepers," but there was no peace to keep.* Instead the UN set itself the task of placing ethnic minority populations in "safe-havens" in Bihac, in Gorazde, in Srebrenica and in Zepa. During the summer of 1995, in the face of a determination among Serbs to take Srebrenica, and an equal determination among Moslems to take Bihac, it became clear that the UN could not even do that. The land belonged to those who were willing to kill to take it and to hold it. In July 1995, thousands of Bosnian men were massacred in Srebrenica with UN troops stationed just a few miles away. Thousands more fled in terror. At the height of the pre-cease-fire land grabs the UN could

---

* In this Rwanda and Bosnia share a sad reality—UN troops deployed to stabilize safety for others, were under orders ultimately to prioritize their own safety above that of the local people.

exert so little military power that the troops based in Gorazde decided in secret to pull out completely overnight, on August 30. The land they vacated belonged to the attackers. At the same time, these disastrous changes in land holdings were among the key factors that made it possible for the leaders seriously to consider making peace.

According to Bosnian Serb troops, Muslims captured in the area are being summarily executed. One soldier, reporting to his commanding officers in Kasaba, said a group of more than 50 Muslims who were armed…are still hiding in the hills around the village of Cerska near Zepa.

On September 8, at "pre-negotiation talks" in Geneva, Balkan foreign ministers gathered to make their first agreement— Bosnia would remain as a single federated state. Follow-up negotiations in New York led to an agreement on September 26 that there would be a joint government for Bosnia. Many more detailed and hard decisions remained.

The soldier proudly declared that his unit had captured seven of these Muslims last Saturday and killed two. "We're going back to catch the group tomorrow," said the soldier. "We just talk to them and then shoot them."

New York Times 8/18/95 p. A4

And still the fighting had not stopped. Serbs kept shelling Gorazde, the one remaining Bosnian enclave in the South. Well into October, the Moslem population there lived under threat of a massacre similar to the assaults on the people of Zepa and Srebrenica. When the cease-fire finally came, Gorazde, just a few miles from the Bosnian capital Sarajevo, discovered it had escaped—saved, perhaps, by proximity to the capital. On October 11, despite a last ditch effort by the Bosnian government to capture still more land by force, all parties agreed to a 60 day cease-fire, making space for the big negotiating push at Dayton.

The agreements

The Dayton Agreement on Bosnia consists of a General Framework and eleven Annexes. They take up the land issues in Annex Two, which contains four items—(1) the specification of an inter-ethnic boundary, (2) the reunification of Sarajevo and an assertion that the city should be "open" to everyone in Bosnia, (3) the creation of a land corridor to Gorazde and (4) a decision to delay the final status of the city of Brcko until the conclusion of an arbitration process, a year hence.

The status of Eastern Slavonia was also postponed for a year. Both Eastern Slavonia and Brcko were dynamite, important enough to destroy the peace-making effort but also unsettled enough to force further delays. Most serious peace agreements contain elements like these, issues that are just too contentious to be settled in the earliest, most precarious times. Yet any delay can just as easily contain the seeds of destruction as allow the breathing room that makes agreement possible. For Bosnia, the risky decision to postpone these issues paid off, but that story only played out fully several years later. For the men gathered at Wright Patterson Air Force Base, Brcko and Eastern Slavonia were pressing reminders that peace-making itself is also dangerous.*

Even the choices that are not necessarily dangerous, are rarely straightforward. After some early reviews of the settlement maps, the Presidents decided on a line for the interethnic boundaries between Serb, Croat and Moslem regions within the Federated Bosnian State. But nothing is ever simple in peace talks. When technicians fed these lines into the Wright Patterson computers, it was revealed that Serb control had slipped from 49% to 45% of the territory. Abruptly, deadlock threatened: Milosevic could not be seen to accept a loss of that size. To regain the momentum, Bosnian Croatians gave up some of their land and the Bosnian government gave up land as well, and so they managed to rebalance the tallies. The story that everyone tells after a peace process must be simple and positive, good enough to convince both the negotiators and their audience that the warriors have not lost more in the peace than they lost in the war.

Each of the four Dayton land agreements carried within it ongoing obstacles to an enduring peace. For example, reunification of Sarajevo and free passage between Sarajevo and Gorazde would involve moving Serbs out of some of their most strongly held positions. Furthermore, Bosnian Serb headquarters in Pale were just a few miles from the center of Sarajevo. How did such concessions come to seem "reasonable?" One of the critical reasons is that Serb military leaders most affected by the reallocations, whose headquarters were in question, were excluded from the process. The President of Yugoslavia, Milosevic, was speaking for all the Serbs and Milosevic proved

---

* In the Israel Palestine agreement, leaving the final status of Jerusalem to be decided later represented a similar, much more serious risk to the long term stability of the Oslo peace accords.

willing to bargain away the very territory the generals inside Bosnia had fought so hard to preserve.* But here again, the negotiators were on risky ground. Generals whose desires are left behind by politicians regularly make attempts to restart the combat, and in the immediate aftermath of the Bosnian talks, such dangers threatened day after day within the Serb zone. Indeed, even eight years later, neither of the two key Bosnian Serb leaders, Mladic and Karadzic, had explicitly come forward to say that they accepted the agreements and supported the peace.

The three Balkan Presidents were there to make agreements. They would take ultimate responsibility for the decisions, but mediators, the international allies and military technologists spoke up at key moments too. Sometimes they helped settle particular details: Wesley Clark, the leading American general, is said to have used mapping computers to persuade Milosevic that the corridor connecting Sarajevo to Gorazde must be at least five miles wide since the local topography made nonsense of anything narrower. When events called for brinkmanship that might put the entire agreement at risk, US Secretary of State Warren Christopher laid down a final deadline although the decision about Brcko remained unresolved. In the end it was Tudjman of Croatia who persuaded Milosevic of Yugoslavia: Brcko could wait.

● Now, largely cut off from the rest of the world, Pale is enveloped in resignation and lassitude. Three young women who paused to chat along a roadside described their lives as a succession of long and empty days.

"Until this war, we were normal, happy people," one of them said. "We looked forward to every day. Now we're miserable. We're desperate for someone to do something to bring this all to an end."

Scott Kinzel, *New York Times,* July 1, 1995, p. 3

* The long term prospects for peace depended on the generals accepting what had been done to them, on their behalf. International forces on the ground overseeing the implementation of Dayton struggled repeatedly with Bosnian Serbs challenging the peace. By the end of 1997, the "peace-keepers" had taken control of local media, had played a decisive role in the outcome of elections, and had also been forced to acknowledge failure in key areas, most noticeably trying to enforce the peace terms which allowed for the return of displaced people to their pre-war homes.

危

The Dayton Accords open with an entire section devoted to the methods by which the various armies would disentangle themselves from each other. Warring soldiers everywhere were to be ordered to lay down their arms, and for this to proceed safely, procedures were needed to prevent the purposeful or accidental firing of shots. Serb soldiers would leave Sarajevo and other occupied areas that were no longer theirs to guard. Croats and Bosnian government troops would reciprocate. The troops would pull back and leave a 2 kilometer-wide corridor all the way along the interethnic boundary, to be patrolled by multinational forces. Prisoners of war and refugees were to be returned home, across interethnic boundaries still brittle with hostilities. The Red Cross was to oversee an exchange of prisoners. This last, often a dangerous process, went well. By January 19, 1996, the pull-back in the rural areas was complete, and had apparently taken place peacefully.

In Sarajevo and other cities, including Vukovar (the site of Croat-Serb fighting in 1991) and Mostar (where Croats and Bosnians had engaged in fierce battles during the fall and winter of 1993-94), the question remained whether it was possible to return to the pre-war condition of mixed ethnic populations. On March 20, 1996 the last Serb forces were to pull out of Sarajevo, and when the date came very few of the 5000 or so Serb civilians who had spent the war in the city were still there. "Pulling out" was both ugly and painful. For the Serb residents, it came to mean their forcible evacuation, at gunpoint, under orders from their fellow Serbs in the army. Civilians were compelled to leave their apartments and homes regardless of whether they wanted to leave or to stay. Fearing murderous attacks from their own forces and revenge from the incoming Bosnian government troops, most Serbs left quietly in the weeks leading up to the hand-over. The city never had a chance to test ethnic coexistence. Troops on the ground showed the world the actual meaning of the agreements made at the negotiations. The risks were immense. The evacuations were so uneasy, even sometimes violent, that they seriously endangered the precarious calm that had fallen on Sarajevo when the bombing ended all those months ago.*

---

* The war in Rwanda also ended with massive and serious dislocations of the different ethnic groups. In that case, most of the Hutu who fled remained outside the country as the war ended, and their return, like the Serb departure from Sarajevo, also posed an immense risk to the peace.

Near Brcko, in contrast, relations between combatants and peace-keepers remained remarkably amicable. American forces helping with the removal of land mines found themselves working in harmonious interethnic conditions, side by side with Croat and Serb forces, who met each other, as the newspapers described it, with "greetings and handshakes more befitting long-separated friends than enemies."

> Admiral Smith declared that the presence of foreign forces was a "serious violation of the Dayton Accord." Secretary of State Warren Christopher had earlier warned the Muslim-led Bosnian government that continued ties to Iran and other Islamic extremists could jeopardize a $500 million American program to train and arm the Bosnian Army that is meant to level the playing field in the Balkans.
>
> Scott Peterson *Christian Science Monitor,* Feb. 21, 1996 p. 6

Dayton, which could do so much to settle the specific details of boundaries on the land, could do nothing to guarantee a stable return to constructive political relations. The negotiators spelled out the political arrangements for Bosnia in annexes setting a timetable for elections and describing new constitutional arrangements. No one had any hope that elections could happen immediately, and in fact the democratic processes remained patchy for several years after the end of the fighting. The republics in the Federation of Bosnia-Herzegovina held elections within a year, as prescribed, but political life was profoundly affected by the presence of thousands of NATO-led troops, and layers of international bureaucratic machinery. Over the next five years, the NATO commanders scheduled and canceled elections, disallowed the results of some balloting, took control of the broadcast media, and even threatened politicians with arrest and deportation to the International War Crimes Tribunal in The Hague. Everyone understood, at the signing in Dayton, that rebuilding and reconstituting Bosnia as a viable political and economic entity would take time, international infusions of cash and external enforcers. The newly rebuilt state would still be vulnerable to renewed fighting should the international forces decide precipitously to withdraw. The long-term hope for a complete renewal of the political process seemed postponed beyond the foreseeable future.*

---

* The outcome of future elections to the Parliament in the North of Ireland also threatened serious challenges to the peace. In that case, referenda on whether or not to accept the basic outlines of the agreement led to such overwhelming victories for peace that the agreements themselves were strengthened in the ballot box.

International support

Setting the right political tone for international support to undergird the peace process was also highly complex. Commentators and journalists use the phrase "international community" freely and vaguely, but identifying which "community" would actually be responsible for peace-keeping and economic development in Bosnia represented a significant challenge. Whose troops should be deployed? NATO had the nearest effective forces, but needed to ensure that Russians, strong allies of the Serbs, were included and that the only Moslems in NATO (the Turks) were well represented too. Furthermore, NATO had no jurisdiction outside its borders, so its troops would have to be deployed under UN authorization. Both NATO and the UN were too big, as international institutions, to oversee the intricacies of the actual negotiations for the Balkans, so diplomats invented a new, extra-legal entity "the Contact Group" (United States, Russia, France, Germany and the United Kingdom), which fostered the actual negotiations. The Contact Group and the European Union's own representative provided the official context for the discussions that took place in Dayton, and the final agreements were initialed by the three Balkan Presidents and the six Contact Group representatives.

Furthermore, in Dayton, the agreements could only be initialed rather than signed. This illuminates an additional complexity of place in the conduct of peace talks, this time a complexity bonded to international issues. The official signing took place in Paris a few weeks after Dayton, because Russia and Europe would have found it impossible to take on responsibility for the success of the agreement had the talks been completely dominated by the United States. The Dayton talks were clearly US-driven. Holbrooke, who got the men together, was an American. The hospitality at the American military base and its technical facilities contributed noticeably to the success of the negotiations. US Secretary of State Warren Christopher had spoken up at a key moment. Still, by moving the final signing ceremony to Paris, to the mirrored halls of Versailles, the Americans were able to slip somewhat into the background, ensuring that later on the other members of the international community would continue to invest to keep the peace.*

---

* The reverse dynamics applied in the Israeli/Palestinian settlements in 1993. The first negotiations were housed outside the United States , mostly in Oslo so, to get American support for the ongoing process, the final signing took place at the White House.

Moral ambiguities

The Dayton Accords stopped the shelling on the Sarajevo market place, and they saved the men of Gorazde from the traumas inflicted on the other "safe havens." The Accords could not, however, reverse the drive towards regional ethnic "purity" which had inspired the war in the first place. By the war's end, Croatia had expelled the vast majority of its ethnic Serbs and the Serb army had driven non-Serbs from the lands that bordered Serbia, making them in effect, if not legally, the "Greater Serbia" that had been the original Serb war aim. The Bosnian government may have fought in the name of an ethnically diverse state, but at the end of the war, its second city, Mostar, was rigidly divided along ethnic lines, and Sarajevo's Serbs had melted away leaving a city dominated by a single cultural community.

No one was awarded a Nobel Peace Prize for ending the Balkan war in 1995. Still, if one looks at a peace agreement as a reward, then clearly the Balkan agreements signed in Dayton did the worst the critical pundits had feared: the agreements rewarded the aggressors; they rewarded the ethnic cleansers. But in truth, Dayton was not a reward. Dayton was an attempt to create an enduring cease-fire, an agreement out of which it was conceivable that a long term peace could be re-established. Dayton offers evidence that peace and moral absolutes do not necessarily go hand in hand.

Bringing peace entails ending a war, which is impossible unless matters are resolved to the satisfaction of the parties, within the actual context in which the fighting took place. In Bosnia and Croatia, the troops on the ground had fought themselves to dispositions that had just enough justice in them to make a settlement possible. In the next case, the war in Israel/Palestine, land is obviously critical as well. From the Jewish settlements in the West Bank, to the devastating overcrowding of Palestinians in Gaza, from the multiple layers of sacred associations in Jerusalem, to the limitations on access to drinking water, it would be hard to find more contentious and more valuable land. And yet, if there was a hope for peace in the region in 1993, the hope did not rest on new deployments on the land. The hope rested on the vision of a few men in key leadership positions.

israel/palestine

SOME KEY DATES   CEASE-FIRE SEPTEMBER 1993

1979 • Israeli PM Begin and Egypt's Sadat make peace at Camp David.

1987 • Palestinians launch the Intifada.

1988 June • King Hussein renounces sovereignty over West Bank in favor of the PLO.

Dec. • Arafat accepts Israel's right to exist and renounces violence but does not change the PLO charter.

1990 • PLO recognizes Iraqi invasion of Kuwait as legitimate.

1991 Feb. • Iraqi Scud missiles attack Israel.

Oct. • Palestinians in joint delegation with Jordanians send representatives to United States/Soviet peace talks at Madrid.

1992 Feb. • Yitzhak Rabin becomes leader of Israel's Labor party.

June 23 • Rabin elected Israeli Prime Minister.

Nov. • Secret talks begin in Oslo between Yar Hirschfield and Abu Ala.

Dec. • Israeli parliament narrowly passes bill to legalize contact with PLO.

1993 Aug. • Shimon Peres travels to Oslo to approve agreements directly.

Aug. 30 • Oslo agreements become public.

Sept. 13 • Oslo agreements signed at the White House.

Oct. • First Palestinian prisoners released by Israel.

1994 Feb. • Israeli "settler" Baruch Goldstein shoots 30 Palestinians at Hebron mosque.

May 4 • PLO and Israel sign Cairo agreement giving Palestinians self-rule in Jericho and Gaza, with further self-rule to be phased in over the next few years.

July 1 • Arafat returns to Gaza.

Oct. • Hamas bomber kills self and 22 others in a Tel Aviv bus.

1995 Nov. 5 • Yitzhak Rabin assassinated by Yigal Amir.

1998 June • Wye Agreements negotiated between Clinton, Barak and Arafat.

1999 May • Date for declaring Palestinian Statehood passes without Arafat action.

2000 Sept. 28 • Ariel Sharon marches onto the Dome of the Rock. Second Palestinian Intifada erupts.

2001 Feb. 6 • Sharon elected PM, and Hamas steps up violent attacks inside Israel.

Sept. 11 • Attacks on the World Trade Center and Pentagon. War in Israel/Palestine intensifies.

THE WAR IN ISRAEL/PALESTINE

Passions and people entangled on sacred land

The astonishing array of dignitaries gathered on September 13, 1993 in the White House Rose Garden were there simply as witnesses, but their presence signaled that the event they were there to see was a momentous one. The signing of the Oslo Accords was recognized worldwide as a dramatic break-through in the direction of peace between Israel and the Palestinians.* Every-one of importance, past and present, seemed to have been invited. Former US Presidents Carter and Bush sitting next to Hilary Clinton, former Secre-taries of State Vance and Kissinger, and the world's assembled ambassadors from Saudi Arabia to Norway. The world's media, cameramen to the fore, were also there to broadcast this momentous event world-wide and to record it for posterity. In Israel and Gaza, on the West Bank and in Beirut, people gathered around televisions and radios wherever they could find them, even stopping to watch TV sets displayed for sale in store windows. While the signing was actually happening it was easy to recognize the magnitude of the achievement. This was the first ever agreement of any kind between the State of Israel and the Palestinian people.

That day, on the White House lawn, the leader of the Palestinian Libera-tion Organization, Yassir Arafat, and the Prime Minister of Israel Yitzhak Rabin, and their two "Foreign Secretaries" Shimon Peres and Mahmoud Abbas signed a document officially called a Declaration of Principles, which begins:

> The Government of the State of Israel and the Palestinian team represent-ing the Palestinian people agree that it is time to put an end to decades of confrontation and conflict, recognize their mutual legitimate and political

---

*Notice the word "accord" not "treaty" once again.

rights, and strive to live in peaceful coexistence and mutual dignity and security to achieve a just, lasting and comprehensive peace settlement and historic reconciliation through the agreed political process.

At the stroke of a pen the PLO had abandoned its public claim, written into its 1964 charter, that its purpose was to abolish the State of Israel. In like vein, the government of Israel was agreeing publicly for the first time that Palestinians had a representative organization—the PLO—and that the PLO should become the core of an interim governing agency for Gaza and for the city of Jericho on the West Bank.

It is easy to forget just how dramatic a turn those two statements represented, particularly since the two sides returned within a few years to a precarious and then a seriously hostile relationship. But this was truly a momentous event, and even the later return to war took on a different cast because these two had spoken as they did that fall day in 1993. Until then, Israel had always insisted that the PLO was a terrorist organization, and indeed had designated all face-to-face meetings between the Israelis and members of the PLO illegal. For Israelis, no Palestinian had a legitimate claim to standing as a political leader of a Palestinian governed territory, and yet that fall they were agreeing to "peaceful coexistence." For Palestinians, the abolition of Israel, and a return to the world as it was before the 1947 UN partition of Palestine, had always been a given. Nothing less was adequate compensation for 50 years of exile. And yet, a Palestinian was signing a document that recognized Israel's "legitimate and political rights." There they were, the Israeli Prime Minister and the head of the PLO, talking and signing, and the whole world was watching.*

Their mutual refusal to acknowledge the other's right even to exist reverberated at the very core of all Israeli and Palestinian disputes. So, the significance of the Oslo Accords, in the context of decades of violent struggle over land each had claimed to be *either* Israel *or* Palestine, is that, for the first time, each group was willing to label maps of that particular piece of land one part

---

* Bill Clinton even managed to set things up so that the two men were forced to shake hands. The key handshake, body to body contact between enemy leaders is another very important part of the peace-making process, one which often shocks partisans on both sides equally. Direct contacts between Nelson Mandela and Frederick De Klerk had a similar impact in South Africa.

Israel *and* one part Palestine. A key first step in making peace is to admit that the enemy exists. A second step is to acknowledge that the enemy has a claim to participate in disposition of powers and resources for the disputed territory.

Norway had hosted almost all the secret talks which led to that historic day, and the United States played almost no direct role, so as late as the end of August, US officials seemed unready to respond to the new reality. Less than two weeks later, Yassir Arafat stood with Clinton and Rabin on the White House lawn, all three looking as though they agreed that each of the others could be the head of a state. Reaching the White House lawn had depended heavily on the standing and values of Yitzhak Rabin and Yassir Arafat themselves. Both men, for different reasons came to a realization that it was worth trying to break out of the endless cycles of confrontation.

The leaders

Rabin's leadership was essential to making the peace palatable to Israel. Like Nixon when he opened US relations with China, and Reagan during his peace overtures to the Soviet Union, Rabin's hawkish credentials were undisputed. Were Rabin an advocate for peace, people were unlikely to doubt that he had the fortitude for continued war. This was not the action of a weak or defeatist man. And Arafat, even though he lived in exile in Tunis, was the only leader the Palestinian people had known. There was no chance for peace without his support. The pressures on them both prior to that first encounter at the White House tell us a good deal about a leader's route to becoming a peace-maker.

Yitzhak Rabin entered politics after a long career in the military and five more years as Israel's ambassador to the United States. He served a term as Defense Minister and so, during the Palestinian Intifada, 1987-89, it was he who faced the challenge of designing combat tactics for a war between stone-throwing young men and the Israeli army. Fierce policing, deportations and a high tolerance for casualties all failed to stem the violence, and Rabin came to understand that he could not depend on military force to govern the occupied territories. After the Oslo Accords were signed, commentators singled out several other events, which had more recently deepened Rabin's motivation to consider the benefits of separating Israel from Palestine. A rash of

The first contacts—in Oslo and Paris and, it is thought, other European locations as yet undisclosed—were no more productive than the increasingly bad-tempered formal talks.

But at the end of March, in the aftermath of a brutal wave of murders, the Israeli Prime Minister, Yitzhak Rabin, ordered the closure of the occupied territories to protect Israeli lives.

It was a typically irascible reaction, but it had far-reaching consequences. This time, it was made known, the closure was not a temporary collective punishment, but an attempt at permanent separation. Israel would have to learn to live without 120,000 cheap labourers from the territories. The Palestinians would have to find other means of providing for their families.

Derek Brown, *The Guardian*, September 13, 1993, p. 6

murders on Israeli lands in March 1993 impelled the government to try to seal off the land known as the Occupied Territories from Israel with fences and guards. For the Israelis, this sudden experience of a more tranquil life gave them a sense of the security benefits that might result from living in a state quite separated from the Palestinians.

Political rivalries mattered too. Rabin's attitude to peace is said to have been softened because he had finally triumphed in his competition with Shimon Peres for Labor Party leadership. Peres was the man who had the bigger claim as an advocate for peace, but now Rabin had the power. During Rabin's 1992 election campaign to be Prime Minister, he was quite explicit about his willingness to trade land to some kind of Palestinian governing power in return for peace. Indeed, this is what the Israeli public expected when he came into office in June 1992. The big question still remained, How? By September 1993, Rabin had become convinced that Oslo's provisions were the right place to start.

Rabin was 70 when he became Prime Minister. His entire life in Israel had been spent living through various kinds of overt and low intensity war. When he reached Washington for the formal signing of the Oslo Accords he made it quite clear he was tired of life in combat and he knew his people were too. As he put it during his speech: "We, the soldiers who have returned from battles stained with blood; we who have seen our relatives and friends killed before our eyes; we who have attended their funerals and cannot look in the eyes of their parents; we who have come from a land where parents bury their children; we who have fought against you, the Palestinians—we say to you today, in a loud and a clear voice: enough of blood and tears. Enough."

Yassir Arafat needed peace urgently too, but for quite different reasons. At the formal signing, his speech was forward looking and hopeful: he had found a way around intense pressures that had been coming in on him from two quite different directions. One was economic and external; the other was over power, and was building up from within the Palestinian community. The economic pressures had become difficult because Arafat sided with Saddam Hussein during the UN war against Iraq in 1991. Immediately, the leaders of the Gulf emirates and the government of Saudi Arabia expelled many thousands of Palestinian workers. Later, these same governments sharply reduced their cash subsidies to the PLO, subsidies that had served for decades as the PLO's primary source of income. Arafat had less and less money to spend just has he faced the challenge of housing more and more people. And the political contest for power was mounting at the same time.

New leaders from the occupied territories had been selected to serve as diplomats to other Middle East peace talks, while Arafat was still in exile in Tunis. Young kids with stones from the Gaza refugee camps were holding the Israeli army in check, and Arafat had no control over them. More seriously, an upstart organization, Hezbullah, was achieving high status among local Palestinians for its attacks on Israel from Lebanon. Inside the Occupied Territories, another new organization, Hamas, was drawing allegiance, because it consistently provided both leadership for, and investment in community-based health and education projects. Hamas seemed to have strong connections to committed adherents to Islam, and a clear-headed willingness to use force when necessary.

For these reasons, both financial and military, Yassir Arafat, still based a long way from the Palestinian homelands, found his position becoming precarious among younger Palestinians. He had been promising a Palestinian State for so long. The talks in Oslo became the opportunity to make such a state a reality, and these same talks guaranteed that he, rather than the other peace negotiators, or Hamas or any other rivals, would be at the center of all future discussions about legitimate authority in such a state. Arafat's speech on the day of the signing made clear that the road ahead would be hard: "[T]he difficult decision we reached together was one that required great courage. We will need more courage and determination to continue the course of building coexistence and peace between us. This is possible. It will happen with mutual determination and with the effort that will be made with all parties on all tracks to establish the foundations of a just and comprehensive peace." Both Arafat and Rabin were clearly ready publicly to assume direction of the peace-making process.

Secret negotiations

The fact that these two leaders and their negotiators had succeed in crafting an opening between Palestinians and Israelis for the birth of mutual tolerance was sprung on a wider world completely unprepared for the news. Beyond leadership commitment, another critical factor in making peace is that the pivotal transformations can often only take place beyond the purview of public scrutiny.* Until August 30, 1993, the negotiations had been totally secret. Until August 20, even the handful of people who knew that talks were happening could still not be sure that an agreement was even possible.

On August 30, 1993, the first day the negotiations became public knowledge, the US spokesman at a State Department briefing, Mike McCurry, still seemed to be close to the old state of denial about the PLO. "We have made our concerns about the PLO well known, and our policy, which is based on concerns we have raised here,... has not changed." While there was talk at that briefing about a visit by Prime Minister Rabin, when a journalist asked: "Is there any US...reason, legal or otherwise, that Yassir Arafat could not be here [in the United States] as part of a tripartite arrangement to formalize this agreement? Is there any barrier to his presence that you know of?" McCurry replied: "I would have to check and see what type of restrictions there are on travel that might be proposed, but I wouldn't want to indicate that there is anything other than a great deal of hypothetical quality associated with that question."

The Oslo Accords, and the US attitude to them, are explained in part by understanding their place in the broader context of another "Middle East Peace Process" occurring at the same time. Since 1991, those concerned

---

* The talks between Nelson Mandela and the Nationalist government which resulted finally in his release from prison, and the release of other ANC leaders, also took place in total secrecy. Even for the talks whose existence is public, like the Dayton negotiations, the details must still unfold in secret.

about peace among the peoples of the Middle East had had their eyes on an extended negotiating and public process in Madrid, jointly co-sponsored by the Soviet Union and the United States. Those talks had begun as a direct result of the aftermath of the war against Iraq, which seemed to open a window of opportunity for change in Israel and among Palestinians. In Madrid, five delegations—from Jordan, Syria, Lebanon, Israel and the Occupied Palestinian territories—had been meeting for two years, but by the summer of 1993, the general consensus was that the talks were stalled. Warren Christopher, the US Secretary of State had been spending the summer of 1993 on "shuttle diplomacy" trips in the Middle East. His travels were directed towards peace between Israel and Syria, in the hopes that a breakthrough over the Golan Heights, the pivotal issue in the Israeli-Syrian relationship, would stimulate progress in other areas. But nothing seemed to break the deadlocks.*

The Madrid talks were conducted under constant public scrutiny, and they perpetuated the United States and Israeli denial about the significance of the PLO. The Palestinian delegation, while truly made up of Palestinians, and of serious diplomats, was forbidden even to consult with the PLO. By the fall of 1993, close observers had begun publicly to wonder whether this peace process, like so many that had gone before, was doomed to failure. The talks may have gone some way to tempering the sense that Israel/Palestine was doomed always to remain a war zone, but they failed to prevent further acts of war.

The violence had never stopped. In 1992, the Israeli border with Southern Lebanon was particularly dangerous; Israelis bombed Hezbullah headquarters in February, and retaliatory attacks rained in on Israel in May and again in October. Then 3,000 Palestinians in Israeli jails went on a hunger strike, and as the year ended Israel deported literally hundreds of legal Palestinian residents out of Israel proper and into Lebanon. Meanwhile, Jews continued aggressively to build West Bank "settlements" on what they claimed were their "traditional" lands. In Madrid the Lebanese could talk directly to the Israelis but their negotiations offered little sign that they might bring about a peace.

---

* Christopher also appeared in the Bosnia story, in which his interventions had exactly the opposite effect. His ultimata were critical to bringing the talks in Dayton to a successful conclusion.

"Try to move your foot," the doctor tells the boy. There is no discernible movement.

Like Mohammed, thousands of Palestinians have been crippled, maimed, blinded or otherwise wounded by Israeli gunfire...a devastating toll of potentially permanent disabilities....

Israelis also have been killed and wounded, including three children from the same family whose limbs were severed by the terrorist bombing of their school bus.

The Palestinian casualties, however, represent a much higher percentage of the overall population and will incapacitate a large number of youths likely to become a burden on a society ill-equipped to handle their rehabilitation.

Tracy Wilkinson,
The Los Angeles Times, Dec. 26, 2000, p. A1.

The heads of the Israeli and Palestinian delegations to the Madrid talks were so startled when they heard that negotiations elsewhere had actually succeeded that, when the Oslo agreements were first being announced, journalists almost persuaded Madrid's diplomats publicly to repudiate the results. The men and women talking peace in Spain had never even heard of the others who were talking peace in Norway.

An informal meeting between a Norwegian academic, Terje Rod Larsen and Yosse Beilin, a prominent member of Israel's Labor Party, in early 1992, marked the beginning of the Oslo process. At the time, Labor was still in opposition in the Israeli Parliament, the Knesset. The Norwegian Larsen's, offer of "contacts with Palestinian officials" was interesting, but nothing was so interesting as the fact that Parliamentary elections were being called for June of that year. Still, Beilin asked an Israeli academic and friend of his, Yair Hirschfeld, and a journalist called Ron Pundak, to stay in touch with Larsen. Another meeting in Israel after Labor's victory in the elections allowed the Norwegian government to make a more official offer—that they serve as host to enable the formal opening of a secret connection between the PLO and Israel. Three months later the first official, though of course unofficial, meeting took place. Yair Hirschfeld was soon sent to the first meeting, at a London hotel, which began with him alone in the room with Terje Rod Larsen. Mid-way through the conversation Larsen got up and left to be replaced by Abu Alaa, a senior PLO official in charge of finances. Technically, that meeting was a violation of the Israeli law that forbade direct contact between PLO members and Israeli citizens.

In Israel, much had changed in the months since the first contacts. Yitzhak Rabin's Labor Party had won the Israeli election in June, and one part of their platform pledged that Labor was willing to trade "land for peace." In January 1993, Labor repealed the law banning contacts with the PLO, so, by the time the Hirschfield/Abu Alaa talks moved to Norway on January 20, 1992, they were nearly legal.

An important facet of the art of negotiation is to avoid over-committing leadership to something which might still fail, so although the talks had been "approved" high up, the early framework for the discussions was set by Hirschfield and by Abu Alaa, with Norwegian Foreign Minister Johan Jorgen Holst providing hospitality and mediating skills as needed. Beilin was now Deputy Foreign Minister, and Foreign Minister Shimon Peres had been informed very early on, but the latter never relayed the information to the cabinet because the talks were not official Israeli policy. Rabin soon gave his blessing and Yassir Arafat knew that discussions were under way, but he too kept far away from any official endorsement. Still, Hirschfield and Abu Alaa worked well together, and quite soon after they began, they were ready to create the plan for PLO control of Gaza and the city of Jericho, both of which were key territorial elements in the final agreement.

In April of 1993, Abu Alaa began to press for more official representation in the Israeli delegation. So, although Hirschfield remained at the talks, Shimon Peres became more directive and the Israelis sent new men to Oslo, including Uri Savir, the foreign ministry's Director General. The PLO's representation also expanded with Arafat's chief deputy, Abu Mazin, also known as Mahmoud Abbas, constantly involved.

The problems that remained unresolved that spring were enormous, and some issues soon began to seem beyond the scope of these particular talks. The control of border crossings between the West Bank and Jordan would have to wait. Much more seriously, so would Jerusalem. Other issues could be written into the agreement only by giving a time table for future negotiations: this was how they handled the challenge of drawing the many intricate boundary lines and the precise schedules of the phased Israeli troop withdrawals. In Oslo, they managed to settle Jericho and Gaza, and they made decisions about the timetable for further talks.*

---

* The Bosnian talks were able to get much further in their agreements about boundaries. Since boundaries are integral to state sovereignty, the failures here must have raised alarms on all sides.

In later years, analysts debated whether setting so many key issues aside doomed the peace from the first. A few had argued this position the moment the plans were announced in 1993. We will never know, but true or not, leaving some issues till later is inevitable in the first phases of peace-making. In no way does this, by itself, diminish the seriousness of the commitments that were achieved. Both leaders clearly hoped they were on the path to an enduring peace. And by the summer of 1993, negotiators faced the task of finding a solution to the most important charge of all: finding the wording to signal each side's recognition of the other's right to exist. This, too, they managed to resolve.

On August 20, 1993, Shimon Peres flew to Oslo. The talks were finished, and he faced his first ever official meeting with a member of the PLO. Peres's presence in Oslo inevitably became public knowledge. Indeed, while there, he gave interviews to the press about the deaths of nine Israeli soldiers killed in an ambush while on patrol in southern Lebanon. However, his meeting with the PLO was so secret that when it came time to initial the agreement, the negotiators, Savir and Alaa, were given the pens. Peres could not act for the Israeli government; the Israeli Cabinet had still not heard about the deal, let alone given its approval. Leaders on both sides spent the next 10 days cementing official acceptance of the Oslo Accords, and informing the American government of the outcome of the talks. Then of course, there were all the preparations for a really public announcement.

The talks were given the name "Oslo Accords" because in serving as host and mediator, Norway had provided complete cover, protecting the leaders in Israel and in Palestine while they undertook a profound change of heart. Norway generously funded the housing, telephones and meals and enabled 14 secret meetings to occur in and around Oslo between January 20 and August 20, 1993, at which the participants could talk uninterrupted. The country could act as go-between and host because neither side carried any deep fears of Norwegian bias towards the other. In this, Norway's stance was markedly different from that of the United States or of the USSR, the official sponsors of the Madrid talks. Furthermore, Norway was an ideal geographical setting in which to work. The negotiators could come and go discretely without being recognized at airports or seen by wandering journalists.

Norway's foreign minister set aside many of his other commitments to devote himself to supporting the negotiators for months on end. Later reports even described the foreign minister's small son as an agreeable distraction from time to time. Designing a deep transformation in perspective of the kind that Oslo represents is virtually impossible in the midst of press interviews, political diatribes and international lobbying. Till the end, although Peres's presence in Oslo was public knowledge, Norway was able to keep its role in the Middle East peace-making secret from all but a few people.

Norway provided the setting to which Arafat, Peres and Rabin could send their trusted confidants to negotiate. Junior officials conducted the actual talks, but the final decision rested with Arafat and with Rabin. After Washington, Arafat was finally allowed to take up residence on Palestinian land, and he staged a triumphant return to Gaza. It has been his home ever since, despite Israel's passion to drive him out. On May 4, 1994, Arafat and Rabin traveled to Egypt to sign a further agreement, which specified in detail the times and places for Israeli troop withdrawals. The germ of a Palestinian state lay in this second document, and although the timetables would stretch out over a number of years, it still seemed that peace was possible.*

While the signing of the Oslo Accords evidently marked a major turning point in Palestine/Israel relations, it soon became obvious that this turning could not, by itself, end the serious tensions in the region. Violence so easily diminished trust in the peace. In February 1994, an Israeli "settler", Baruch Goldstein, had fired on Palestinians at prayer at an ancient mosque, killing 29 and wounding 125. Later in 1994, Hamas began a campaign of local bombings, leading to the worst attack of all in February 1995 when 20 Israeli soldiers and one civilian died in a single assault. Meanwhile the struggles over land ownership on the West Bank reached such intensity that many began to wonder whether this really was the way that land and peace should be traded. Palestinians might be gradually gaining control of parts of the West Bank, but at the very same time Israel was building roads from Jewish settlement to Jewish settlement and thereby splitting these same Palestinian lands into tiny

---

* By 2001, war had once more created intense turbulence in the region. The long term consequences were as unpredictable as the earlier war against Iraq, which been one of the stimuli to spur the 1993 accords.

parcels, while the Israeli government claimed long term military jurisdiction over the transportation network. Palestinians began to fear that their "control" might lead to no more than a series of isolated "oases" in the midst of a Jewish state. Jews, meanwhile, were demanding and being given the right to build more and more housing on contested acreage.

Many Palestinians and Israelis were doubtful of the wisdom of the Oslo Accords even in 1993. Over the next two years, the doubters grew in number, and anxieties on all sides intensified. Still, talks and withdrawals continued. They signed Oslo II, which would move Palestinian authority into another six cities (including Hebron) on September 28, 1995. Finally on October 6, 1995, the Israeli Knesset voted to accept the Oslo Accords, although the final margin had only one vote to spare.

And then disaster struck. In November 1995, Yitzhak Rabin was assassinated by one of his own, Yagil Amir, an orthodox Jew who was determined to stop any further trading of lands for peace. Rabin's death seemed briefly to cement the desire for peace, and in the next few weeks the hand over of the six West Bank towns went ahead even faster than officially scheduled. But in the long term, the forward momentum on the Oslo Accords died with Rabin. Shimon Peres was Prime Minister, and though personally committed, he could not govern without calling new elections. In February 1996 his Labor cabinet was out, replaced by one under the leadership of Benjamin Netanyahu, a man who had reviled the Oslo Accords from the day they were signed. Israel now had a Prime Minister who said his policy was "security before peace." By the end of 2000, the Oslo peace was all gone, blown to bits by suicide bombers, by Ariel Sharon, by US funding for Israeli weapons. Its last fragment was demolished on September 11, 2001.

A year after the Oslo Accords were signed, in 1994 the Nobel Peace Prize Committee offered their award to Rabin, Arafat and Peres, rightly believing that Oslo represented a huge change in Middle East relations. The Nobel Peace Committee dreamed that these three men would, like Sadat and Begin before them, craft a specific peace between Israel and a neighboring state.

The Middle East had indeed been permanently changed by the Accords signed that September day. The PLO and the Palestinians now "existed" as they never had before, in official Israeli eyes. Palestinians had even developed most of the attributes of a State. On maps of the West Bank a few years later, the PLO was officially in control of a significant amount of territory. Palestinians conducted elections in their new territories, fielded their own police force, were issuing passports, and beginning to collect foreign aid and investment. They were also still talking about the next stages of the withdrawal as mandated by the Oslo Accords, though there was no chance of meeting the May 4, 1999 deadline promised in the original agreement as the date for a Permanent Agreement. Arafat had hoped that he would declare an independent state that May, if necessary without a Permanent Agreement, but the date passed without any action.

Oslo could never have served as more than a the first of a series of stepping stones towards a final agreement so as to make peace an enduring condition in Israel and in Palestine. With the final status of Jerusalem set aside till later, more talk was inevitable. And yet Oslo's achievement remains significant even in these war torn times. If peace is to become possible between two parties, each side must admit that the other actually exists, and even has legitimate political rights. Though there remain many Israelis and many Palestinians who still refuse to accept this reality, in 1993 Yassir Arafat and Yitzhak Rabin stood on in front of the White House shaking hands, each making physically manifest the existence of the other. And this seed for peace is still in the ground, agreed to by all but the most radical extremists on both sides.

south africa

SOME KEY DATES   CEASE-FIRE DECEMBER 1993

1986 June • President Botha declares a state of emergency.

Sept. • US Congress overrides President Reagan's veto and imposes strict sanctions on South Africa.

1987 Feb. • The government effectively bans 17 opposition groups.

July • Botha invites Mandela to the president's office for a conversation.

1989 Sept. 14 • Frederick De Klerk becomes President of South Africa.

Oct. • De Klerk frees six of Mandela's ANC colleagues imprisoned for more than 25 years, including Walter Sisulu.

Dec. • De Klerk meets Mandela at the president's office.

1990 Feb. 10 • De Klerk releases Nelson Mandela. By the end of the release process 1000 more prisoners have been released.

1991 June • Major apartheid laws are repealed.

1992 Mar. 17 • White voters overwhelmingly approve the changes in a referendum.

May and June • constitutional talks failing, and increasing violence against Blacks. Mandela breaks off talks.

1993 Feb. • ANC and Nationalist government agree that the transitional government will be for "national unity," continuing the White presence in the government.

Nov. 18-23 • All parties to the constitutional talks agree a format for elections and the transitional government. The transitional government is to last five years.

Dec. • Mandela and De Klerk awarded the Nobel Peace Prize

1994 Apr.26-29 • South African elections and the first ever opportunity to vote for Blacks.

May 2 • Mandela declares an ANC victory.

1995 Dec. • First meeting of the Truth and Reconciliation Commission.

1998 Dec. • Final report of the TRC hearings. Final disposition for thousands of amnesty requests remained to be completed.

1999 • First regular election. Nationalists defeated and out of the government. Thabo Mbeki chosen as President.

THE WAR IN SOUTH AFRICA

Alone, making peace and making justice

One of the striking features of the Dayton Accords for Bosnia, 1995, and the Oslo Accords for Palestine/Israel, 1993, was that negotiators felt able to leave finalization of many, if not most details of political organization and the structure of government for a later time. In Dayton, they did set the schedule for internationally supervised elections in Bosnia. Still, with the Serb sector under the control of Generals Karadijc and Mladic, the leaders who dominated the war, few people left Dayton under any illusion that Bosnia's political evolution would move steadily ahead. Israel/Palestine negotiations had charted even less of a political framework. The 1993 Oslo Accords were explicit that the permanent political agreement had yet to be drafted, though they declared the hope that agreement would take only five years to complete. Bosnia in 1995 and Israel/Palestine in 1993 are reminders that when enduring peace first becomes genuinely possible, a full and solid peace is still far away.

This telling of the South African story will center on a much later stage in the process, the point at which government and electoral systems and permanent political processes are actually finalized. In South Africa, the pivotal time was December 1993. The document to which the participants were putting their signatures was a new constitution, in which the country was setting itself irrevocably on the path towards a whole new identity as non-racial state.

South Africa remained strife-torn, even after the new Constitution was accepted, in part because of the dreadful burdens of exploitation and colonization, which some might say reached their worst extremes during that last half century of avowedly racist government. But the war was finally over. In December 1993, apartheid ended for good. As the new country came into

Mr. Mandela said…that the move to democracy in eastern Europe had been started by Mr. Gorbachev, not by Western governments. "He is the only statesman I know who has had the courage to confess that there were deficiencies in the system to which he committed his life. As far as the West is concerned, I have never heard a single one saying 'We were wrong in introducing colonialism.'"

John Carlin, *The Independent*, Feb. 15, 1990, p.12

being, the Nationalist government was declaring its own willingness to abolish itself. As if this were not achievement enough, the new country also made the radical assertion that it planned to find healing ways to recover from the dreadful damage of the war years. One way this commitment was officially implemented was through the hearings and amnesty provisions for the Commission for Truth and Reconciliation.

The last chapter of the story began in 1993, just a few months after the Israelis and Palestinians finalized the Oslo accords. South Africa bears some surprising resemblances to Israel/Palestine. Timing is just one. For each, the process was shaped by a very small number of key leaders and their immediate surrogates. In both cases a pivotal moment came when the opposing sides each realized that peace depended on their willingness to acknowledge the continued, legitimate existence of the other. There were resemblances too in their respective histories of government terror campaigns directed at their own oppressed populations, of resistance through the bombing of civilian targets and youth violence, and the fact that key leaders were in exile or in prison for decades in the name of "preventing terrorism."

But in the way they approached peace-making there were enormous differences, one of which I will argue lies at the center of the differences in their chance for an enduring peace. South Africa decided to deal explicitly with matters of justice and accountability, as one step on the path to recovery after decades of war, brutality and horror.

The South African story also shows how long the buildup and conduct of a war can last. Understanding this peace depends on knowing, at least in outline form, some history of the conflict between White Nationalists and Blacks in South Africa. The most powerful of the Black political organizations, the African National Congress, became visible on the international scene for the first time in 1919, as spokesman for the rights of Africans at the Versailles Peace Conference, which ended World War I. When South Africa gained independence from England in the 1930s, these same activists became immersed in a struggle for the reins of their own government.

During the 1950s and 1960s, the White Nationalist party in South Africa, which had captured the government in 1948, began imposing massive and harmful civil restrictions on Blacks and others on the basis of race. These were the very kinds of restrictions the winners of World War II had just repudiated in the war against Nazi Germany. South Africa instituted a second class of citizenship for Blacks, aiming to separate them physically and legally from the economic and social opportunities available to Whites. Legislation requiring all people to register on the basis of race passed in 1950, to which was added restriction on places that Blacks could live. By 1952 the Nationalists were reducing the Blacks' right to travel and designing systems for segregation in educational and other public facilities. In 1955, the African National Congress, in collaboration with other groups adopted the Freedom Charter, repudiating all of these measures, and calling for equal political rights regardless of race.

The South African government had been using force to further its racist aims at home from the beginning. In 1960, it "banned" the ANC and all the other opposition groups that had protested police actions at Sharpeville—an incident in which the police killed 69 unarmed protesters. Through banning and police violence, the South African government was making official the process of denying its Black opposition legitimacy, specifically by institutionalizing the denial of the Blacks' right to exist in the political realm.* In the 1960s, the government also began sending troops into neighboring countries, notably Rhodesia (later Zimbabwe), South West Africa (Namibia) and Angola (until 1975 a Portuguese colony), to shut down the African liberation movements in those regions, lest their successes spill over and increase resistance in South Africa itself.

A year after Sharpeville, the ANC began recognizing that if it truly hoped to achieve a non-racial government, it too must become willing to use force.

---

* Once the ANC had been designated an "outlaw," it became impossible for the government to be seen to negotiate peace with them. Here one can see the beginnings of the very same process the Israeli government had to back down from in relating to the PLO, and the British government had to back down from in negotiations with the IRA for the Good Friday Agreement.

危

The young Nelson Mandela, later to become a world-renowned leader, the embodiment of gracious statesmanship, was the person who proposed and pushed for this violent strategy. Once his plans had been accepted by other leaders, the ANC authorized Mandela to establish the military units, and he began working "underground," traveling Africa in search for money for his campaign, training himself and others in the military arts and beginning to select the targets for attack. Like the government forces, the ANC also moved into other countries, training its troops in Ethiopia and Mozambique, preparing for combat against South African military forces in Zimbabwe as well as at home.

The ANC used force for the first time on December 16, 1961. With that, the two sides were well and truly "at war." In 1964 Nelson Mandela and several other leaders were captured and sentenced to life in prison. The rest of the ANC executive went into exile. For 30 more years, apartheid rule lived on.

The war between the Nationalist government and the ANC continued despite the physical absence of the elders in the leadership; from time to time the outside world even heard about it. The Soweto "riots," eight months of intense confrontation, which resulted in the deaths of over 500 Blacks in 1976 were widely covered in the media prompting huge dismay both in South Africa and abroad. In 1977, Steve Biko, an internationally known resistance fighter died, evidently murdered by his South African jailers. In 1986, Prime Minister P.W. Botha, responding to a re-energized ANC campaign, engineered the passage of three successively more draconian declarations of a "national state of emergency," which allowed him to take extraordinary "security" and "enforcement" powers into his own hands.

Seemingly, these were not auspicious times for peace. The Whites looked quite invulnerable. The government, elected by such a restricted franchise, was never in danger of losing its majority, and the countryside provided almost all the resources that a modern nation state needs to withstand external economic pressures like sanctions. Key opposition groups, including the Pan African Congress and the African National Congress were banned, and the Blacks' most idolized leader was in prison for life, hidden away in a maximum-security cell, cut off from contact with the outside world.* Or at least, that is what the outside world knew about the situation.

In fact, just when emergency measures were being intensified, Nelson Mandela was beginning his first, secret talks with members of the Nationalist government, meetings conducted with Mandela still in his prison cell. The decision to talk grew out of the very same heightened tension in Nationalist/ Black relations that had led the government to clamp down on rights and to declare the state of emergency.† An active search for peace is just as likely to begin when violence escalates into crisis, as it is to start when a war has reached a stalemate, or one side suffers defeat.

Around the world, criticism of the South African government's position was beginning to harden. In 1984 Bishop Desmond Tutu of South Africa had been honored with a Nobel Peace Prize, the award serving as international recognition of the legitimacy of the Black's quest for justice. International stigma against apartheid became even more visible in 1986, when the United States joined other nations to impose economic sanctions on the country. Some Nationalists began to experience their isolation, on a continent on which, one by one, all the other White-dominated governments had fallen. Still, the basic dynamics between the two sides had not changed. Whites had absolute power, and the most important members of the Black leadership were in exile, in hiding, or in prison.

So, it was a stunning surprise when outsiders learned, just before his release, that Mandela had in fact been in negotiations with the enemy for nearly five years. His first meeting with a government minister, Justice Minister Coetsee, occurred in the fall of 1985, those talks so secret that almost no one but the two men in the room had the any idea they were even happening. Mandela's ANC colleagues only learned later of the first few encounters. One seemingly insurmountable barrier to progress was that Mandela refused to renounce violence, refused unilaterally to end the war. He held to this position, despite many offers to trade it away in return for his personal freedom. Finally the Nationalists realized that his release, and freedom for the

---

* Initially Mandela, and the others sentenced with him, notably Walter Sisulu, were imprisoned on Robben Island, a jail in Capetown Bay. He, and the other key members of the ANC leadership were moved to Pollsmore in the spring of 1982, most probably to cut down on the activism and organizing that took place on the island, with its large political prisoner contingent.

† See Mandela's words which open the next chapter describing the dangers and dynamics of peace-making.

other great ANC leaders, would have to come first.* Mandela himself came out of prison in February 1990 and the men in exile, including the great Oliver Tambo were allowed home at the same time. These releases and returns indicated that the Nationalist government had finally become able to acknowledge the ANC as legitimate, as the force with which they must negotiate if they were ever to find a permanent settlement. Later that year on August 6, 1990, the ANC and the Nationalist government officially suspended their own violence against each other, agreeing to a cease-fire in a document known as *The Pretoria Minute.*

Two unconnected episodes of ill health played a critical role in furthering these events. The first was some relatively minor deterioration in Mandela's own health. Though not serious, each situation required that he be given treatment in a hospital. The hospital rooms and his subsequent return to a different cell away from his ANC colleagues allowed Mandela to meet privately with Nationalist officials. This they did. Not often, and not easily, but the talks continued erratically over several years. Then, in January 1988, P.W. Botha, the President and Prime Minister since 1978, was felled by a serious stroke. Botha was a man much more associated with fierce escalation of the war to preserve apartheid that with serious peace making, though it must be acknowledged that the first outreach to Mandela happened during his years in power. Still, despite a strong desire to hang on to this power, Botha was forced to resign permanently in 1989. His early retirement opened new avenues for the peace talks.

Botha's replacement, F.W. de Klerk, perhaps recognizing how far the preliminary talks had gone, began actively to take political steps that would facilitate public social encounters between Blacks and Whites, just a little. The changes ranged from opening all beaches to people of all races, to disbanding Botha's special emergency agency, the National Security Management System. De Klerk's immediate willingness to look towards reducing the strife came as a surprise. He had risen to the top of the party hierarchy without giving any clues that he might be willing to take such radical steps.†

---

* The Israelis and Palestinians had talked in secret, too, but the secret part of their talks lasted only a year.

† The events of 1989 and 1990, exemplify once again the pivotal importance of the characteristics of the particular leaders in charge.

In December of 1989, Mandela wrote De Klerk in preparation for their first face to face meeting that: "A mutually agreed-upon cease-fire to end hostilities ought to be the first order of business, for without that, no business could be conducted." By this time, Mandela had received extraordinary powers from the ANC executive personally to conduct negotiations. Though traditionally a "collectivist" organization, the ANC was willing to allow one man to lead. When the whole process was over, looking back on Mandela's release, it is that single most important act that symbolized the inevitable end of apartheid.

> Since the ANC...agreed to suspend its "armed struggle," political violence has claimed more than 1500 lives.
>
> At about 2am, Saturday, unknown gunmen cruised past the house of Rachel Ncube where 300 mourners were holding an all-night vigil...The opened fire...Piercing screams punctuated brief silences in the relentless gunfire.
>
> We were preparing to bury Christoffel [Nangelembe]." said a dazed Mrs. Ncube. "Now, we have many more to bury."
>
> John Battersby, *Christian Science Monitor*, Jan. 14, 1991, p. 4.

The South Africa talks between 1985 and 1990 were, as Mandela and the ANC called them, "talks about talks." More talks about talks followed after his release. The "real talk," to formulate the political structure of a non-racial South Africa lasted three more years, years of continued strife and difficulty. The struggle centered on a deep and widespread unwillingness among Whites to abandon apartheid, and also on the fact that the ANC had never been the only voice speaking for the rights of Blacks in South Africa. A few in the Black community had even found ways to benefit personally from the apartheid system, benefits they were loath to lose. In both communities there were spoilers lurking, ready to damage the peace-making project.

Making a constitution

On December 20, 1991, the "real talks" began. Negotiators from a wide variety of political groups convened to design a new constitution for South Africa. They met, as they would off and on for nearly two years, in the World Trade Center convention hall in Kempton Park, located in a formally all-White suburb of Johannesburg. Later, in a book about his life, Mandela described the scene: "There was not only a sense of history at the World Trade Center, but of self-reliance. Unlike the negotiations preceding new dispensations in African states like Zimbabwe and Angola, which required outside mediators, we in South Africa, were settling our differences ourselves.... The National Party's chief delegate to the talks, Dawie de Villiers, even offered an apology for apartheid." (*The Long Walk to Freedom*, p. 663)

By the time they met that day, all parties were already ready to agree to a document the two sides called their *Declaration of Intent*, in which they committed that South Africa would once again be a single, unified state. Its constitution would be protected by a judiciary and all civil liberties would be guaranteed by a bill of rights. During the first part of 1992, the delegates to the final meetings were to gather in smaller groups, to reach agreement on dozens of other critical issues. Among the most difficult was to settle the future of the previously all-Black homelands, a key bone of contention for Inkata, a Zulu party and one of the most powerful rivals with the ANC for power in the Black community. The major task, though, was the creation of an interim government, to oversee the first few years of post-apartheid rule, easing the tradition to an ordinary democracy governed by majority rule.

The ANC and De Klerk's delegates were still very far apart when they reconvened as a large group in May 1992. The Second Constitutional Conference quickly deadlocked over whether Whites could have a veto over the constitution, over the powers granted to the regional authorities, and over whether the constitution they were designing, which guaranteed ministerial posts even to minority parties, should also serve as the framework for the permanent constitution. In the summer and early fall, it began to look as though the progress was slowing catastrophically. As always, in South Africa's system of peace building, there were secret talks as well as public talks spurred on by catastrophic violence in the form of government killings of protestors. By late summer, the leaders were willing to take decisions on behalf of the peace, which would have seemed impossible just a few months earlier.

On September 26, de Klerk and Mandela signed a *Record of Understanding*, in which the government agreed to vigorously investigate the two recent heavy and violent police attacks. The two sides also agreed on the shape of a constituent assembly to come into being after all-party elections, to govern the country on an interim basis, its main purpose would be to adopt a permanent constitution. Later in the fall of 1992, the ANC executive designed a plan for power-sharing after that first election, so that parties polling as low as 5% of the vote would have cabinet level representation in that government of national unity. De Klerk's party was satisfied that this would give it a substantive role, while the ANC remained confident that it would have the dominant authority. By February of 1993, the government and the ANC had crafted the key elements of a new regime, to serve for five years in the transition to majority rule. Even though they were nearing the time when Mandela's ANC would clearly be designated the absolute winner of their war, neither side could afford to brush off the needs of the other.*

Mrs. Faith Mashiloane, pointing out that the massacre happened 24 hours after an agreement was reached on power sharing before next April, accused renegade elements in the National Party. "I don't mean the government, who are negotiating, but the people who don't want South Africa to take on a new face, who are afraid of changes."

Alec Russel, *The Daily Telegraph*, Sept. 10, 1993, p.11.

These proposals did not pass unchallenged. And, inside the constitutional sessions, South Africans were discovering that although making peace surely depend on bringing everyone to the table, not everyone would necessarily feel obliged to stay, or to support majority decision-making. Inkata and the Pan African Congress both found fault with procedures whose effect seemed designed to diminish their own standing. Both continued, at times violently, to threaten the stability of the new governing structures, right up to the day of the voting began for the new National Assembly.

Resistance among Whites took a more shocking and an equally violent turn. On June 3, 1993, the Constitutional Convention decided the date for the first ever South African multi-racial elections: voting would begin on April 27, 1994. Just a few days later, extremist Whites, having commandeered an armored vehicle, literally crashed through into the World Trade center where the delegates were meeting. This attack made everyone fear for the safety of the elections themselves. Could a small, extremist minority destroy the entire quest for peace? In the event, they did not, and neither did Inkata, which talked boycott until the very last moment.

---

* In imaginary stories about war, winners can impose their harshest demands on the loser, who has no recourse. In reality, even in a setting like South Africa where the final outcome was complete victory for the Blacks, the only way to construct a society at peace was with the active consent and participation of the losing White minority. No war can end unless the loser agrees.

Matters moved forward over the summer of 1993, with delegates approving a list of civil rights for all races, and setting standards for the new Constitutional Court, and designing a federalized government centered on nine provinces, each with a locally designed constitution. The President would come from the party with the largest number of votes and Vice-Presidents from parties getting more than 20% of the vote. The interim National Assembly would have 400 members and the Senate 90. Finally, the South African Army would become the National Defense Force, with a newly designed mandate to limit its powers over its own population.

Each clause represented a body blow to the structures of apartheid, though most also represented compromises as well for the ANC. To make peace together, each side had to shift their positions noticeably. The Presidency would definitely go to a Black, and yet the Nationalist party was also guaranteed power, if only for the next five years. Nine new provinces meant the abolition of the Black "homelands" created by apartheid, and in 1993, the abolition of these states also meant the abolition of governments that were already in the hands of Black homeland leaders. This was what Inkata hated so much. Still, in agreeing that each province could write its own constitution, the ANC had conceded that these powers should not be suspended completely. Above all, by getting an agreement on universal suffrage, the ANC had won its central goal, a non-racial democracy, and the White Nationalist administration had had to cooperate in their own ultimate, if not immediate defeat. Difficulties were still likely with older Whites, who remained obsessed with protecting themselves from accusations about the past. A younger generation, which included Roelf Meyer and Leon Wessels, was looking ahead, ready to construct a new South Africa with a future for them all.

In the midnight hours of November 17/18, after yet another stint of behind the scenes, bilateral ANC/government talks, the delegates approved a new constitution that would provide the framework for a five-year-long, transitional government. While most of the delegates spent the rest of the night dancing, laughing and celebrating their achievements, even then a few left in disgust. The next week, the United States government lifted the last of its economic sanctions, representing the wider world's recognition that the war between Blacks and Whites in South Africa was truly over, with final victory for the Blacks guaranteed. A month later, on December 22, 1993, the sitting members of South Africa's all White Parliament assembled to approve the interim constitution, and thereby to vote themselves out of existence.

The following year in April 1994, South Africans went to the polls over a period of three days. The voting was joyous and remarkably peaceful. On May 2, De Klerk made his concession speech (it had taken several days to collect and count all the votes), and on May 10, 1994, Nelson Mandela was sworn in as the first freely elected President of South Africa. De Klerk, representing the Nationalists, and Thabo Mbeki, representing the ANC were sworn in as Vice-Presidents. The PAC ended up with much less than 5% of the vote and no cabinet position at all. Eighteen months later, at the very end of 1996, Mandela went to Sharpeville, the first of the major "battle sites" in the war, and there he signed a permanent constitution. This document replaced all of the "power sharing" provisions of the 1993 agreement, with true direct majority rule. The first elections under the new constitution took place in June 1999. The war, and the peace-making process were finally over.

Reconciliation: truth and amnesty

That final transition to permanent peace in 1999 was not merely a political and legal achievement. It was also a signal that one of the unique parts of the South African peace-making process, its intensive focus on memory and justice, had successfully completed the first phase of its work.

While they were designing their interim constitution in 1993, the delegates spoke to another issue as well. "There is a need for understanding but not for vengeance, a need for reparation but not for retaliation," as they phrased it later in legislation establishing the Truth and Reconciliation Commission. They needed understanding because the history behind them left agonizing scars all over the people of South Africa, most severely among Blacks who had worked actively for justice and peace. Some of the scars were very recent. Even during those ten years of peace talks, all parties to the war continued their violence; at times it was dreadful violence. The police massacred children in the townships. The ANC killed and maimed in bombings designed to make South Africa ungovernable. Police officers arresting dissidents committed dreadful torture and carried out brutal killings, while resistance fighters also acted brutally against those they designated traitors to the Black cause. While trust was building between one part of the government and the ANC, others in the government, through their supportive relationship with the Zulu-dominated Inkata Party, actively fanned the flames of Black on Black violence. By far the most serious destruction was done by the apartheid government forces but no faction was totally free of responsibility.

Violence between peoples who are destined to continue to live in the same place cries out for judicial reckoning, for some system of punishment or reparations and yet it must not be a system that destroys their ability to coexist. At the end of World War II, the Allied winners, using a hastily concocted amalgam of national laws, prosecuted what they called "war crimes." They tried, convicted and sentenced key German and Japanese war leaders to die. Soon after, these same prosecutors started contributing actively and significantly to the economic recovery of both regions. Later, the first German government after the end of Allied occupation took steps to acknowledge itself that Germans had acted in a deeply wrong manner, so officials in Bonn set up a system of cash reparations, sending money to all those who went into exile and lost assets because of Nazi racial policies. In the ongoing story of World War II, all of these kinds of actions continued to resonate, but it is not clear even today how or whether the directly judicial proceedings made peace-making in Europe or Asia any easier.*

Neither major trials nor sizeable cash reparations were an option in South Africa, and large-scale external economic assistance was never forthcoming. After all, South Africa had no beneficent occupiers to give them money.† Even the faintest whisper of the threat of widespread trials would have guaranteed an end to the constitutional negotiations. Whites, who had to consent to the abolition of their own power, could not have done so had they then faced the risk of criminal prosecution, even death, as a result of their years of "government service." South Africa could not consider cash

---

* This whole issue, whether to sponsor war crimes trials or other proceedings as a war comes to an end, is covered in depth in the last chapter of this book.

† Mandela, above, conveys his pride in doing the negotiations without external mediators. Evidence from the other wars suggests that large amounts of economic aid risks itself becoming a cause of strife, thus hindering peace-making more than it helps.

payments either. The victims were so numerous, and the money so desperately needed for other government programs for education, housing and health care in the very parts of the country most damaged by apartheid's policies.

Instead, the new, mixed-race South African Parliament created a Truth and Reconciliation Commission. The Commission would take testimony about the deaths and the massacres, the torture and the disappearances, and would grant amnesty to those applicants who volunteered full disclosure of their actions. Applicants would also have to prove that their actions were prompted by government or organizational policy. No amnesty was offered for merely personal or gratuitous violence. Members of the ANC and other Black resistance groups were entitled to and subject to the same terms as government employees. They could come forward to receive amnesty for their attacks on the government and the White population.

As far back as May 1990, the South African administration had begun passing stop-gap measures, known as "Indemnity Acts," as a means to gradually release the ANC and other political prisoners, imprisoned for actions that were now recognized to be acts of war and not crimes. Their release was a sign the war coming to an end.* Several hundred Blacks soon petitioned for indemnity, forgiveness in exchange for a full acknowledgement of their actions. However, few from the White security forces came forward, presumably hoping to avoid the issue of responsibility for everything. Even the Commission suffered a dearth of White participation, but its existence did encourage confessions from many Black perpetrators on both sides and testimony from thousands of victims. These hearings also compelled the entire white community to learn, through broadcasts of the testimony, what many of their race had done; it offered to Blacks excluded from indemnity a forum in which to argue for their own release.

The bill for the Truth and Reconciliation Commission was introduced in Parliament in November 1994, and signed on July 19, 1995. It began work on December 1, 1995, with Archbishop Desmond Tutu in the chair. While the Commission's actual impact on gathering the truth and promoting reconciliation will be uncertain for years, that first constitution which anchored the

---

* This provision resembled decisions made during negotiations over Israel/Palestine and the North of Ireland

peace in South Africa could neither have been signed, nor taken hold without the promise of a procedure for dealing with the history. The Commission offered a clear strategy for owning the profound political, physical and emotional damage done under apartheid while managing to avoid institutionalizing a cycle of vengeance for the generations.

The Commission's contribution to peace-making is a very important strand of my thinking on peace-making. Woven into a larger discussion with the newly-founded International Criminal Court and with ancient traditions of mercy and justice, the Commission will take center stage in the last chapter of this book. This South African story ends once more in Oslo, with yet another Nobel Peace Prize.

The Nobel Peace Prize Committee had spoken twice before about South Africa, and in the fall of 1993, with the new South African constitution nearly complete, the prize was awarded to Nelson Mandela and Fredrick De Klerk. While one could argue that it was inevitable that Nelson Mandela might one day be released from prison, it was never inevitable that Blacks and the White government would be able to reach a negotiated agreement for the creation of a non-racial government. Perhaps more than anything, their success resulted from South Africans doing the work themselves. In South Africa, numerous divergent groups together negotiated a constitution, looked their horrifying history in the eye and managed a complete transfer of power from White to Black control. In this, as in their design for the Truth Commission, South Africa differed markedly from the Balkans and Israel/Palestine. There were no outside mediators and there was precious little financial or economic aid. The ultimate success of the negotiating process owed much to Frederick De Klerk. Nelson Mandela explained his feelings about the Nobel Prize this way: "I was often asked how I could accept the award jointly with Mr. de Klerk, after I had criticized him so severely. Although I would not take back my criticisms, I could say that he had made a genuine and indispensable contribution to the peace process." And so did many others on all sides. Peace in South Africa was a long time coming. Efforts to bring it into being did not falter despite the many chance interventions that endangered the project. And both these particular peace-makers engaged with their enemies. They did not merely defend against them.

the north of ireland

SOME KEY DATES   CEASE-FIRE APRIL 1998

1985 • Anglo Irish agreement signed giving the Irish Republic a role in shaping policy in the North of Ireland.

1992 • Intensive bombing all year long. 15 episodes in London alone.

1993 • Downing Street agreement announces Anglo Irish cooperation for peace talks.

1994 Aug. 31 • Unilateral IRA cease-fire.

1995 Nov. • George Mitchell appointed to International Decommissioning body.

1996 Feb. • IRA cease-fire ends with Canary Wharf bombing.

June • Manchester Arndale center destroyed by a bomb.

1997 April • Bomb hoax ties up motorways in the Midlands.

May • Labor defeats Conservative party in UK national election. Tony Blair becomes Prime Minister.

July • IRA cease-fire resumes.

Aug. • Gerry Adams meets Mo Mowlam Secretary for Ireland at the Ulster Parliament.

1998 April 10 • George Mitchell announces an agreement on Good Friday.

May 22 • Referendum on the agreement, which passes by huge margins in both North of Ireland and in the Republic.

June 25 • Elections for the North of Ireland assembly held.

1999 Dec. • New government installed with David Trimble as first minister and Martin McGuiness as education minister.

1999-2001 • Direct Rule from London reimposed several times and withdrawal of Unionists from the peace process due to IRA slowness in decommissioning arms.

2001 Sept. 11 • Attacks on New York and Pentagon mean renegade dissidents lose credibility. United States support for IRA dries up.

Oct. • IRA announces that some weapons are permanently beyond use.

THE WAR IN THE NORTH OF IRELAND

Peace-making: a choice between weapons and power

The first two of these stories about peace-making centered on a single series of negotiations which culminated in an initial framework for peace, one in Bosnia and the other in Israel-Palestine. The South African story was focused on the ending stages of the process. This story about events in the North of Ireland sketches out a longer picture, stretching over several years, both before and after the signing of a another pivotal document. The Good Friday Agreement was first presented to the public in 1998; the journey towards it had already been long and distinctly treacherous. The years afterwards were equally volatile. Hopes burgeoned and wilted repeatedly. The events in the North of Ireland illustrate that crafting an enduring peace is an intricate process, that "the devil is in the details," and that the very details which are supposed to nurture the peace can equally well poison it.

Several factors converged in 1998 to support the negotiators as they made their way towards definitive settlements. First, the Irish peace movement had never really disappeared. It continued its organizing, a steady reminder that the support for more war was neither solid nor unified. Though the political leaders and negotiators may never have been in the same room as the activists making speeches and running workshops, the activist commitment to change was a reminder that reconciliation between Protestants and Catholics was conceivable. A second factor was that the earliest high-level debates about political settlements had been successfully hidden from public view, mostly in private houses, so secret that almost no one but the direct participants knew that the discussions were even taking place.*

---

* This is similar to the secrecy of the Oslo talks and the early Mandela/government talks in South Africa.

When she heard that the Protestant guerrillas, following the lead of the I.R.A., were going to call their own cease-fire, she hoped it would not be on Oct. 13, the third anniversary of her husband's killing, but it was announced on that day

"It didn't feel right," she said. "I was praying for peace, but I didn't want it on that day." Now, she said, she faces the prospect of seeing representatives of the guerrillas became celebrated personalities as they approach formal negotiations with the British and Irish Governments and the other political parties in the North.

"I don't like the idea that after they've killed so many people, they'll be sitting down to say what the future will be, when people like these destroyed my children's future. But if it stops people being murdered, I've no objection."

James Clarity, *New York Times*, Mar. 7, 1995 p. A11

Another propitious sign was Tony Blair's election as Prime Minister of Britain in 1997. The Labor party came into power for the first time in 18 years, and while not inherently more peace oriented than the Tories, Blair at least had no personal political capital invested in victory over the violence in the North of Ireland. Last but not least, even militia members had been behaving for several years as though peace was in the air. Both Protestants and Catholics pronounced their own cease-fires in late 1994 and, although violence broke out again within eighteen months, the notion that the war might end had mostly been very well received. However, anyone who imagines that peace-making ought to emerge gradually from incremental steps, faces rude contradiction in Ireland. This process wheeled and surged again and again, veering from rejoicing to terrified doubt and back again.

The first moments of rejoicing had come in the summer of 1994 when the Catholic militias announced a unilateral cease-fire. Their decision grew out of groundwork laid at two levels. In a private house in London, two Irish Catholic men, Gerry Adams, a Republican militant, and John Hume, a moderate MP, had secretly been talking for years. They explored all manner of questions about whether and how Catholics, militant and moderate alike, might achieve a just society even if they could not achieve complete independence from Britain. At the same time, in official buildings, administrators from the London and Dublin governments were meeting to construct their first united approach ever to ending the constitutional and military stalemate. Their inter-governmental collaboration was made public in the Downing Street Declaration in 1993. The next year the Hume/Adams secret talks paid off and on August 31, 1994 in Belfast, Gerry Adams and the Catholic side renounced violence for

the first time in 30 years. Belatedly, the Protestant Unionist militias announced their own cease-fire on October 13, 1994.

Neither the private talks nor the official ones conceived of themselves as
the final arbiter of peace. Gerry Adams put it this way: "We note that the
Downing Street Declaration is not a solution nor was it presented as such by
its authors. A solution will only be found as a result of inclusive negotiations....It is our desire [through this cease-fire] to significantly contribute to
the creation of a climate which will encourage this. We urge everyone to approach this situation with energy, determination and patience." Yet even at
this optimistic time suspicions also remained high. *The Economist*, the
weekly British news magazine, greeted the IRA announcement with a cover
photo of a sinister man carrying a large gun, his face hidden behind a dark
woolen mask. Polarized reactions flared up repeatedly. If an optimistic mood
dominated somewhere, the pessimistic was nearby; whichever mood had
center stage, the other was ready to take over at the slightest prompting.

The governments in Dublin and London both quite quickly lost their
focus on peace. By late 1994 they were swept up other activities that weakened their commitment. Ireland's leader, Albert Reynolds, had been forced to
resign in the wake of a financial scandal. In London, John Major's miniscule
majority in the House of Commons was getting even smaller, and he found
himself increasingly dependent on fiercely anti-Catholic, Irish Unionist MPs
to sustain his parliamentary position. Within a year, politics in both capital
cities was more damaging to the peace than helpful.

And yet, just as optimism was fading in Eire and in Britain, it was on the
rise in the United States. At the height of the war years, when the sound of
Gerry Adams' speaking voice was banned from British radio and TV, the
British government also managed to keep his physical presence out of the
United States. However, in the spring of 1995, with a US visa in hand, Adams
set off on a tour of key Northeastern cities, feted everywhere as a major political leader. Because of this visit, Anglo/American trust plummeted. John
Major found it hard to forgive Clinton's decision to confer the credibility of
a visa and a visit on a "terrorist"* The whole episode fit with the traditional

---

* Note the similarities here between Ireland and Israel. Peace-making in both places was severely im-
peded by a sitting government's insistence on labeling the leadership on the opposing side "terrorist."
The designation is all it takes to prevent officials even considering negotiations.

American approach to intervention in Ireland, deeply friendly to the separatists, but still concerned about the war. Gerry Adams' visit caused no qualms in the United States.

Back in Ireland, among the militant members of the IRA, Gerry Adams's travels were not reassuring, and the slow pace of the peace process meant that credibility and power were shifting back to those who had never wanted peace in the first place. Impatient, in February 1996 they opted to set off an enormous bomb at Canary Wharf in London. The IRA cease-fire was over. For more than a year the future once again looked quite grim. In April 1997, the IRA managed to tie up the freeways across the whole center of England with a bomb threat later shown to have been a hoax. The war did not even have to kill anyone to turn existence on its head. Still, the vestiges of a peace process remained alive and finally, at the end of July 1997, a new cease-fire was announced and the critical talks began.

Though it had begun to seem routine for the warring parties to agree to a cease-fire, placing their weapons permanently beyond reach and decommissioning them for good was about to prove the most persistent toxin contaminating the peace. And like so much in Ireland, the toxin brought along its own antidote, in the person of retired Senator George Mitchell. Mitchell had been nominated by President Clinton to serve as the US representative to the international military decommissioning body. He was the perfect man for the job, and when the talks resumed in 1997, Mitchell focused attention on constitutional and power sharing arrangements as much as on weapons. He is justifiably credited with enabling the 1998 talks to reach a successful conclusion.

Even with Mitchell at the helm, progress was deadly slow, and in the winter of 1998, word got out to the public that the negotiators could not possibly meet their deadlines. Once again the mood swung abruptly to pessimism. And then fear changed to delight with the announcement that the negotiators had indeed reached an agreement. Good Friday 1998 was a day for joy, instead of a day for mourning. For the next few months, the peace seemed to grow ever stronger, winning overwhelming support in popular referenda in Northern Ireland and in the Republic of Ireland. Even the bloody bombing in Omagh described in the Prologue turned out to deepen the very commitment to peace it had been designed to end.

Good Friday, like Dayton and like Oslo, was only a beginning; it could not create a full foundation on which to stabilize peace. Necessarily, it left key issues till later, specifically issues about procedures for governance and deadlines for the destruction of weapons. So the peace continued to be volatile. During 1999, both the IRA and Unionists engaged in small scale but shocking acts of violence, which made agreements about weapons increasingly urgent. The summer of 1999 was particularly discouraging. George Mitchell returned once again in September 1999, allegedly to review the settlements, but actually to mediate further discussions to revitalize them. That November, Adams and Trimble announced another break-through, but once again the agreement faced a threat, this time from the Unionist side. Finally the London Parliament voted a bill to devolve government powers to a regional parliament in Belfast, giving the North of Ireland substantial control over its affairs for the first time since 1972. On December 2, the new Northern Ireland Executive Authority met. That same day the IRA sent a representative to the weapons decommissioning body. The war, it seemed, was finally over.

Three months later, London abolished the autonomous government, and the peace was in crisis again. The IRA was in violation of its commitment to adhere to the established decommissioning rules. Disarmament procedures crafted to strengthen the peace, by drawing so much attention to the IRA compliance, had also acquired the power to harm the peace; the mechanisms by which Protestants and Catholics were to share power in the new government were also proving challenging. These patterns repeated themselves year after year. And the violence, while it faded to a much lower level of intensity, never quite managed to stop. Was the war in Ireland over? Who knew? All anyone knew was that the talks which culminated in the 1998

Belfast is coming alive, due to an optimism activated by men like Hume. The center, once claustro-phobic with checkpoints and British soldiers, is filled with shoppers and 20-piece orchestras playing on sidewalks battered by bombs a few years ago. Fear has found a worthy opponent in a growing economy....

The short news conference concluded and Bono, Hume, and Trimble disappeared through a stage door of Waterfront Hall, where they remained invisible until an hour later when all three stood on stage as U-2 sang "Give Peace a Chance" while a Catholic grasped a Protestant's hand in a simple sign of alliance.

Mike Barnicle, *Boston Globe*, May 22 1998, p. A14.

Easter Accords represented the first real chance to make a durable peace in nearly 30 years of war.

In the years after 1998 three key factors each exerted both beneficial effects on the peace and pressures against it: (1) the continued violence, (2) new constitutional realities and (3) weapons decommissioning. The biggest stumbling block, the factor on which peace seemed so regularly just about to founder for good, was decommissioning.

And everything was easily tainted or blessed by rhetorical flourishes, and by the meanings each so often read into the others' particular words. Words mattered. At every stage, from the Anglo/Irish Downing Street Declaration of 1993, through the agreement in November 1999, Sinn Féin kept demanding that meanings be "clarified." In their turn the Unionists constantly denounced IRA statements about "unequivocal" support for peace as mere equivocation. The terminology used in each announcement was liable, in its own right, to prompt yet more hostility over issues which were already challenging enough.

Special complexities emerged each time people talked about prisoners. Were they "criminals" or "POWs?" The word "prisoner" was given substantive meaning in the Good Friday Agreement, when the British government listed 253 specific people convicted during the years of strife who were to be released regardless of the remaining length of their sentences. This list nearly caused a crisis at one point amidst pointed debates about the unwise release of known murderers, but Mo Mowlam, Northern Ireland Secretary, reaffirmed the high political status of the "prisoners" by making an unprecedented official visit to the Maze prison to reassure people that the release program would proceed. The cease-fire had been about to collapse, but with support from those in jail they found their way back to the negotiations once again.

Threats and counter threats over "decommissioning" haunted the peace, with British and Unionist leaders using the term repeatedly to imply that the IRA alone was responsible for the violence. And "decommission" was not the only difficult term. Tensions also revolved around the word "complete" and its close relatives—"permanent" and "final." What did they mean? Melting down the weapons or turning them over to a third party for protection? The answer finally was to lay them out in a bunker and pour concrete over the top.

The other truly pivotal term was "government." Would Sinn Féin get ministerial assignments, or not? It all came down to which came first, "government" or "decommissioning." The meaning of both terms came ultimately to depend on timing. The November 1999, Adams/Trimble breakthrough crafted words to signal making a simultaneous start on both on the same day. But still the question would not go away. Even on the one day, which must come first? Long after the worst memories of the violence were beginning to fade, threats embodied in words remained.

Violence

Cease-fire is the time to stop the violence. In the North of Ireland, all sides kept their hands very close to their weapons even when officially under a cease-fire. The British doubted their troops could safely patrol without bullet proof clothes and armored trucks. Republican and the Unionist militias still targeted key opposition leaders for execution, and both groups continued to compel loyalty in their own forces by brutally and physically punishing those suspected of drifting towards reconciliation projects. One of the clearest signs that the peace process was really at risk in the summer of 1999 was that the Protestants were once again threatening violence during their summer parade at Drumcree, a traditional battle zone. In July, British forces began reinstalling their razor wire and water cannon to keep the two communities apart. Still, even violence had unpredictable consequences for peace, sometimes strengthening it and sometimes hindering it.

For example, in September 1997 an IRA splinter group set off a bomb in the town of Markill to prevent the "all-party" negotiations starting their final push towards peace. Unionists did stay away from the talks that first day, but that particular bomb also gave Gerry Adams an opportunity forcefully to speak out against more violence. A week later, on September 17, 1997, the Unionist leader, David Trimble, arrived for his first ever meeting with Adams. Finally, Trimble could be in the same room as Adams, in part because the violence of others on the Republican side had temporarily removed the taint

Under orders from a government-appointed Parades Commission, British security forces erected extensive barricades to block the July 5 march. The ensuing standoff has brought rioting to Northern Ireland for the third consecutive summer.

Police and soldiers came under gunfire but no casualties were reported as they confronted mobs early today in Protestant east Belfast; the Protestant section of Antrim, west of Belfast; and Newtownards, east of Belfast.

Shawn Pogatchnik,
The Columbian, July 8, 1998, p.1.

of violence from Adams himself and from Sinn Féin as well. Markill even forced one of the splinter IRA groups to join the cease-fire, to step out of the way of the peace process.

Killings continued and mostly they worked against the passion for peace. During 1997, a British soldier, a woman police constable and a police officer were killed by Republicans, reawakening English qualms about even trying to make peace. Republicans mounted a huge display of anti-British feeling at the funeral of their comrade Sean Brown. In the main councils of the IRA a meeting occurred at which key leaders argued the peace process was futile, that the only path forward was violence. Gerry Adams rebuffed them, and the talks continued, but so did the violence.

The Unionists favored killings one by one over large scale bombings, and almost always they attacked in the North. They also favored confrontational, violent parades and marches across Catholic communities every summer. In fact, a Unionist parade had set off "The Troubles" in the first place, back in 1969, when the Apprentice Boys circled the walls of Derry to intimidate the local Catholic population. In that year so long ago, the Catholics had responded with violence, and every summer thereafter the marches had renewed the Unionist call to arms. For a few people, after the first cease-fire, the marches also became a way to show the opposite, that change could happen. Scout troops from Protestant and Catholic communities walked together in Armargh in honor of St. Patrick's Day.

The Protestants did not confine themselves to marching. Well after the cease-fire, Unionists carried out one of their most spectacular murders, the cold-blooded killing of Rosemary Nelson, a prominent lawyer with Republican associations. Once again, violence had unintended consequences. Nelson's death failed to prompt retaliatory violence. Instead, since she herself was held in such high regard, leaders on all sides were once again calling for calm and a renewed commitment to peace. Violence both poisoned the peace, and kept it on track. Much the same can be said of the attempts to create a new constitutional framework for Ireland.

Constitutional arrangements

Each time someone planted a bomb in Ireland, or burst into a pub and started shooting, they justified their actions in constitutional terms. They called themselves Republicans, as in "the Irish Republican Army" if they wanted to unify with the southern part of the island, Eire, the Republic of Ireland. They called themselves Unionists if they wanted to preserve the status quo, as part of the United Kingdom of Great Britain and Northern Ireland. Governments also centered their confrontation on constitutional dispositions. Eire had a clause in its constitution claiming sovereignty over the whole island. When The Troubles first began, the Irish leader, Jack Lynch, maintained he was entitled to call for UN intervention, much to the fury of the British who called the whole matter their "internal affair." The government in London claimed repeatedly that Northern Ireland was legitimately part of the United Kingdom, because under the parliamentary system the only majority that counted was that of the voters of the six counties, Protestant and likely to remain so for the foreseeable future.

During 25 years of war and five years of peace-making, the conviction that the constitutional choice must be between *either* Ireland *or* Britain began gradually to transform into an option to be *both* Ireland *and* Britain.* Changes in the configuration of the European Union, a new governing party in Britain for the first time in 18 years, a change in the Irish constitution and massive alterations in British governance structures combined to make this possible.

When the war began in 1969, national identity in the region had only one dimension. One was either Irish or British. The rhetoric of war supported undivided and simple allegiances, but in reality, national identity was becoming more complex as time went on. Membership in the European Union forced changes in British government handling of Irish prisoners

---

* While the land issues in Ireland were nothing like as burdensome as in Israel and Palestine, peace-making in the two places made a similar shift from seeing options as mutually exclusive to seeing them as complementary.

because they now failed to conform to European human rights rules limiting preventive military and judicial actions in the face of threats of violence. When British Prime Minister John Major and Albert Reynolds, Taoiseach of Ireland were working on the 1993 Downing Street Declaration they collaborated with ease. Their years as colleagues at EU meetings reaped dividends. Even though both later lost office, the soundness of their relationship is widely acknowledged as a key stepping stone on the path to peace. But the bonding was personal, not national and later struggles between Reynolds' successor, John Bruton, and Major played an equally important part in weakening the peace process. The failings of Bruton and Major, as much as anything else, caused the IRA to end their first cease-fire in 1996.

Elections in Britain by turns helped and hindered establishing an enduring peace. Conservative John Major came into office with a strong boost from Margaret Thatcher, and at first he used this momentum for peacemaking. But as the years passed his power base collapsed, and finally Major could not stay in power at all without taking the Unionist side. His passion for peace faded. Then on May 1, 1997, Tony Blair became Prime Minister. Labor had won a huge parliamentary majority; their Northern Ireland policies were now invulnerable to Unionist threats. Blair's Northern Ireland Secretary, Mo Mowlam, made regular use of this power to bring the British government into direct contact with key figures on all sides. For the first time since 1994, the London government was free to take active and courageous positions.

Wider British constitutional reforms also made a positive contribution to the peace process, at least at first. Labor had run for election on a "Devolution" platform, repatriating selected political powers to Scotland and Wales. Popular referenda in Scotland and Wales voted in favor of Regional Parliaments with taxing authority and control over local judicial, health care and educational systems. Inside the UK national identity was being reshaped. The powers and resources that a government in Northern Ireland would acquire suddenly seemed really worth having. So, when serious negotiations began in late 1997, all sides could consider options for internal and intergovernmental decision-making that would have been literally inconceivable when the fighting first broke out. Ireland (Eire) could safely end its constitutional claim to the northern counties, confident that the North of Ireland would have substantial authority to chart its own course. Mirroring the existing transnational government bodies in Europe, the peace negotiators could opt for transnational bodies for the whole of Ireland to collaborate over tourism, transportation and the environment. Again following a European model, votes in parliamentary elections could be carefully apportioned, ending a long history that guaranteed Protestant control, and quite literally ending the "tyranny of the majority." Lastly, since Britain had set a precedent with referenda over joining Europe and over devolution, the negotiators were confident they had the right to hold parallel referenda about their plans in Ulster and in the Republic, ensuring that the voters of Ireland as a whole decided whether to accept these new arrangements.

As is often the case in complex negotiations, the broad outlines were clear but dangerous "details" remained unresolved, liable still to derail the peace roller coaster, instead of bringing it safely to ground. Did it help the peace to have the constitutional stakes so big? Did the possibility of this kind of power make Trimble and Adams more willing to make concessions, or did the later collapse of their shared government create disappointments and distrust so large that in the long term, the peace was bound to fail? Even without large constitutional changes, there might have been enough incentive to keep working towards a solution. In the context of struggles over weapons, an ample supply of political power did not turn out to be adequate by itself to stabilize the peace. The peace talks nearly disintegrated in the summer of 1999, in part because the United States intercepted a shipment of weapons destined for the IRA. How could anyone believe Republican protestations that the war was over if military branches of the Republican movement were still importing more arms? The Unionists would join a government that contained Republican officials only if the IRA took tangible steps to disarm. The IRA kept backing away even from the smallest tangible steps.

Weapons and "decommissioning."

As months and then years under cease-fire passed, one issue arose again and again—weapons. The really serious difficulties always came back to the question of decommissioning, who would do it and when they would begin. In this war, much more than in any of the other cases, the demilitarization of the war zone kept emerging as the key issue, and yet the challenge was one of rhetoric more than one of security. The word "decommission" went onto the negotiating table first, and it was still there long after they had settled the political, the economic and the social arrangements for peace.

All parties to the war in Northern Ireland were armed most of the time. The Irish government guarded its frontier with the North. The guards on the other side of that frontier were British troops, and many more were scattered in barracks and patrolling the streets, armed in bullet-proof vests and travelling in armored vehicles. The Unionist militia were armed too, with guns for targeted killings, and with bottles and stones each time there was a march or a riot. For the British and the Unionist negotiators the only decommissioning process which mattered applied to the IRA. Republicans of course were always concerned about weapons on the other sides, particularly the heavy British military presence in the province. The international decommissioning body formed to discuss weapons, deployments, policing and the armies on all sides was still at work long after the parties to the Good Friday agreement had signed their documents and gone home.

Decommissioning was one arena in which words mattered as much as action. Gerry Adams would say he could not speak for the IRA, that they were the ones with weapons. The Unionists would then say they could not work side by side with Sinn Féin until Gerry Adams spoke for the IRA and provided a specific IRA action plan to turn in weapons. The British press kept on doubting the peace process, because the Republicans would not talk about turning in weapons. The Republicans on their side were waiting for the British to discuss troop withdrawals. The British refused, arguing that their forces were "peace-keepers," not "combatants," so decommissioning did not apply to them.

In some situations, a war is hard to end because the causes that started it in the first place remain profoundly unresolved. The war in Israel/Palestine is such a war. Sometimes a war is hard to end because of damage done during the fighting. The catastrophe in Rwanda is such a war. The war in Ireland has proved hard to end because one term, written into the very first attempts to make peace, "decommissioning," itself proved a stimulus for more conflict. Still change was in the air, and while peace remained uncertain, the new men running the North of Ireland most often seemed willing to continue to trade weapons for power.

In 1998, new leaders working from within new constitutional frameworks in Britain and Ireland made proposals that inspired a search for peace, proposals that would have seemed outrageous when the war began. Even in 1998, those suspicious of the peace managed to keep its success in doubt for a long time. Putting pressure on the leaders on their own sides, these spoilers publicized their mistrust. And from time to time someone would be killed, deepening doubts that the violence would ever stop. Like the war in Israel/Palestine, the war in the North of Ireland kept refusing finally to end.

Peace in Ireland differed from Israel/Palestine in that the leadership that made the peace was not the same as the group that had invested everything in the war. When Gerry Adams and John Hume began talks in the late 1980s, they represented a new generation of leaders. The subsequent elections of David Trimble to head the largest Unionist party in 1995, of Bertie Ahern to head Ireland's Fianna Féil party in 1996, and of Tony Blair in 1997, produced new leaders for all parties to the war. With George Mitchell and Ireland Secretary Mo Mowlam as leaders in the face to face talks, patient, imaginative and courageous people were in charge.

Ultimately, only John Hume and David Trimble were recognized for their work when Oslo announced the 1998 Nobel Peace Prize, but the award recognized Easter 1998 as the turning point, the first real chance for an enduring peace in the North of Ireland in 30 years. Like all crucial moments in peace-making it was replete with both danger and opportunity.

chechnya

SOME KEY DATES   CEASE-FIRE AUGUST 1996

1985 • Gorbachev appointed Soviet Premier.

1989 • Berlin Wall comes down. Cold War is ending and Soviet Baltic Republics also press for independence.

1990 May • Boris Yeltsin elected head of Russian Parliament.

Aug. • Iraq invades Kuwait.

Fall • Soviet/United States collaboration in war against Iraq begins.

Nov. • Dudayev, Chechen leader calls for complete sovereignty.

1991 Aug. • Coup attempt against Gorbachev fails thanks to Boris Yeltsin.

Oct. 27 • Dudayev is elected Chechen President, without Moscow's approval.

Dec. • Soviet Union disbanded by Russian President Yeltsin, and the Presidents of Ukraine and Belarus. Other republics now find themselves independent. Chechnya still part of Russia.

Dec. 25 • Gorbachev resigns as Soviet leader.

1993 Dec. • New Russian constitution gives Yeltsin sweeping powers.

1994 Dec. • Yeltsin sends Russian troops into Chechnya to crush independence revolt.

1996 April • Dudayev is killed.

Aug. • Chechens capture Grozny from Russian troops.

Aug. 28 • Brief agreement signed between Russian Alexander Ledbed and Chechen leader Maskhadov.

1997 Jan. 28 • Alsan Maskhadov elected president of Chechnya.

May 12 • Yeltsin and Maskhadov sign peace treaty.

1999 Aug. 9 • Yeltsin appoints Vladimir Putin as acting Prime Minister.

Sept. • Bomb attacks around Moscow lead to the resumption of war in Grozny.

Dec. 31 • Yeltsin resigns in favor of Vladimir Putin as Russian President.

2001 Sept. 11 • Attacks on New York and Washington lead to support for Putin's war aims in Chechnya.

THE WAR IN CHECHNYA

An unequal contest and a minimal peace

The particular part of the war in Chechnya that serves as the core of this story lasted from 1994 to 1996, and ended with a cease-fire agreement in late August 1996. In May the next year, Russian and Chechen leaders signed an apparently more binding agreement. Though the second document was a mere four sentences long, it took only very few words to reveal that there had been antagonisms between Russians and Chechens for centuries. And yet, for a brief moment in time, it looked as though the time had finally come to make peace. The larger meanings, embedded in the first part of the Russian/Chechen story are: (1) a very small force can keep very large armies entangled in a war for very long periods of time, and (2) the impetus for, or failure to make peace may have more to do with the purely internal domestic politics of one of the two sides, than with their combat or the justice of the cause.

Five years after the 1996 peace agreement, following the 2001 attack on the United States, this small, local war suddenly broadened in meaning. This story now ends, therefore, with a much wider view and a more confusing picture than it originally seemed. We will begin, though, with the narrow picture, since it has an important bearing on peace-making in its own right.

Like the war in the North of Ireland, the Chechen war was replete with stories of ancient hostilities and brutal government actions. For Chechens this had entailed a period of forced exile from their homelands. Still, in some senses the war in 1994 had a much shorter time frame, and was a direct outgrowth of the break up of the Soviet Union. The Soviet Union collapsed as a single governing entity during the waning years of the Cold War after 1989. Many Soviet Republics had gained independence from Russia peacefully; some plunged into their own civil wars, and a few discovered that Russia itself would not allow them independence. The Chechens were in the last

Dozens of dead Russian soldiers lay heaped behind the pockmarked presidential palace. Occasionally a stray dog slipped up, worried at a body and made off with an entrail. Many of the dead had been left to die by a demoralized and confused army—four Russian divisions that seemed incapable of subduing a republic the size of Connecticut. The job of removing the Russian dead fell to Chechen fighters who had held the nerve center of their resistance despite a four-week Russian offensive.

Rod Norland, *Newsweek*, Jan. 16, 1995. p.28.

group. For them, independence was declared out of the question. In late 1994, Russian President Boris Yeltsin sent the might of the Russian army against the "rebels," expecting to bring about their speedy defeat. Instead, what Yeltsin's government found was their own version of the Vietnam War, a television war, whose carnage was visible to the Russian people day after day, and whose outcome was murky at best.

Ordinary people began gradually to understand that, although thousands of Russian dead were being sent home in zinc coffins, the enemy was showing no sign of collapse. While casualty figures cannot easily be assessed, one report indicated that out of 30,000 dead, only 4,000 were Chechens. While the Russians had the vastly larger numbers, they had not been well trained for urban warfare, and were simply no match for Chechen snipers and marksmen. Each time Chechen fighters encountered vehicles moving in a column, they would simply knock out the head and the rear, and then deal with everyone else trapped in the middle.

By the summer of 1996, the bitter combat had lasted 21 months and Yeltsin's first opponent, the Chechen's original leader, Dzokhar Dudayev, had been killed. Grozny the capital city, was a shell of its former self, buildings gutted and a large percentage of the population gone, sheltering in the mountains out of reach of Russian tanks. The whole area was a physical disaster zone.* Its politics seemed considerably stronger.

By comparison with what we will soon see were the wildly fluctuating power politics in Moscow, the political leadership in Chechnya was remarkably stable despite the 10-year-long struggle. Dudayev had been elected to the Presidency of Chechnya on November 1, 1991, when the republic gave itself

---

* "It is hard to imagine the intensity of the barrage [against Grozny] except to say that at the height of the shelling of Sarajevo there were thirty-five hundred detonations a day, while in Grozny the winter bombing reached a rate of four thousand detonations an *hour*." (emphasis in the original) Remnick, David, "In Stalin's Wake," *The New Yorker*, New York City, July 24, 1995, p. 48.

state sovereignty. He remained in power despite the war, and despite local challenges in Chechnya, until the day he died, killed by a Russian rocket, April 22, 1994. His successor, Aslan Maskhadov was also a Chechen military commander. During the war years, there were no elections, but in the wake of the Russian Chechen peace, he was formally elected President of a semi-autonomous Chechnya in January 1997, and was still in power in late 2001 when events in this obscure Russian republic began suddenly to take on such global significance.

By contrast, despite the long-running Presidency of Boris Yeltsin, Russian politics in Moscow were distinctly unstable. At the time of Chechnya's first Declaration of Sovereignty, Boris Yeltsin was just completing his triumph over Gorbachev, to become President of the Russian Federation. The first period of Yeltsin's government, a reformist period, lasted nearly two years. After an electoral scare in 1993, Yeltsin himself began to act in a more authoritarian manner. One part of his new posture was that the Russian President decided he could no longer ignore the challenge to Kremlin power represented by Chechnya. At home in Moscow, Yeltsin began playing an ever faster and faster game of political musical chairs, moving in and out of the Prime Minister's job a succession of men, each of whom saw themselves and who were seen as possible candidates to be Yeltsin's successor.

The story behind Russian-Chechen peace-making in 1996, and their return to war in 1999, pivots around the lives of two of the Russian pretenders for Yelstin's Presidency: General Alexander Ledbed, former security chief, who made peace and lost power and Vladimir Putin, a former leader of the KGB, who returned to war and thereby won power. It would be a mistake to conclude from this summary that the Russians could not give power to a peace-maker. When Ledbed stepped in he became, if only briefly, every ordinary Russian's hero. Few would have guessed in 1996 that these same ordinary Russians would, three years later, greet Putin and the return to war with equal enthusiasm.

The agreements made by Ledbed and his Chechen counterpart, Maskhadov, represent the minimalist version of peace-making. The two men had hardly met each other. Since the violence on the ground in Chechnya was so ferocious, it was not a congenial environment in which to talk. It was also so ferocious that no outsiders, with the exception of a handful of international humanitarian aid workers, would contemplate coming to help. The two men signed their initial cease-fire agreement at the end of August 1994, and nothing in either its terms, or the plans for future agreements gave any particular confidence that the fighting would really stop. In the event it did. The Russians acted very fast to withdraw their troops. During the war in Vietnam, Americans often heard it suggested that the United States should simply declare victory and leave. The Russians did just that in September 1994, except that they did no more than declare a cease-fire and begin the troop pull-out at once. It seemed almost possible for the Russian people to forget that the Chechens had routed their army in Grozy in just a month earlier. Ledbed was a hero and the war was over.

Ledbed and Maskhadov's agreement committed the two sides to work towards a peace treaty establishing a new constitutional framework for the Chechens, but by mid-October 1996, a mere three months after his great triumph, Ledbed was gone, ousted by accusations that he was planning a coup against Boris Yeltsin. Ledbed did indeed want to be President, but rather than staging a coup, he retreated to the Krasnoyarsk region of Siberia, to run for election to Governor. He won the election and disappeared from serious contention for the Presidency of the whole Russian Federation.

Meanwhile, it was Yeltsin himself who signed the final agreement with Maskhadov in May of 1997. This document also represents a minimalist approach. Neither side could do more than promise, in bald platitudes, to set aside violence "forever" and to settle their disagreements using the recognized norms and principles of international law. They could not even agree on the name of the document. The Chechens wanted to call it a peace "treaty," which the Russians refused to accept because the term implied Chechen sovereignty.* Two annexed agreements were intended to lay the groundwork for economic cooperation and for the repair of the destruction of the war, but the details were never spelled out. They gave themselves until August 2000 to complete that task.† And yet this minimalist peace had remarkable durability despite the

---

* As with the Irish case, the words on the documents themselves became an additional source of contention between the two sides.

† Once again, a peace process willingly left important issues to be resolved later.

political turmoil inside the Russian government. It took little more than a promise and a handshake to stop the killing for three whole years.

Domestic politics in Russia

Inside the Kremlin, the turnover of Prime Ministers was speeding up. Since the job was the stepping stone to the favored position on the Presidential ballot, and the election was most likely scheduled for the summer of 2000, it was an anxious period. Victor Chernomyrdin, Ledbed's nemesis, lasted only until March 1998. His successor, Kiriyenko, lasted three months, gone by June 1998. The next man, Primakov, lasted until August 1999. When the surprise winner of the game, Vladimir Putin, was appointed in August 1999, most people were stunned. Relatively obscure politically, his most obvious qualifications for the job were his years in the KGB. The summer's surprise turned into a New Year's amazement when Boris Yeltsin announced, on the first day of the new millennium, that he was stepping down. As of Jan. 1 2000, Putin was Acting President of Russia. The long awaited elections would be held in March, instead of waiting until June. On March 26, Putin won, easily defeating, among others, Alexander Ledbed.

More surprising, given the widespread relief which had greeted the 1996 peace, Putin won in part because it was he who was leading a renewed assault against the people of Chechnya. This time, the war was widely accepted as necessary, indeed urgent. The trigger event, and it really was a trigger, was a bomb which exploded in a Moscow apartment building on September 13, 1999, the third apartment building bombing inside three weeks, and by far the most destructive. Though cynics had their doubts, most Russians accepted the government claim that Chechens were responsible. The dead numbered between 70 and 100 people. President Yeltsin announced on nationwide television that "Terrorism had declared war on Russia…That enemy does not know conscience, pity or honor. It has no face, ethnic origin or faith." While Russian generals were assuring the press that they had learned the lessons of the last Chechen war, their Prime Minister Vladimir Putin was swearing to "pursue terrorists everywhere."* Domestic power politics in

---

* The language in reports of these bombing attacks bore such a close resemblance to the words spoken by President George Bush after September 11, it is hardly surprising that Russia became one of the firmest supporters of the United States in its war aims in Afghanistan. Such language is also a key impediment to peace.

There is no sign that the rebels will give up. On the contrary, Russia is still losing dozens of soldiers a week, even by its own official estimates. On July 24th, three Russian soldiers were killed and 24 injured when rebels attacked a military convoy, in the capital Grozny, in broad daylight... A Russian general, Alexander Popov said... his checkpoints came under fire as often as 20 times a day.

Anon, *The Economist*, July 29, 2000. p. 51

Russia brought a fragile peace to Chechnya in 1996. Domestic politics ended the peace in 1999. Yeltsin made a conscious decision to make the apartment bombings the beginning of a crusade. It was always a matter of choice, and there were even some who accused the President's own security men of carrying out at least the last of the attacks. Yeltsin, Putin and others seemed to have become confident that another war would help to ensure Putin would win the Presidency.

This Chechnya "case-study," as it was originally written, focused on the war largely in the context of Russian politics. As we have seen, those politics did explain both the search for cease-fire in 1996 and its collapse three years later. For the most part the war stayed out of the international news. Despite its brutal consequences for the Chechen people, no outsiders felt able to intervene, either to mitigate or to end the fighting. UN leaders declared it a domestic matter for the Russians. Before a gathering of the G8 leaders in Genoa, amidst furious anti-globalization protestors, President Bush astonished and silenced other major leaders by offering an enthusiastic endorsement for Putin's war, despite the fact that some Russian commanders had just described its tactics as "lawless." Humanitarian aid workers were too terrified for their own personal safety to mount any campaigns to halt the fighting. Worst of all, nothing in the fighting itself seemed likely to stir the urge for peace. The first war had pulverized so much of Chechnya. The second simply reopened pre-existing wounds. No new pain could feel any worse than the already existing situation.

And then, the scope of the Chechen war was dramatically transformed on September 11, 2001—by terrorists mounting attacks all too easily compared to the bombings in those three Moscow apartment buildings. Suddenly the war in Chechnya was seen as a bond between Presidents Putin and Bush, who declared themselves united in a worldwide war against terrorists. Chechen Muslims were to be seen in the same light as the radicals behind the September 11 attacks. The Presidents had found common ground despite the fact that the Sufi Muslim beliefs in Chechnya share little with the Sunni branch of Islam espoused in Saudi Arabia, the heartland of the September 11 attacker community. And Presidents Putin and Bush were not merely imagining a non-existent linkage. During the 1990s, complex interlocking networks of personal relationships, shared training and mingled distribution systems for money and weapons did indeed come into being. Among the wars in this book, Chechnya, Iraq, Israel/Palestine, Bosnia, and even Ireland, were all impacted by the networks and their money to some degree. In Israel/Palestine and in Chechnya, the networks would also have a significant effect on the chances to make peace.

Vladimir Vakhayev, 36, escaped with his wife and three children during the fighting. Since the Russian flag was hoisted over Grozny, he has repeatedly visited the city to see if it is feasible for his family to come back. And today he turned away in disappointment. "They have cleaned up the streets a bit, but there is no attempt to restore the city," he said.

Michael Gordon,
New York Times, April 27, 2000, p. A3

Crafting an enduring ending to the war in Chechnya had become much more unlikely, after September 11, 2001. A local conflict, over which the Russian government and its Chechen opponents could have the last word, had become a global issue.

Still, it remains worth remembering the dynamics of the 1996 peace process, and its break-down in 1999 from its local perspective. These events provide clear examples of one important strand of peace-making processes, the power of domestic politics to shape war and peace-making. And indeed, for well over two years, it did look as though the 1996 cease-fire had ended the war. In mid-1998, Gail Lapidus, a US expert on ethnic conflict in states of the former Soviet Union, published a post-mortem on the Chechen war. In it, she proclaimed that "a renewal of large-scale violence is unlikely in the foreseeable future" even though she acknowledged that settling the remaining constitutional questions would prove very difficult. In the event large scale war did break out again, within a year. Those Russian words, "a war against terrorism," which re-ignited the war against the Chechens, guaranteed that when the United States too "went to war against terrorism" in the mountains of Central Asia, Russia would be encouraged to fight on indefinitely.

rwanda

SOME KEY DATES   CEASE-FIRE JULY 1999

1993 • Tutsi from Uganda attack. Peace agreement mediated by UN at Arusha giving the Tutsi a base in the NW corner of the country and mandating power sharing.

1994 April 6 • President Habyarimana assassinated in a plane crash. Genocide begins in Kigali the same day.

UN peacekeepers from Belgium captured, tortured and killed.

Tutsi forces inside the country and in Uganda declare war and begin an assault.

Massacres in Kigali, Kibuye and Muyaga and throughout the country. More than 400,000 killed in three weeks.

UN cuts its peace-keeping forces to 270 troops.

May • Refugees begin flooding into Tanzania, Zaire and Uganda.

June • French peace-keepers arrive and establish a "safe haven" in the SW region of the country.

July • RPF return to capture Kigali

July 18 • RPF Tutsi declare a cease-fire and form a government in Kigali.

Nov. • UN Security Council establishes the War Crimes Tribunal for Rwanda.

Dec. • Hutu refugees in eastern Zaire announce a government in exile.

1995 April • Zaire begins a forcible repatriation of thousands of Hutu refugees.

Nov. • First indictment signed in the International Criminal Tribunal for Rwanda.

1996 Mar. • Final 679 UN peacekeepers leave Rwanda. Government denies them a mission extension.

Oct. • War breaks out in eastern Zaire, as Zaire tries to expel its own Tutsi population.

1997 Feb. • President Mobutu of Zaire goes into voluntary exile in France.

Oct. • Killings of Tutsi by Hutu returning from the refugee camps.

THE WAR IN RWANDA

Genocide and military conquest

Rwanda is a verdant country, its terraced slopes covered in banana groves and small fields, with more people more densely packed together than any other country in Africa. 7.1 million of them once lived in a country about the size of Maryland. During two months in the spring of 1994 hundreds of thousands of Rwandans died in a murderous war, killed by their friends and neighbors, even by their own relatives. The assault, directed by the ruling Hutu against their fellow Rwandans of the Tutsi community, was genocidal in purpose, and a disaster of global significance.

Rwanda has a nickname, "Land of a Thousand Hills." In 1994, the local name for those thousand hills, Mille Collines, echoed everywhere, the call sign for the radio station the governing Hutu used to broadcast their genocidal mania out into the countryside, nationwide. Vile radio speeches and threats day after day gave the oncoming catastrophe an air of inevitability. In the capital, Kigali, officials filled in the last names on their lists of Tutsi to be destroyed before sending their orders out for execution to local governments in villages and towns dotted all over the hills and the valleys. Local gendarmes (police) and militias formed up, and on April 7, 1994, the slaughter began. Within a month, most of the 800,000 or more doomed men, women and children were dead.

By early May, thousands more had become refugees, fleeing Rwanda for UN sponsored refugee camps in Uganda, Tanzania and Zaire. Were these Tutsi, fleeing for their lives? No, most of refugees were murderers not victims. They were Hutu, convinced that it was they who were now at dreadful risk, under threat from an advancing Tutsi army. This army, the Rwandan Patriotic Front, had launched Rwanda's other war just as the genocide began. The second war is best described as a conventional struggle for control over the government between two ethnic groups. An earlier cease-fire between the RPF and the Hutu government had been on the verge of collapse, so as the genocide against them began, the Tutsi army responded with a conquering march across the country.

A mere 20,000 strong, the Tutsi army planned to capture the whole of Rwanda. What is more, within three months they had succeeded. In fact, they almost took control of the capital within the first few days of the war. Starting out from bases in northwestern Rwanda, the troops' first destination was the airport at Kigali. Then they left the city, and marched on to take the southeastern regions. By May, they had turned west, aiming towards the land that bordered Zaire (later to be called the Congo). On July 18, 1994, the RPF army finally returned to Kigali and took over the entire city, ready at last to establish their own, Tutsi-dominated government. At that moment in July, the Hutu had killed 800,000 Tutsi and, in fear of the Tutsi response, well over a million Hutu were now refugees.

Like the wars in Ireland and Chechnya, Bosnia and South Africa, both Rwandan wars had a long history behind them, sharpened by some very recent history, which was driving the opposing sides into action. The old history, described as an "ethnic rivalry," originated in colonization, first under Germany and then under Belgium. The European governors turned Rwanda's existing economic and social division between agriculturists and cattle herders into a race-identifier system, thereby creating the social hierarchies they needed to maintain control of a distant colony. All the while, Hutu field workers and Tutsi cowmen could and did marry into each others' families, live under the same legal system and respond equally enthusiastically to Catholic missionaries. Still, relations between the two groups had become tense by the 1950s, when the independence movement spread across Africa. Rwandan independence came burdened by a history that linked the Tutsi to the Belgian colonizers, and thus to a role in depriving oppressed Hutu of political power. Soon after the Belgians left, this story became the justification for a civil war, which ended with many thousands of Tutsi in exile in Uganda. In 1973, Juvenile Habyarimana, a Hutu, became President of Rwanda, and the country seemed basically to be at peace, the old history resolved by a new power structure which gave the Hutu all the power but left leading Tutsi living beyond Rwanda's borders.

The more recent history began to unfold in the early 1990s, when a new generation of Tutsi exiles, English speaking since they had grown up in Uganda, began to press for the right of Tutsis to return to Rwanda. The exiles mobilized an army and made successful inroads in the northwestern part of the country in 1991, which sent shock waves through Rwandan society. UN mediators stepped in two years later to broker a cease-fire and a power-sharing agreement between the Hutu government and Tutsi returnees. Hutu repudiation of that agreement prompted the catastrophic outbreak of war in 1994.

Among the most startling features of the combat between April and July 1994 is that, despite the human catastrophe—800,000 dead and well over 1 million refugees from a total population of 7.1 million, both wars simply stopped once the Tutsi forces returned in triumph to Kigali. The Tutsi army won the contest for control of political power in a rout so the leaders of the genocide fled the country. The new conquerors even promised a revival of the power-sharing model of government. And yet, the Tutsi rout lacked general consent from the various factions of society for its political settlements. It also lacked mechanisms to repatriate hundreds of thousands of refugees and lacked the justice system needed to deal with those who committed the genocide. Victory under these conditions represented far less than a complete end to the Hutu/Tutsi wars. The two peoples were still far from peace. The ending of war in Rwanda would depend finally on whether the Rwandan people could recover from their traumatic experience. To understand the peace, it is necessary to offer a brief sketch of the disaster as it unfolded.

The war years

There were three parties to the fighting in Rwanda—the Hutu, the Tutsi and the French, who deployed their army under the label "peace-keeping force." The complex and somewhat questionable activities of the French will be covered more fully in the cease-fire chapter that synthesizes this story with the six others. Here, our focus is on the two indigenous communities, so I will do no more than say that the French forces invaded, held about 25% of the territory for two months in the second half of the war, and withdrew at

危

After weeks of decay in the tropical heat, it is difficult to distinguish where one body ends and another begins in the chaotic mounds of death. Clearly visible at other locations is the newly turned dirt indicating the existence of mass graves, where the victims will never be counted.

The killers in Rwanda, however, are discovering what the Nazis discovered half a century before them: The truth of this ultimate crime against humanity can be difficult to keep buried. Random arms and legs, demanding attention, have somehow managed to pop up through the loose soil of Rwanda's newly dug grave pits.

Roger Winter,
The Washington Post June 5, 1994, p. C1.

once when the Tutsi had established full control. A significant number of Hutu who had participated in the genocide were sheltered by the French.

These indigenous Rwandan wars both started as a result of the same event, the assassination of President Habyarimana. A missile downed his plane as it was coming in to land in Kigali. Habyarimana was killed because he was trying to stabilize the UN mediated power-sharing agreement. His assassins were adamantly and publicly opposed to this, convinced that the Hutu could continue to hold sole power provided they exterminated enough of the Tutsi. By nightfall the next day, Hutu forces had rounded up and killed most moderates in Kigali who supported Hutu/Tutsi political power sharing. Many were murdered with machetes or by a single bullet. Later, in the countryside, most died the same way, though some Tutsi were herded into buildings, which were then set on fire, killing all inside.

From their bases in the northwest, Tutsi could hear Mille Collines broadcast genocidal threats as well as anyone, so the moment they heard the President was dead, they were also ready to act. Despite being equally quick off the mark, both the Hutu charged with genocide and the Tutsi charged with conquest faced weeks of struggle. The intricate, hilly geography of Rwanda prevented them from projecting local successes into the distant corners of the country. They had to traverse the actual terrain to achieve their goals.

The Tutsi army trying to reclaim power and the Hutu army and militias trying to exterminate the Tutsi fought valley by valley, village by village. So well organized were the Hutu lists and plans that it took only two weeks for them to massacre 250,000 Tutsi. After one more week, the mass executions were over and nearly 2/3 of the victims were dead. Still, the lists showed that thousands remained to be killed, and during May and June Tutsi went on dying, 10-20 at a time.

In the same two weeks, the Tutsi forces drove the Hutu government out of Kigali and captured most of the eastern part of Rwanda. Then they moved south, until their forces came up against the barrier created by the French. In the last phases of the war, RPF troops from the far northwest of the country battled for the rest of the western region in a rather strenuous campaign fought in the midst of massive floods of people trying to escape into Zaire. While the total number of Hutu dead is hard to calculate, many, many thousands were undoubtedly killed in reprisal for the genocide, and the scale of the refugee exodus defies the imagination. On a single day in May, 250,000 Hutu refugees streamed over the main bridge into Zaire.

Quickly, international refugee aid workers staffing the camps in Zaire and Uganda realized, to their chagrin, that they were feeding and housing genocidal killers. The refugee camps were even providing an opportunity for the Hutu to regroup and plan a renewed attack on the country.* In the first few months after the fighting ended, the prospects for an enduring peace looked grim.

From conquest via justice to peace

As the horrors of the war in Rwanda poured out all over the newspapers of the world that spring, Southern Africa presented two deeply contrasting pictures of humanity. As a *Los Angeles Times* front page story put it on May 8, 1994: "From South Africa, aerial photographs of whites and blacks standing together patiently waiting to vote, in lines that seemed to twist and turn for miles, conveyed hope and the promise of a new era. From Rwanda, scenes of a sea of brutalized and terrified refugees fleeing from genocidal violence spread despair and fear of an unfolding apocalypse that could engulf much of the continent." *The Times* did not have the story quite right, because the Rwandans in flight were the genocidal killers themselves; their intended

---

* Those who intervene in war often find they are confronted with a choice about whether to work in alliance with someone who has done serious wrong in the past, in order to ease future pain. While the United States has become an enthusiastic participant in the prosecution of Slobodan Milosevic for war crimes, one would be hard pressed to guess that from reading this book. After all, when we last met Milosevic he was an honored guest of the US government in Dayton, a leading negotiator setting the terms for peace in Bosnia.

victims were mostly already dead. Still, these refugees did represent one of three very serious impediments to transforming the July 1994 RPF cease-fire into an enduring peace. The other two impediments were the complexities inherent in forming a viable power-sharing government made up of both ethnic groups and, most serious of all, rendering justice in response to the genocide.

In Zaire and Uganda, hundreds of thousands of Hutu found shelter in refugee camps. Overseas aid flowed in, in vast quantities, keeping the camp residents clothed and fed for two years. And yet, the camps themselves desta-bilized the peace in several ways. One challenge was to persuade the Hutu to return home peacefully but while Zaire was governed by President Mobutu, their hosts put the Rwandans under no pressure to leave. All the same, in 1996, disturbances were building in Zaire, and when Rwanda's government helped insurgent Laurent Kabila to oust Mobutu, threats of forcible refugee repatriation by Kabila, combined with Rwandan army shells landing on the camps, persuaded many refugees to leave. They traveled in streams almost as large as the ones in which they had fled two years earlier and within a mat-ter of weeks the camps were empty.

Neither the overthrow of Mobutu nor the surge in Hutu refugee repa-triation ended the dangers to Rwandan peace from outside its frontiers. Most Rwandans went back home, but no one knows how many thousands were still hiding out in the bush in the eastern Congo (the new name given to Zaire when Kabila came to power). Indeed, continued grassroots uprisings in the Congo threatened to engulf the whole of Central Africa in war. Rwanda, Uganda, Burundi, Tanzania and even Zimbabwe began sending troops into different parts of the Congo. Alliances proved hard to stabilize. Laurent Kabila was assassinated and succeeded by his son. Those refugees who had not returned to Rwanda became entangled in a new war in the Congo, and the war they had originally exported from Rwanda threatened to return home once again. The Hutu outside the country still represented an ongoing threat to the stability of Rwanda. In the camps, with little else to occupy them, many began to organize into militia and opposition political cadres whose leaders were the same men who had been architects of the earlier genocide. In 1997-98, many actually made several serious assaults on

Rwanda intending to destabilize the government and regain sole power.

The decisive Tutsi military victory could not establish a stable peace, in part because of the difficulties in power sharing inside the country. Even in 1994 when the camps were at their fullest, most Hutu were still living in Rwanda and when the Tutsi dominated government took power, a considerable number of the men named to the highest posts were Hutu, including the President, Pasteur Bizimungu. The most important man was a Tutsi, Vice-President Paul Kagame. Their blended multi-ethnic government began work at once, but the massive genocidal killings had left Rwanda with a much reduced professional community and few experienced people in either ethnic group were available (or perhaps courageous enough) to serve. Lawyers and judges, doctors and administrators had been right at the top of the lists of people the Hutu ordered assassinated, and many in the capital Kigali had been killed within a day. Still, the power sharing government survived until early in 2000, even though by then a number of the Hutu had begun to resign.*

However, the biggest problem in Rwanda, both for the government and for ordinary people, was prisoners. Within weeks of the RPF victory, 125,000 people were in jail, many having surrendered themselves seeking protection from revenge attacks by their victims' families. Each prisoner was suspected of playing a significant part in the genocidal war. At the same time, far away in New York City, the United Nations was arranging for the creation of an International War Crimes Tribunal to take responsibility for the prosecution of the most important leaders in the genocide, almost all of whom had left Rwanda. The UN claimed the right to try the key leaders among the Hutu from Rwanda. One by one the indicted leaders were arrested and delivered to Arusha, in Tanzania, where the UN court was established. In January 1997, the UN Criminal Tribunal was at last ready to begin its first trial, but their cases went forward dreadfully slowly. After three years UN officials managed to complete only seven trials, six of which were still on appeal, with a mere 44 more defendants in custody. There was also a problem about sentencing. The UN Tribunal, largely under the influence of European jurists in The

---

* It makes sense to see those first few years in Rwanda as similar to the interim government in South Africa. In the immediate aftermath of the agony, it is easy to recognize the importance of conciliatory acts. After a while divisive pressures increase and the need for collaborative solidarity decreases.

Mr. Barayagwiza was headed for trial as the mastermind behind genocide propaganda when appeals court judges at The Hague ruled in November that he should be released. They said his rights had been violated by sloppy prosecutors and incompetent court clerks, who let him spend 330 days in prison without charges and waited 98 days to bring him before the court.

Farah Stockman,
The Christian Science Monitor Feb. 24, 2000, p.7

Hague, had agreed that the death penalty would not be imposed even on those convicted of genocide. Rwanda, by contrast handed down the death penalty 300 times prosecuting lower level officials. No one knew how far the UN tribunal would try to reach, but the Rwandan government knew it still had over 2,000 key perpetrators it wanted to see held accountable. It gradually became clear that this particular approach to justice might hinder peace-making more than it helped it.

In addition, 120,000 or more of the lower level perpetrators were still in custody. The Hutu who had surrendered probably never imagined that they were subjecting themselves to indefinite detention. Although Rwandan justice, despite a decimated judiciary, was moving much faster than the international, they were able to handle only 2,000 convictions in the years between 1994 and 2000.* The remaining caseload was staggering. Neither the international nor the Rwandan government systems of justice were up to handling the vast numbers of people. So, five years after the war ended, the government decided to send most of the prisoners back to the communities from which they had originally come. To end the war they had fought village by village; the country would try to bring justice and thus peace village by village.

Proposals to use a more local and traditional Rwandan system of justice began to gather momentum in 1999. Known as "Gacaca," this system would entail setting up as many as 10,000 local tribunals, each one to handle the cases from their own community. Those in favor of this kind of process believed it would force each town and village to come to grips with their personal experiences with the genocide. People would have to admit, say, that every fifth house on the street had been vandalized while the remaining four were left untouched by the war. They would have to look at the teenager who

---

* This is another area of stark contrast with South Africa. In only three years, ending in December 1998, the South African Truth and Reconciliation Commission had heard testimony from well over 20,000 people and was close to finalizing the disposition of all 7000 of the cases before it.

was 10 years old during the war and now faced the rest of his life without the arms hacked off by his neighbors. They would have to walk to the church-yard where hundreds of people from the surrounding area had been burned to death, and the man who was mayor at the time would have to admit to allowing the catastrophe to proceed. For those against such trials, the fact that Rwanda was now even more disproportionately Hutu than it had been before the genocide meant that the guilty in each village would still have plenty of supporters while those bringing accusations would continue to be at risk. The trials would be a charade and villainous assassins would escape punishment.

In October 2001, the Rwandans elected 26,000 judges to sit, three to a tribunal, hopefully to dispose of all but the few ring-leaders who remained in Rwandan jails awaiting more formal justice. The Gacaca, like South Africa's Truth and Reconciliation Commission, would depend for its success on truth-telling by the perpetrators. As with the TRC, hearings would take place all over the country, allowing the local people to describe their suffer-ing and perhaps also allowing the perpetrators to repair some of the damage by traditional means—an apology, a cow, a local gift of some kind. If all went according to plan, the tribunals would have their work completed in three or four years, leaving the country's capacity to make peace considerably strengthened.

Clearly both South Africa and Rwanda recognized that the resolution of claims for justice would have an important impact on determining whether the new peace represented a permanent end to the struggles or merely a break in a longer war. But Rwanda faced burdens which a regionally more dominant South Africa could avoid. Rwanda's war spread beyond its own frontiers, enmeshing the Congo, heightening Hutu/Tutsi tensions in Burundi, and leading to armed confrontation with former allies like Uganda. Ultimately, Rwanda's long term peace would be dependent on them too. Furthermore, South Africa had been able to devote nearly four years to de-signing a constitution for a transitional power-sharing government, on the road to true majority rule. The very speed and decisiveness of the Tutsi victory in Rwanda left the winners to decide for themselves whether and how much to share power with the losers. The faltering of the power-sharing

危

regime in 2000 was a reminder that merely winning a war, no matter how decisively, is not enough to secure an enduring peace. In Rwanda, the capture of Kigali, the capital, was enough actually to stop the killing. But stopping the killing did not end the political conflict, and ending both of these was never going to be adequate to salve the wounds of the genocidal war. For that, Rwandans concluded, the right kind of justice would be critical, both to the long term health of their country and to their peace.

We turn now to the last of the stories about peace, to Iraq in 1991. The war that year was supposed to have ended in a victory by the UN Coalition over Saddam Hussein, a victory even faster and even more decisive than the Tutsi victory in Rwanda. But in Iraq, the "loser" never did accept that he had lost, and so in fact the war never ended. US troops came home in triumph but it was a hollow triumph, and 12 years later they were back on Iraqi soil, killing and muscling their way through the desert, aiming once again for that final victory so thoroughly and effectively repudiated by Saddam years ago.

機

rwanda • 143

SOME KEY DATES   CEASE-FIRE STILL TO COME

1990 • Aug. 2 Iraq invades Kuwait, seizing the emirate within 24 hours.

Aug. • Saudi Arabia requests U.S. military aid. Operation Desert Shield begins.

Nov. • The Bush administration adds troops to make an offensive combat capability to eject Iraqi Army from Kuwait.

1991 Jan. • Secretary of State James Baker meets with Iraqi Foreign Minister Tariq Aziz in Geneva but their talks fail to produce an Iraqi pullout from Kuwait.

Jan. 17 • Operation Desert Storm begins. Allied air strikes in Iraq and Kuwait.

Feb. • Ground war starts with Marine Corps in southern Kuwait.

Feb. 28 • Coalition announces suspension of ground combat operations.

Mar. 3 • Formal acceptance of UN cease-fire conditions by Iraq.

Shiite rebellions in southern Iraq, put down by Iraqi military units.

Apr. • US Operation Provide Comfort to aid Kurdish refugees in northern Iraq.

May and June • UN Security Council passes Resolutions about weapons of mass destruction and war reparations, rejected by Iraq. Embargo, Res. 661, stays in effect.

July • Iraqi deadline to disclose nuclear materials passes. Embargo remains in effect.

1992 • "No Fly Zones" instituted, first in the north and then in the south.

1993 Jan. • Crisis in Northern Iraq leads US ground forces into action in the region.

1992 • Iraq accepts UN proposal for limited oil sales in return for allowing import of food and simple medical supplies.

1998 • Iraq expels UN weapons inspectors permanently.

2001 • Oil for food program arousing international criticism from France and Russia. United States and Britain seek resolution compelling Iraq to allow inspectors to return.

2002 Fall • United States and Britain lobbying at the UN for a resolution allowing military force in Iraq if inspections do not resume. Resolution passes, and inspections resume.

2003 • Inspectors make monthly reports to the UN Security Council. France promises to veto a resolution authorizing force.

March 19 • US and British Forces attack Iraq with support from Spain and others.

THE WAR IN IRAQ

False endings or the war that never ended

In August 1990, Iraq invaded and then took control of Kuwait. Within days the UN Security Council responded with Resolution 661, imposing a comprehensive embargo on all Iraqi exports, including oil, and on all imports, even including food and medicines. Soon after, a coalition of UN sponsored military forces under US leadership began to assemble, mostly in Saudi Arabia, preparing to recapture Kuwait from Iraqi troops. Some hoped that the UN embargo would be enough to force Iraq to withdraw, without the opposing armies actually going into action. The embargo never showed any signs of that kind of success and, throughout the fall of 1990, more and more soldiers continued to assemble, all of them preparing for an active campaign.

By the time the first UN coalition bombs exploded onto Baghdad on the night of January 16, 1991, 500,000 Americans and thousands of others were fully deployed, ready for action. Night and day over the next six weeks, the UN forces pounded the Iraqi military from the air with a combination of B52's "carpet" bombing Iraqi divisions and precision assaults on specific Iraqi military sites and weapons factories. Yet more bombers and cruise missiles were sent to destroy Iraqi power plants, oil industry operations and other sites designated by targeting experts as "military infrastructure." The UN-Coalition forces flew 109,876 sorties and dropped 88,500 tons of bombs. The Iraqis responded with small, sporadic counter attacks. The total tonnage of bombs dropped during the six week period was, according to one calculation, as much as six Hiroshima bombs. It was a ferocious assault.

The widespread scope of the damage was very carefully hidden behind controlled media coverage during this phase of the war. On "home fronts" worldwide, millions of people watching a sanitized version of combat on CNN were led to believe that the UN forces were virtually "surgical" in their

A week into the Persian Gulf war, one aspect of the most intensive bombing campaign in history is becoming clear: it is hitting the underpinnings of Iraqi society as well as the planes, tanks and soldiers of the Iraqi armed forces....

While assessments differ on what impact the 14,000 bombing sorties are having on the civilian population, few dispute that with water, communications and other basic necessities being temporarily or permanently disrupted, the war is reaching into the homes of thousands of people.

Peter Grier and Scott Armstrong,
Christian Science Monitor, Jan. 25, 1991 p.1.

restraint. For one brief and terrifying moment in the middle of the war, when Iraqi missiles began landing on Israeli territory, the scope of the threats had evidently broadened, but even that crisis was over within days. Then, in late February 1991, thousands and thousands of US infantry and tank troops began their long-awaited ground offensive. Their period of danger only lasted a few days; it was over so fast it came to be dubbed the "100 hour war." On February 28, the US President, George Bush, made an announcement that a cease-fire had gone into effect.

This was the official narrative of the "Gulf War" which, through tight management of public information, told of an unambiguous, restrained and yet seemingly unmitigated triumph of military strategy.* The wider world continued to watch events in Iraq for a little while longer, and at first the official story of the "six week war" held up. The leaders of the UN coalition had some justification for believing that they could end the war whenever they chose.

On March 3, 1991, an intermediate cease-fire agreement was signed during a meeting between UN coalition and Iraqi generals in the Iraqi desert. The agreement covered the exchange of prisoners and the disengagement of forces.† Iraqi troops were in retreat. UN troops, which had advanced well into Iraq, drew back to Kuwait, and to their bases in Saudi Arabia. Iraq handed back its handful of Coalition prisoners (though they held on to 20,000 Kuwaitis for much longer) and the UN forces repatriated their 70,000 captives. In the UN offices back in New York, planners were beginning to

---

* One way the American military system manages to avoid endowing its enemy with legitimacy is by labeling wars with anything other than the name of the people under attack. The "Gulf War' was always a war against Iraq and against no one else. Its other name, "Operation Desert Storm," allowed people to forget it was even a war. If one is not at war, then there can be no need to make peace.

† Like the agreements making peace for Bosnia and Ireland, the opposing sides here understood the need for common standards on prisoners and the disengagement of forces. Unlike those other negotiators, at the end of the Iraq war, the UN simply imposed the political conditions. Clearly these were not "peace talks."

design the destruction of Iraq's remaining missiles and its known reserves of toxic weapons. American troops returned home to heroes' welcomes. President George Bush and the other Coalition leaders exulted that fewer than 300 of the UN forces had died in combat, and for several months it remained possible to bask in the sense that the UN Coalition had won a complete victory, after an amazingly short war.

Those who still wanted Iraq punished for its "aggression" could rely on the UN Security Council, where the winners were passing resolutions and setting out the details of Iraq's obligation to pay reparations and a system of UN control of Iraqi weapons. "Defeated," Iraq would obviously have no choice but to comply. It seemed so simple.

Initially the UN voted three resolutions. In R687, Iraq was told it had legal responsibility to compensate for the economic losses of its war victims. In R699, Iraq was ordered to offer up, for their complete destruction, the remaining components of its missile, nuclear and bio/chemical arsenals. In R715, Iraq was informed it must agree to ongoing monitoring of its weapons production by a UN group to be known by the acronym UNSCOM. Furthermore, until these provisions were complied with, the UN Security Council authorized a continuation of the August 1990 embargo, supervised by the UN's 661 (Sanctions) Committee. The war, they assumed, had ended and the winners were establishing clearly what Iraq, the defeated power, was now to do.

The official story seemed watertight. The only problem was that it was wrong. Saddam Hussein had said so quite explicitly. As the allied forces pulled out of Iraq, it was clear that as far as he was concerned the war was not over, he had not suffered a defeat. American news commentators were shaking with laughter. His refusal to admit his defeat was taken to be yet another sign that he was delusional, not a political leader worthy of the name.

The story I have to tell here offers a much more complex narrative than both the official US/UN version and Iraq's bald claim to have ended the war without defeat. From the perspective of a peace-maker, it is clear that the war between Iraq and its two prime opponents, the United States and the United Kingdom, never did end. No one on either side ever made even minimalist statements like those of the Chechens and Russians, declaring they would never again resort to force. Rather than engaging together in serious negotiations about powers and resources, the Iraqis, the UN and their respective military agents simply spent the next 12 years issuing and following up on violent threats and counter threats.

Now, in the week in which I complete this manuscript, massive numbers of bombs are exploding in Iraq once again. Key buildings in Iraq's cities are being smashed to the ground by American and British planes, while tanks and guns advance on the capital Baghdad. Even if Saddam Hussein himself does suffer a defeat, and if the Iraqi people turn out to be grateful for some degree of political liberation, this war will certainly have implications for peace, or the lack of it, in Iraq itself and on a larger scale around the world. Who knows how and when peace will return to the United States or to Iraq, that place I learned, as a child, to call a cradle of human civilization.

With hindsight, one can see that the fiction that the war had ended actually first became clear in the passage of the very first UN Resolutions against Iraq. The Security Council thought it could *force* Iraq into submission to its demands, when Saddam Hussein had repeatedly and strenuously vowed to resist. He would not pay reparations, even if his people starved. He would not facilitate the destruction of his own arsenal. Again and again he would challenge the UN's weapons monitors, even at the risk of UN military reprisals. The UN might talk as though the war was over. Saddam Hussein knew it was not, and he was ready to show the world one of the key realities of war and cease-fire: the fighting cannot end until *both* sides agree that it is over.

With hindsight, we also know that the official description of a precision-targeted, six-week "Gulf War" was and always had been an illusion. The war was more encompassing than that, both in its duration and its physical scope. War, real war, started with the embargo months before the January 1991 bombings and for the next 12 years US and British bombers, under UN authorization, were in regular hostile engagements with the Iraqi military. To comprehend this unending war fully entails recognizing its onset in August 1990 as a modern and massive siege war. The full tally of acts of war after February 1991 is immense, including UN control of key parts of Kurdistan, air combat over much of Iraq's land area, UNSCOM's weapons destruction project and continuation of the state of siege/embargo.

The consequences for Iraq were massive human suffering and the collapse of a modern, oil-export-based industrial infrastructure. The costs to the United States and its allies have traditionally been measured in terms of money and the sums are large but not overpowering, up to $1 billion a year for the United States. The moral costs may turn out to have been much greater when a full accounting is done, because a siege such as this can only be understood as total war, with the accompanying costs born largely by Iraq's civilian population.

From the beginning, the siege was intensified by repeated armed raids inside fortress Iraq. Saddam Hussein was engaged in war too, and bears his share of the responsibility, but the United States and its allies have always tried to blame the entire war on him. That is wrong. War is interactive and is the result of the actions of combatants on all sides. With the passage of time, more and more of the UN's own leadership began seriously to question the ethics of their actions. Leading members of the Security Council, in particular France and Russia, urged ending the sanctions entirely. Their stance gained support when senior UN humanitarian employees resigned in dismay and despair about the human costs of the war. The situation finally erupted once more into all out war on March 19, 2003. No matter what happens, the moral justifications for 12 years of siege war need to be very strong, and the UN's reasons to postpone a lasting peace began to look less and less commanding several years before the 2003 assault.

Each of the other cases has been devoted to the steps taken to ending a war. This case, sadly, is a story of steps taken to continue it. This is what some people whose hearts and minds have been altered by war become able to do. My comments at the end about possible paths towards a true cease-fire are, and must be, purely speculative. In 2001 the US government had fallen once more into the hands of the particular people and political families who prosecuted the onset of the war. Iraq was still under its own war-era leadership. By the end of that year, US shock and outrage at the World Trade Center attack was bringing down on Iraq yet another round of unproven accusations of terrorism. It was hard to imagine then that there would soon be the critical changes of heart and leadership needed to make the end of this war possible. At the same time, it was also still possible some event would prove this pessimistic speculation wrong.

Two kinds of war—military engagement and embargo

To see the whole Iraq war clearly we must start again at the beginning. The first action taken against the Iraqis after they invaded Kuwait—the world-wide embargo—ensured Iraq was totally cut off economically, and encircled by hostile forces. Iraq could neither sell the oil, whose revenues were the basis of its modern urbanized/industrialized state, nor import any goods from overseas. The embargo was enforced by armed military forces; military ships intercepted and boarded traders, planes prevented unauthorized flights and frontier guards on the ground cut off supplies. Survival quickly became precarious for many Iraqis. The 1998 *World Disasters Report* issued by the International Red Cross report explained why:

> [Iraq was not] a low-income rural country of small farmers able to eke out an existence from the land if necessary. It [was] an urban country and had an economically buoyant economy ….
> [Pre 1990, their oil] income paid for $2 to $3 billion of annual food imports to meet two-thirds of its needs, [and for] thousands of foreign workers, $30 per person a year drug supplies, cheap or free health care, an effective education system, and plenty of jobs in ministries, military forces and state-backed enterprises. In this urbanized society, three-quarters of the 22 million population were dependent on the complex lifelines of towns and cities, from electrical power to piped water.

As a consequence of bombing and the ten-year-long blockade, education, health care, oil-production facilities and power and clean water supplies deteriorated sharply. Iraq's GNP fell by 75% from its pre-war levels. Saddam Hussein's government was routinely castigated by its enemies for its priorities in spending the money it did have, but in truth it acted as any government must when under siege. It fed and supplied its military forces first. It was they, after all, who provided the country's defense against ongoing UN military action and its last bastion of fortification against total subjugation to the UN's edicts.

Combat engagements 1991 - 2000

Back in 1990 when strategists framed the military options available to the United States as a choice between "embargo" or "war," one available choice was to intensify the existing siege through a direct assault on Iraqi fortifications, with the attendant risk that the UN forces might suffer thousands and thousands of casualties. The other choice was to wait. In January 1991 when the assault took place, the extent of the risk turned out to have been vastly exaggerated. The UN coalition was easily capable of bursting into fortress Iraq. Still, in a break with siege tradition, those in command opted not to occupy the capital city. They turned down the option to take responsibility for the long-term control of the administration of Iraq. Instead, the Coalition forces returned to their siege stations. Finding itself under continued embargo, and facing UN mandated destruction of its remaining power weapons, Iraq realized it was still a nation at war.

For five full years after the official cease-fire in 1991, the country managed to rebuild only a small fraction of its damaged infrastructure, a few of its electric power plants, water pumps and sewage treatment facilities. Throughout the period between that nominal 1991 "cease-fire" and the massive onslaught in 2003, Iraq suffered air attacks, naval seizures and even ground incursions by UN sponsored forces in Kurdistan.

UN forces were confident that they were entitled, by Security Council Resolutions, to control sea-going traffic in Iraqi waters, monitoring all ships leaving port, and checking the ships arriving to deliver goods. The first embargo enforcement fleet deployed in the late summer of 1990. The apparent cease-fire in February 1991 made no difference at all to the number of ships stopped or seized. All ocean-going vessels in the Persian Gulf were subject to challenge by the UN sponsored Multinational Interception Force. A December 2000 report announced that the interceptors had sent radio queries to more than 28,000 vessels and boarded more than 12,000. 700 were allegedly

> US carrier task forces on station in the Persian Gulf are free to use military power against Iraq or any state that threatens them. Carriers are not subject to the political limitations of air bases on foreign soil.
>
> The recent stand-off between the United States and Iraq illuminated an enduring truth: Sea power means not having to ask permission.
>
> Norman Friedman, *Naval Institute Proceedings*, Feb 1998 p.91.

in violation of UN sanctions. The sea was an active theater of war.

Land and air were equally engaged. In the months immediately after the end of the 1991 assault on Iraq, rebellions broke out against the Saddam Hussein government in the Shiite dominated south and the Kurdish north. US troops, representing the UN, went into northern Iraq immediately, on a mission to protect the Kurdish community from Saddam's retribution. While ground troops remained only a few months, air patrols soon replaced them, and in October 1992 the Iraqi government was forced to sign a statement that UN relief workers and armed forces would hence forth be in charge of food distribution for Kurds. From April 1991 onwards, the British, French and United States claimed authority over a "no-fly zone," banning all Iraqi military air patrols over the northern third of Iraq. From August 1992, they took control of the airspace over the southern third of the country as well. Though most outsiders quickly forgot the Kurds, the 1992 UN management mandate remained in force, and when food distributions finally began, the UN routinely allocated the Kurds somewhat more of the total ration than their population numbers could justify.

The UN's decision to provide long-term support for Iraq's Shiite and Kurdish people clearly represented a military challenge to Iraq for control over its own land and people. It has been harder for non-Iraqis to recognize the UN's decision to demolish Iraq's missile and toxic weapons arsenal as an act of war, and to see the UNSCOM weapons "inspectors" as agents of war.* And yet their task was to destroy weapons, the central strategic function of combat in war. UNSCOM was just like a Trojan Horse inserted to destroy the country's military power from within. Saddam Hussein perceived in UNSCOM the UN's chosen means to complete Iraq's military defeat, to finish the job that the United States and allies had left unfinished after the first assault.

Although at first the weapons inspectors expected to stay only a few months, they soon realized they were in search of a large, complex and skillfully hidden arsenal. So they were in Iraq for years, both enduring and

---

* This statement applies even more to the early months of 2003, when inspections were put forward as an alternative to war. Within the analytical framework I present here, the inspections are not an alternative to war, only an alternative to a violent and direct military assault on the cities and people of Iraq.

provoking repeated violent and hostile clashes with Iraqi troops and officials. Finally, in December 1998, Saddam Hussein managed to force UNSCOM to leave. Commentators everywhere had laughed derisively when the Iraqi President first announced to his people that they had not been "defeated," indeed that they had "won." If one recognizes the weapons destruction project as part of the war itself, and then sees the victory in Iraq's expulsion of UNSCOM, his claim begins to seem much less laughable.

The weapons-destruction was not a military success. Indeed, the withdrawal of UNSCOM provoked an escalation of the war in another arena: air combat by more traditional means. Immediately after the inspectors left in 1998, cruise missiles rained down on Baghdad and the town relived 1991 once again. In fact, the basic framework for ongoing air warfare had been set much earlier and revolved around the northern and southern "no-fly zones." The British and Americans sent out sorties two to three times a week, most of which were ignored by press and public. US aircraft flew over 200,000 missions in the first eight years. Later, the scale of operations became even larger. Between December 1998 and March 2000, there were "actions" on 159 days and the British defense minister announced that the Iraqis had fired on "coalition" aircraft 550 times. In March 2000, a Russian Federation official at the UN stated that during those first three months of 2000, US and British forces had conducted over 20,000 bombing strikes in the no-fly zones.

A simple summary of these UN sponsored military engagements and assaults during the years between 1991 and 2000 demonstrates clearly that Iraq and the UN were at "war" the whole time. The UN Marine Interception Force intercepted nearly 30,000 ships, boarding thousands and detaining hundreds. UNSCOM destroyed thousands of ready-to-use weapons, and several thousand tons of chemical and biological reserves. UN-mandated aircraft flew thousands of missions each year, regularly attacking Iraqi

> The United States and Britain staged air strikes against radar stations and air defense command centers in Iraq today, including targets around Baghdad, in what President Bush called a necessary response to Iraqi provocation.
>
> The raid—carried out by more than three dozen aircraft shortly after night fell in Baghdad— represented an escalation of the long-running, low-level skirmishes between American and British jets and Iraqi forces.
>
> James Dao and Steven Meyers, *New York Times*, Feb. 17, 2001 p. A1

military facilities, fighter planes and helicopters with live ammunition. Iraqi officials lost control of Kurdistan as well. The government of Saddam Hussein was encircled, at war. The war's biggest casualties were a sophisticated civilization and hundreds of thousands of ordinary people, in particular the children of Iraq. And the worst of the damage was done by twelve years of an embargo that was still in force right up to the onset of the 2003 assault.

The embargo 1991 - onwards

When the bombs were falling during the height of the 1991 UN assault on Iraq, military spokesmen kept assuring an anxious public that the targets were all "military." American and British bombers and cruise missiles were aimed at air-force bases and tank factories, no doubt. They also attacked nuclear facilities and damaged chemical weapons factories. Coalition citizens watching the news at home did not discover until some months after the assault was over that targeting planners had placed electricity and water pumping stations on their list of "military targets." Civilian Iraq had been cut off from imported food and medical supplies in August 1990 and now its urban infrastructure had been devastated as well. Accustomed, as the country once was, to exporting billions of barrels of oil each year to maintain its modern society with mass education and health care, Iraq suddenly found itself without the ability even to maintain the most basic feature of an advanced civilization: a steady supply of clean water.

Such a consequence is perhaps to be expected in a war. But when the war is said to be over, rebuilding should be allowed to begin. At the end of World War II, the United Nations helped pay for the reconstruction of the industrial and social base they had just purposively destroyed in Germany and Japan. Of course, Iraq had never acted as the defeated should towards the victorious; even in the spring of 1991, mutual hostilities remained so intense that a restorative collaboration was impossible. The UN's leaders were willing, even in 1991, to allow minimal Iraqi oil sales under highly controlled conditions. Iraq, repudiating the "defeated" status this implied, refused. For the next five years the embargo was total. No oil was permitted to leave Iraq, no food or medicine could be imported. Iraq and the UN could not even agree on the smallest amount of "humanitarian" economic activity. In 1996 there was a breakthrough (literally so, if one is thinking in terms of siege war) and the UN passed Resolution 986, which allowed small but increasing sales of oil to pay for the import of food and medicines. And yet, the costs of the embargo, even after it began to ease, were horrendous.

Before the 1996 oil sales agreement, the situation was particularly dreadful. In 1992 US Census bureau researchers calculated that life expectancy had dropped from 68 to 57 for Iraqi women. In 1996, Iraqi government statistics accepted by the UN showed that malnutrition had risen 400% since 1991, and now afflicted nearly 20% of the population. By 1995, 576,000 children had died as a result of the lack of both food and medication, according to UN Food and Agriculture program estimates. Meanwhile, the World Health Organization estimated that 90,000 Iraqis were dying in hospitals each year, over and above the number that would have died under peace-time conditions. Teachers burned student desks for heat and Iraqi children gathered for class seated on bare stone. The US government acknowledged that the embargo cost Iraq $120 billion between 1990 and 1998. Before 1990, Iraq had depended on oil sales for 85% of its foreign exchange; from 1991 to 1996 the government could muster only 15% of its prior wealth.

During the 12 years of siege, buildings damaged in the bombing, including civilian housing as well as oil-production facilities, went unrepaired. When revenues began genuinely to normalize in 2000, after the UN finally lifted all limits on the amount of oil Iraq could sell, the money still had to stretch to cover not just the everyday pre-war expenditures, but repairs to war-damaged infrastructure, as well as the UN's heavy reparations and administrative demands. The situation was strained well beyond conventional economic endurance.

Although the money had begun to flow, the Iraqi government had only limited control over its revenues. Firstly, Iraq was forced to commit 30% of all proceeds from oil sales to Kuwaiti and to corporate reparations. Another 5% went to the UN to pay for the UNSCOM inspectors and the humanitarian program officials responsible for supervising the spending of the rest of the money. The remainder could be spent on domestic needs, but the UN had to approve every item, so every contract had to wend its way through a

bureaucracy thousands of miles away. Distribution delays and political up-
heavals in Iraq compounded the disaster. The people who paid the greatest
price were Iraqi citizens, particularly the children.

Two resignations of the Directors of the UN's "oil for food" program,
one right after the other, are among the most explicit proof that the UN's
embargo was brutal, the antithesis of humanitarian. The first to leave was
Denis Halliday, who resigned in the summer of 1998 after overseeing two
years of food imports. His successor, Hans Von Sponeck, whose resignation
ended a 36-year UN career, lasted only 18 months in Iraq. Though food was
flowing, thanks in part to Halliday and Sponeck, both reached the same conclusion: that the UN was *causing* and not *curing* the devastation. In December 1999, when a new UN resolution ended the dollar limit on oil sales, Van
Sponeck called the UN's action "a false hope" since the import controls remained in place.

George Bush the elder ordered a halt to the ground war against Iraq,
saying to his colleagues that he hoped to avoid a "sloppy, muddled ending."
In fact there was no ending at all, not even as much as a false hope. In the two
years after the 2001 terror bombings in the US, the risks that Iraq would
suffer further could only increase. Thus the only way for us to explore peace
in this war is speculatively.

Cease-fire: speculation instead of hindsight

In late 2001, with still no change in the war against Iraq in sight and certainly
no visible opportunity for peace-making, the bombing of the World Trade
Center was just the kind of "unexpected" event that might have been expected to make a radical change in the opportunities for peace. The radical
change took place. With ever increasing intensity, the US government took
actions intended to bring about the overthrow of Saddam Hussein, to end
the war by forcing a change of leadership on Iraq. The climax event, all out
war, began on March 19, 2003.*

---

* I abhor the tactic used, but I am forced to agree that for a war to end, either the leaders must change,
or their attitudes must change. One of the most alarming aspects of these recent events is that the US
government does not appear to consider itself obligated to change at all.

Could any other strategy have brought this war to an end? Indeed yes. Other cases suggest questions to explore and places to look. The paragraphs below were written before the onset of the 2003 assault. They were speculative when written and remain so still.

For some Iraqi exiles the dream that they would return in triumph at the head of an international army never died, but the Iraqi exiles were quite unlike the Tutsi exiles who had successfully conquered Rwanda. Geographically dispersed, and politically fragmented into factions, Iraqis could only have succeed if they had depended on overwhelming US military backing, even supposing the UN could be persuaded to support this endeavor. The UN had refused an occupation mission in 1991 and did not seem particularly likely to agree to it ten years later.[5]

It was possible that secret talks somewhere would help, though it was not clear who should participate, who would play host and whether they could possibly be as coercive as the United States was at the Dayton meetings in 1995, or as supportive as the Norwegians were in 1993 in Oslo.

Some change in personnel in the inner councils in Iraq or Britain could have altered the outcomes. The United States, under a new Presidency held by a second George Bush, seemed unlikely to present a conciliatory face. Tony Blair, in Britain, turned out also to be obdurate and the opposition of the other permanent members of the UN Security Council could not deflect Bush and Blair from their planned course of action.

Perhaps some other unexpected natural event, say an earthquake, could also have changed things. Imagine, for example, a major cholera epidemic in Iraq, which inspired the world's health experts to demand an end to the destructive embargo and a release for Iraq's besieged people.

Serious renewal of hostilities between Israel and the Palestinians could also have an impact by fostering Pan-Arab solidarity. This in turn might have led other major oil suppliers to decide to pressure the United States to back down by threatening the loss of access to Middle East oil, the very spur that had pushed everyone into war against Iraq in the first place.

At the onset of the new millennium all sides were still so merciless, so hostile that the prospects for a true and meaningful peace were very dim. America's leaders still wanted to win. Britain's government had a coherent argument which justified their commitment to the cause. Saddam Hussein was no more submissive than he had ever been. This meant that children would keep on dying, rivers would remain polluted and oil fields would remain in disrepair. None of the handful of men who had a say in decisions about Iraq was willing to admit that the suffering was too much.

When a change finally comes, it is unlikely to be the product of the brutal mechanical equation of siege war—the offer of a return to the world market (carrot), plus the threat of embargo (stick)—which the US and the British governments continued to assume would "simply" work. For one thing, Saddam Hussein had yet to agree. On March 1, 1991, the *New York Times* gave us the actual words he used accepting the cease-fire. They make it evident that even then he was convinced the war would continue.

> Many battles occurred in Basra district and other places in our great Iraqi territories after the withdrawal.
>
> Due to faith in our capability that is able to teach the enemy forces lessons that will make them worried militarily and politically if the war continued, Bush announced his decision early this morning.
>
> We are happy for the halt in the fighting, which will save the blood of our sons and the safety of our people after God made them victorious by faith against their evil enemies and save the blood of humanity who suffered due to Bush and his traitorous agents.
>
> Therefore orders were issued to all our units at the battlefront not to open fire. God is great.

A war cannot end until both sides agree it is over.

THE DANGEROUS DYNAMICS OF PEACE-MAKING

Real people, real choices

*Solitude gave me a certain liberty, and I resolved to use it to do something
I had been pondering for a long while: begin discussions with
the government. I had concluded that the time had come when the
struggle could best be pushed forward through negotiations…
It was clear to me that an [ANC} military victory was a distant if not an
impossible dream. It simply did not make sense for both sides to lose
thousands if not millions of lives in a conflict that was unnecessary.
They must have known this as well. It was time to talk.*[1]

This chapter offers a picture of peace-making as a whole, of the people in-volved, the settings in which they meet to negotiate and the risky moments and challenging issues which spur them into wanting peace in the first place. It ends with a brief survey of the equally serious risks and choices that deter-mine whether the first tentative approaches to peace will deepen and be transformed into a real chance to end a war permanently.

Seeking to make peace is a matter of choice. And what is more, the choice is available at numerous points during a war. In South Africa, 40 years passed between the onset of ANC violence and the onset of the Mandela—government talks. A minor illness facilitated their initial contacts. In Chechnya, Alexander Ledbed held power just long enough, after three years of war, to pull the Russian troops out. Israelis and Palestinians had their first chance at peace for over 35 years as a result of a war in which neither was directly engaged. The issue that prompts the start of fruitful talks can be small or large, early or delayed, a small window of opportunity or a lengthy period of time. Whenever it comes, the effort will always entail alarming uncer-tainties, and requires all parties to leave behind the clear moral imperatives of war. Instead of defending against enemies, peace-makers must engage with their enemies to begin building a new world and also to repair the damage done by the war to the old world.

In making peace, everyone faces a huge task: they must construct the framework of a whole new way of describing the world in which they see themselves. Before the talks begin, dangerous enmities could still justify brutal attacks. Once peace talks are underway, people from all the conflicting sides must be included if they are to design the architecture of the new society and to heal the damage done to the old. The earliest and secret talks usually occur while fighters on the ground are still committing violent acts. Defining and constructing the framework of a postwar social system and selecting the first objects for repair entails working collaboratively in the same room as people one once wished dead.

It seems that acting this new way becomes possible only after false starts and dangerous detours. While outsiders and those used to the practices of modern democracy may desire transparency in peace-talks, such an aspiration is counterproductive amidst the huge choices that peace-makers actually face. In December 1993, Mandela and de Klerk were able to appear on a platform together to receive the Nobel Prize. They had come a long way from their first face to face encounters completely out of sight of others. When the world saw Rabin and Arafat manage to shake hands in front of the White House, their uneasy movements towards each other still conveyed suggestions of their history of struggle. This was a moment they must have been edging towards for quite a while, while no one was watching.

We will begin, as peace-making itself does, with the small group of key leaders who have the greatest power to make or break the peace. The middle of the chapter lays out the complex, but still comprehensible mechanisms that determine the dynamics of the interactions among the actual people involved and the decisions they must make about weapons, politics, refugees, humanitarian aid and justice. Next comes a description of the ways that peace expands the size of the community of people who claim a right to make decisions and yet surrounds them with a swarm of moral ambiguities. The chapter closes with a reminder of the considerable power that remains with those leaders who are willing still to use suffering and violence to achieve their ends. No war can end until all sides agree that it is over.

The leaders and the settings for talks

The first decisions about whether to end a war rest with a handful of prominent people. In his earliest talks with the Nationalist government in South Africa, Mandela was the only ANC member involved. Likewise, the initial overtures towards peace in the North of Ireland included only Gerry Adams and John Hume, alone together in Hume's London house. The whole series of Oslo talks involved fewer than a dozen men. Richard Holbrooke elicited agreements to attend the Dayton talks through a series of private meetings, one on one with the regional leaders. Even in 1991, the ceasefire that halted the UN sponsored ground war in Iraq was determined by George Bush and a very small group of his own personal advisors. There was no debate in the Security Council, despite its standing as the body that had first authorized the war. Several able outsiders, notably the mediators Holbrooke and George Mitchell, and the Norwegians who acted as hosts for the Oslo talks, played a critical role in these events.[2] Yet the final authority over whether to accept or to walk away from an agreement remained closely held by leading figures in each of the war-torn communities.[3]

Leadership and change—In the midst of combat, leaders repeatedly repudiate the possibility of negotiation or contact with the opposing side's commanders. Indeed there is a dreadful logic to repudiating any such action. If enemies are killing each other day after day, how can they build enough trust to conduct talks in good faith?[4] Nonetheless, peace is impossible without talk, flexible, imaginative and persistent talk. Certain kinds of talk will already have served as important auxiliaries to the military action during the war years. For example, the other side's leaders must publicly be described as so vile and so threatening they do not merit any response other than violence. Enemy armies are identified as the authors of dreadful destruction and deep suffering, so any hostile and derogatory labels will seem well deserved. Different communities use different derogatory terms; many bring back figures from history to evoke danger and the imperative for continued war.

Americans learned to respond with true fear to the word "Nazi." Thus, the characterization, by both of the Bush administrations, of Saddam Hussein as the modern equivalent of Hitler was an expedient way to ignite and then reinflame support for war against Iraq. Alarmist characterizations can be quite general too. Throughout the Cold War, Americans were highly reactive against a "communist threat."[5] Today's equivalent is "terrorist," a term that played a significant role in strengthening already close connections between the United States and both Israel and Britain, two countries which also conceived of themselves as the victims of terrorism. The term nearly cemented a strong bond between the United States and Russia as well. Another Russian name for the Chechens is "bandits." That word carries associations with random violence at least as far back as medieval times in both Europe and Asia. The Hutu labeled the Tutsi "cockroaches," language that conveyed both disgust for the people and recognition of their pernicious skills.

If ending a war is to become conceivable, such negative expressions will have to fade into the background. When Gerry Adams moved into the political foreground during negotiations over the North of Ireland, his associations with the IRA were downplayed and his place as leader of Sinn Féin, a political party whose objectives were identical with the IRA, gained prominence. Nelson Mandela explicitly refused to agree that he renounce violence so as to secure his own release from prison, and yet his statesmanlike qualities were given much more public attention than his history with the violent wing of the ANC. As a war is coming to an end, those who resist peace make their presence known in part by their refusal to abandon the hostile language.

For peace actually to come into being, the leaders themselves must also change, not just the language describing them. Either there must be a change in the actual people occupying positions of power or existing leaders must radically modify their approach to the war.[6] Tony Blair, the first Labor Prime Minister in Britain in 18 years, could contemplate changes for the North of

Ireland because he came to power without the burden of years of commitment to a certain kind of victory over the IRA to hinder him. As a recently installed President, F.W. De Klerk could begin to ease some of the social restrictions on Blacks that his predecessor Botha, who served in office for 10 years and was the architect of a state of emergency, could not contemplate. Although Botha had initiated the first talks, it took De Klerk to carry through with enough confidence building measures to convince everyone the situation could and must change. In Russia, the first cease-fire in the Chechnya war was made possible by the sudden rise of Alexander Ledbed. Later, of course, the utterly unexpected accession of Vladimir Putin was directly responsible for the resumption of fighting. When leaders like Saddam Hussein and George Bush do not change their minds, the war does not end.

Many among the key participants in these wars have described such changes in books and interviews.[7] Their stories are complex, personal and quite varied. Mandela's description nonetheless manages to convey feelings that were common to most:

> "It would be too strong to call it a revelation, but over the next days and weeks, I came to a realization about my new circumstances…We had been engaged in the armed struggle for more than two decades. Many people on both sides had already died. The enemy was strong and resolute, yet even with all their bombers and tanks they must have sensed they were on the wrong side of history."[8] *

Mandela was shaped by a long view of the future. He could recognize that time was on his side if he made peace and against him if the ANC kept trying to use violence. The next major segment of this chapter takes up the question of timing, to argue that there is no way to predict precisely when someone in Mandela's position might come to such a realization. The central fact at this point is that peace prospects change with changes in the people participating and changes in perception in the leadership.[9]

Secret talk, good hosts—Merely wanting to end a war is never enough. In each of the seven war stories, leaders came to critical decisions in negotiation

---

* Notice also that here again is a leader describing his decision to begin working for peace in terms of the suffering he wanted to avoid. This issue is central to the next chapter on the interactions between the search for justice and the chance to make peace.

with each other, and the settings in which they talked contributed significantly to the outcome. I have mentioned secrecy more than once. Mandela
and the Nationalists, John Hume and Gerry Adams, and the Oslo negotiators
were working in such secrecy that the outside world had no idea discussions
had even begun. Even at Dayton and in Ireland and Chechnya, when it was
known that they were talking, there were no day-to-day news conferences
about the concessions being made and offered.

Beyond secrecy, numerous other features of the settings can also influence outcomes. Clearly the warmth and hospitality in Oslo helped build trust
between the two sides; good food, shared at the same table, is a mundane but
vital confidence building measure. Gerry Adams and Mo Mowlam held their
first meeting in the old Parliament buildings in Belfast, which had been
closed at the outbreak of war. The decision to meet there signified to the
wider world that Mowlam considered Adams a legitimate public figure. At a
later date, she conferred a similar legitimacy and confidence on imprisoned
militia members who had begun threatening the peace process, by choosing
to negotiate with them in their cells. Mowlam's action demonstrated that she
saw them as POWs not criminals, which turned them once more towards
supporting the peace. At a much more mechanical level, the military technology in Dayton allowed all parties to measure accurately the geographical
consequences of the plans they were making. By contrast, the hurried meeting between UN commanders and Iraqis in the desert in 1991 offered none
of these kinds of inducements for the opposing sides to take up complex issues and thus to make a true peace. Those 1991 meetings were simply another sign that the war was not yet over.

Danger and dynamics

Although each of the seven peace stories centered on a single pivotal moment in which commitment was made or reaffirmed, here the analysis must
broaden out. Peace-making is a long and arduous process. Even when leaders opt to consider a first outreach to each other, the process will be anything
but straightforward, so we will turn to examining the risk and timing dilemmas inherent in all attempts at outreach across dangerous boundaries. The
decisions to be made and the decision-makers that claim their own stake in

the outcome are legion, their engagements fraught with violence, hope, fear, complexity and danger. And the uncertainties they bring can last for years.

If there is a single attribute that advances success in such times, it is flexibility. Since the peace-making process unfolds in the midst of uncertainty, any agreements will be resilient when threatened, whether by violence or by floods of desperate refugees, only if they leave room for adjustment. None of the settlements I have described, all of which were pivotal, made any pretense to be the final word on peace. Even the South Africans, who were close to the end of their process, were signing off on an "interim" Constitution, not a document for the ages. All the other settlements were known as "agreements" and "accords" not "treaties."

In each case, the combatants made public their commitment to peace, and set aside their weapons accepting that significant issues remained still to be resolved. In Dayton, they left the final disposition of two highly contentious areas, Brcko and Eastern Slavonia, for the future. In the North of Ireland, they left for another time the mechanisms which would guarantee the decommissioning of weapons. In Chechnya, they put almost nothing definite down on paper. In Israel/Palestine, they delayed till later all talks on the timetable for a new Palestinian State and also on the final dispositions for Jerusalem. In South Africa, their agreements committed to elections for the new government before deciding whether perpetrators of the apartheid-era atrocities would be allowed to participate in those elections. Each of these choices contained enough energy to restart the violence if progress towards peace went awry. And yet, it would have been fruitless to wait for their resolution to stop all violence and to end the war. The essence of peace-making is that it is dangerous and full of uncertainties. Those whose efforts succeed embody two contradictory traits. They are unshakeable in their commitment and yet flexible in their approach. They apply these attributes to a hundred choices.

As I said in the Introduction, prewar speeches are filled with persuasive but fallacious metaphors that convey that ending a war has quite definite attributes.[10] Speech writers' characterizations of peace-making make it seem far too easy. When a leader talks about "victory," he implies that, like a game, winning ends it. If his speech contains words like "carrot" and "stick" or "sanctions" and "economic aid," a listener can infer that the decisions about when to end a war will be calculated with a clarity similar to cost-benefit analysis in an economic decision. When the media headline words like "shock" and "awe," they suggest that sheer brute force is all it takes to compel the other side to surrender, that making peace is a one-sided affair. In fact, the dynamics of decision-making at the end of a war bear little relationship to any of these.

Ending a war is a roiling, uneasy process. If one invokes analogies from the everyday world, they should conjure up chance and uncertainty, danger and opportunity. Ordinary life presents experiences every day that reveal how often drama and uncertainty occur in the same instant. There is the combination of beauty and danger in the unpredictable track of a summer thunderstorm across the sky. And most of us have been swept into a tangle of emotions, both relief and fear, on that terrifyingly lucky day when ours is the car that escapes hitting another by a fraction of an inch. Many Americans watched half fascinated half appalled at the sequence of crises sprung on an astonished nation during the 2000 Presidential election. And all because of a few hundred hanging chads among millions and millions of votes. Each one of these is an everyday example of a "chaotic" event in the technical sense that scientists use the term.

Although modern life encourages people to develop a fascination with control, there remains a very significant chaos in nature and thus in human existence. War does not have, and never has had either the predictable and elegant mechanics of a Newtonian universe, or the clarity of an investment banker's spreadsheet, nor the one-sidedness of a basketball game headlined a "blowout."

Clausewitz was right. War's outcome is one-third chance. And we cannot know exactly where the one third will produce its uncertainties. Therein lies much of the danger in peace-making. Danger and chance go hand in hand in life and in peace-making. In this book danger comes first.

Danger

Each one of the seven stories in this book demonstrates that no attempt at peace-making can be characterized as an unqualified success. Some people would be even more critical. They would, for example, describe the Oslo

Accords as a "failure," because violence flared up so soon afterwards, and because, in fewer than seven years, Israelis and Palestinians were mired once more in virulent and dangerous combat. Indeed, South Africa stands out as the only case in which the war in question is well and truly over. But the tangles and difficulties, crises and violence that ensnared all seven of these regions should not be seen as signs of "failure." Rather, they are signs that the path to peace is always dangerous, that people will die making peace as well as making war, and that the path to peace is very long. Often, even the well intentioned lose their way.

How does the danger manifest itself? In the lives of the leaders who initiated the process; in the challenges inherent in disarming the front-line combatants and releasing the captives; in returning thousands or millions of people to the homes they fled; in receiving and distributing humanitarian aid; and in the reallocation of powers and resources in the disputed territory. In other words, just about every facet of peace-making can be dangerous. This list is much more than a general warning to peace-makers to be careful. It has specific substance behind it. Those who try to craft a peace are putting their own futures at risk, and since the work must be done in a much more ambiguous moral space than the combat conditions of war, peace-makers often give up. They abandon their uncertain negotiations and trust-building efforts for the moral clarity of war, and the hope that a new round of fighting will bring them closer to their ultimate goals.

Spoilers—Any leader who makes the first overtures towards peace is liable to find himself in a precarious position the moment his actions become known. Alexander Ledbed lost his chance at the Russian Presidency within three months. Nelson Mandela risked being called a traitor by his colleagues in the ANC, for his willingness to work in direct collaboration with successive leaders of South Africa's oppressive apartheid government. Gerry Adams risked his own vast political ambitions by advocating a tortuous path that might end in a role for him in a power sharing government. He had available a much more certain, though violent path, that would deliver to him both high

standing among Catholics and a large, if rather unattractive reputation among the Protestant Irish and in England. More seriously, leaders who seek peace risk their own lives. Yitzhak Rabin is dead, murdered by one of his own people who feared the destruction of his West Bank settler community in the event of peace. Rabin is far from the only dead peace-maker, and he would not have been surprised at his fate. After all, President Anwar Sadat had been killed just a few years earlier for the same reason, because he was making peace with Israel.

At the edges of a war, death has always lurked near those who are working for peace. Murderer and victim, as with Rabin and Sadat, are frequently committed to the same cause; the killer best described as a "spoiler" intent on continued war. Spoilers are living, breathing and acting embodiments of the conflicts inherent in any society that has been at war. In combat, the spoilers are integrated into the warrior forces; but they break away once peace initiatives gather momentum. "Peace creates spoilers because it is rare...for all leaders and all factions to see peace as beneficial."[11] The South African tank drivers who tried to destroy the Constitutional talks saw themselves holding up the last bastion in defense of the racially pure society so many had worked so hard to protect and build. Hamas opposed the Oslo Accords the moment they were announced. Their suicide bombers, attacking in the years after Oslo, saw themselves as the only true Palestinians, the only ones still holding fast to their commitment to the abolition of Israel, since Arafat had now betrayed the cause. After Dayton, the two Serb leaders, Mladic and Karadic, with many loyal soldiers behind them, remained committed to bringing about a Greater Serbia, the prize that Slobodan Milosevic had so blithely traded away.* Spoilers hold considerable power because violence and the

---

* Although the United States always wanted to brand Saddam Hussein a "spoiler," he was more accurately described as an enemy leader still refusing to make peace.

threat of violence so easily dominate the public space and define the political agenda.[12]

There is danger too because, once the combat shows signs of ending, the work to be done is risky in itself and often provides an ideal venue for those spoilers still trying to ignite further violence. Among the most difficult tasks is the disengagement and demobilizing of the armed forces. After Dayton, the Serb troops being forced to turn over their captured Sarajevo suburbs to Bosnian Moslems were very happy to create mayhem as they left. Nothing disastrous happened in Sarajevo, but in every war zone, disarming the soldiers and disentangling the opposing armies makes peace vulnerable to delay or worse. In the North of Ireland, Chechnya, Palestine, South Africa and Bosnia, renegade military units killed rather than agree to being disarmed. The risks were even greater on the Rwanda/Congo border, where entire Hutu clans continued living together in refugee camps, where they planned assaults on Rwanda. They carried out several revenge attacks during the winter months 1997–1998, and although the peace "held," the Hutus' inroads on the country served as a stark reminder that it was still anything but stable, a full three years after the Rwandan war had officially ended.

Refugees and aid—Rwanda and the Balkans also reveal, in the worst possible way, the perils in trying to establish peace in those regions where large numbers of people flee their homes during the war. Both were encumbered with refugee populations numbering in the millions and with damaged villages and towns where the remaining intact buildings housed those who stayed behind. [13] Refugees considered themselves entitled to come safely home, yet during the war years neighbors had found other uses for their abandoned houses, farms and businesses. As returnees, the refugees presented unwelcome competition for scarce resources and a huge challenge to the new social order, since compounding the practical difficulties, there were emotional conflicts as well. The returnees were often members of a despised ethnic group. Worse still, some were known murderers, perpetrators of violence that was still evident in the traumatized bodies and minds of the same people who were supposed to greet them as neighbors once they came home.

International humanitarian aid rarely eased such problems, which does

Chechnya is devastated. The few who remain in Grozny apartment blocks are largely ethnic Russians, who don't have a network of relatives in the region to take them in. Without functioning utilities, they carry clean water from hand-pumped wells in buckets to wash by candlelight. Many of their windows were blown out and they worry about the coming winter.

For weeks in August, while Russian bombers flew overhead, the remaining residents lived in neighbors' basements. For many in apartments, food stocks were perilously low."

Ingwerson, Marshall,
Christian Science Monitor, Sept. 3, 1996

not mean that aid should not have been offered. Often, overseas donors and host families away from the war zone saved real people from dreadful suffering and loss. But to the people who never left, returnees commonly stood for cowardice in the face of danger and a callous willingness to go off in search of a better life while others, less privileged and more committed, remained behind. So, a recovering society already divided in the many ways wars can create divisions, between supporter and opponent, fighter and non-combatant, well fed and starved, faced yet another division, between those who stayed and those who left. "Internally displaced persons" (the term is a relic from World War II) and refugees constituted only fifty percent of the risk. The rest emanated from those who stayed behind and lived close to the danger. They expected a lot from the peace.

Economics and politics—Peace-making disappoints all too easily. During the months or years of combat, danger and deprivation are to be expected. The war offers plenty of reasons for pain and the moral fervor for war sustains resilience. But what happens when peace comes and things are no better? When Israeli border guards still treat Palestinians crossing daily at the same check-point to go to work as though each one were a potential terrorist? When block after block in the city of Grozny is still nothing but rubble, surrounded by a shell where once large apartment buildings housed a thriving community? When the international aid budget is being spent on security and building projects favored by the political leadership, but no one seems to remember that the children need a school? War's purpose is to destroy and leave scars behind, and the physics of repair is intractable. While it takes mere moments for a bomb to bring down a building, its replacement will take weeks, if not months to go back up.

All of these difficulties, the returning refugees, the competition for resources and the struggles of daily life in war damaged areas, often do no more than cast a shadow on the peace. Sadly, sometimes a factor in the agreements itself becomes a stand-in for the contentious issues which made the war so intense in the first place. At those moments, peace-making becomes a threat to itself.

The volatile and dangerous nature of events in the North of Ireland was created in part by proposals to demobilize combatants on all sides. Resistors to this "decommissioning" succeeded repeatedly in shaking trust in the new regime. Others, even those leaders officially committed to the peace, also were turned confrontational by the topic. David Trimble, winner of a Nobel Peace Prize for his contributions to the Good Friday Agreement, seemed periodically to lose his faith in talk, negotiation and politics. Rather than threaten violence, Trimble used other threats: that he would resign from and thereby terminate the autonomous government in the North of Ireland. Then London would take back direct rule over the Province, and hostilities were liable to erupt once more. His first resignations spurred talks and more concessions and not more violence, so the government in Belfast would be reinstated once more. But Trimble's tactics entailed serious risks. Suppose there came a time when London, impatient with all sides, publicly refused to restore the local powers to the Northern Ireland Parliament. Without question, that would lead to a Republican revolt, and most probably more violence. Talking back and forth in the North of Ireland was taking years and proving liable to self-destruct. Making peace was the agent of its own instability. Nine years after the first cease-fire the outcome remained, still, uncertain.

A fast, decisive victory would not necessarily have made matters any easier. The Rwandan RPF effected such a victory, but even discounting the tremendous difficulties inherited from the genocidal Hutu war, making peace proved far from easy. The Hutu and Tutsi communities had gone to war in 1994 largely because, despite their power-sharing agreement negotiated in 1993, spoilers among the Hutu found it appalling that they were being required to develop a system that genuinely shared authority among the two communities. After the 1994 war, the new Tutsi rulers took selected Hutu into the leadership unilaterally. The two groups were working side by side, but the one-sided Tutsi victory had allowed them to by-pass engaging their differences as peers in a process specifically directed at peace-making.

Within five years, Hutu leaders were backing away from this way of doing business and danger threatened once again.

The Americans and others on the Security Council suffered a similar frustration despite achieving a great military triumph over Iraq in 1991. The opposing sides never freely negotiated any features of peace-making beyond their prisoner exchanges and troop disengagement. Both Tutsi Rwandans and the Security Council, as winners, acted as though they could impose terms unilaterally. Wise or hostile though their terms might be, their absolute victories created too little incentive to negotiate. The participants in both of these wars proved unable to talk their way through to peace.

Any attempt to make lists of all the dangerous moments in peace-making in just these seven wars would take up many more pages. One list would cover all the ways that peace-making endangered the personal lives and careers of each of the leaders trying to hang onto to their power long enough to make peace. There would have to be another, listing the practical decisions to identify essential physical repairs, characterize the recipients entitled to compensation, locate refugees for repatriation and instigate local processes to bring about reconciliation. Each one of these decisions, literally hundreds of them, carries the potential to ignite another round of fighting. Then there would have to be a list of narrow escapes, of risky decisions that worked out surprisingly well, including the many decisions to delay decisions.

Spectators to peace-making have little basis on which to judge others' breakdowns and violence as "failures." Rather, they are the normal signs that peace-making is proceeding ahead. The challenges and dangers are huge, the opportunities and possibilities really worth the struggle.

Dynamics

Clausewitz—Having looked at the dangers, it is time now to turn to timing and the dynamics of uncertainty. After all, danger and uncertainty go hand in hand. For this we return to one of the most important ancestors of modern strategic thinking, Carl von Clausewitz. He is most widely known for his maxim that "war is merely the continuation of policy [politics] by other means."[14] To Clausewitz, this signified that strategists must repeatedly conduct rigorous appraisals to determine whether combat continues to further political or policy aims. But this particular policy maxim was, according to Clausewitz, only one of three equally important characteristics of war, each of which interacts with the others to make war the complex whole it really is.

His second maxim was that war is inherently interactive, that combatants on one side become able to do things they simply could not or would not have done if they had not had an enemy with whom to interact. Once again, every day life provides an analogy to illustrate the point. Imagine two wrestlers tangled in a complex hold, neither falling to the floor. Alone, neither could hold the position each has individually adopted. Together they can hold, supplying pressure and counter pressure, for an astonishingly long time.[15] I said earlier that, to most people's surprise, there appears to be little connection between the intensity of suffering in a war and the decision to seek peace. The interactivity of war helps explain the absence of any connection. Without an enemy pressing on them, no community of people would tolerate being subjected to that much pain for long. However, since an enemy is right there, a direct threat to something of value, leaders receive support for violent stratagems even after the damage and destruction have begun to make the costs of war apparent. Likewise, ordinary people discover in them-

selves extraordinary power to survive pain and danger they would never previously considered bearable. We will return to suffering once again in the closing chapter on justice, since pain and injury are deeply embedded in memory and reconciliation.

Clausewitz's third maxim to define the essence of war is that "no other human activity is so continuously or universally bound up with chance."[16] Chance is a result of the "fog" of war, "fog" referring to factors that are hidden from view or distorted by the noise and confusion of war. Chance is also a result of "friction," which he explains as follows: "Everything in war is simple, but the simplest thing is difficult. The difficulties accumulate and end by producing a kind of friction that is inconceivable unless one has experienced war...This tremendous friction, which cannot, as in mechanics be reduced to a few points, is everywhere in contact with chance, and brings about effects which cannot be measured, just because they are largely due to chance."[17]

For the purposes of understanding cease-fire and peace, the last sentence is critical. Outcomes in war are not measurable, and hence cannot be foreseen by the ordinary calculus on which we rely to predict mechanical results. All attempts to control precisely and to measure exactly the balance of forces in a war, so as to determine when the optimum time for making peace will come, inevitably fail. War has too much "friction" and too much "fog" to enable such analyses to lead to accurate outcomes.

Uncertainty—In recent years, thanks to a paradigm shift in modern science popularly known as "chaos theory," analysts in a number of fields have learned to use a new language to explore the dynamics of chance. Previously, for more than a hundred years, social scientists had searched for repeating patterns in uncertain settings by using probabilities and statistics. To this day in the United States, a steady stream of such statistics and their accompanying behavioral advice is culled from health studies and then reported widely in the Sunday newspaper. Strategists use similar tools for military research. Both explore "risk factors," "accuracy rates," and "margins of error," a few of the many forms of probabilistic thinking. Any serious student of Clausewitz must have a good deal of respect for careful calculations about the likely outcome of a decision. My only difference with the Pentagon's analysts and their mathematical formulae has to do with the kind of math they use.

Statistical analysis is often taken to be the mathematics of choice in the study of human decisions and the decision to seek peace is certainly a human decision. However, statistical rules create formulae that are only really conclusive about linear relationships. Thus, they are ideal for determining the effectiveness of a medical intervention, for example. The intervention goes into the body, which then responds straightforwardly, at least on average.* In the complex and interactive relationships of wartime, linear models are more deceptive than useful. From the very first assault, a myriad of actions and responses creates confusion if not worse. Above all, though, power in war is intimately bound up with factors more unstable than the mechanical force supplied by weapons, and thus the results of any given action are inherently non-linear and uncertain.†

War includes, among many other factors, battlefield weather conditions that impinge on human morale, which is also affected by the on-site mechanical durability of weapons, in part determined by the leadership's priorities about the spending of scarce resources. And all of the factors, interacting with each other simultaneously, influence the likelihood for peace. "Chaos theory," since it allows analysts to visualize the structure and dynamics of a variety of turbulent systems, turns out to be an ideal tool for understanding the dynamics of war and peace. The US military knows this now as well and has, in recent years, become more interested in applying chaos theory to battle planning and strategic decision-making.[18] However, despite honoring Clausewitz, US military leaders keep "fog" and "friction" well hidden behind the public rhetoric of certainty in war, at least until after the onset of combat.‡

Although chaos theory might seem to suggest a system that has no predictable elements, in fact its models of non-linearity improve the understanding of turbulent processes by identifying a rather small number of clearly delineated attributes of complexity on which to focus attention. Each

---

* Of course there can be complications such as threshold effects, skewed distributions or multi-factor relations. Nonetheless, the mathematical imagery derived from chaos theory is much closer than statistics at illuminating non-linear relationships.

† I have had a good deal of help understanding this scientific thinking from my physicist husband, Rob Knapp. I am as grateful for his skills as a teacher as I am for his cautious approach to the direct application of chaos theory models to human purposes, beyond their original application in understanding in natural systems.

‡ In week two of the second war against Iraq, *The Economist* carried a cover of a soldier in a sand storm, headlined "The Fog of War." March 29-April 4, 2003.

one illuminates where and how war's uncertainties are likely to manifest. It is these specific characteristics that are so useful in understanding sudden, unexpected efforts to make peace.

For these purposes, non-linearity has three key components.* Firstly, non-linearity is the product of disproportionality. In the 1990s, an oft-repeated story explained the impact of disproportionality on a forecaster's inability to predict the weather: a butterfly in China flaps its wings, which starts a small turbulent updraft that has undergone transformation into a thunderstorm by the time the turbulence reaches the sky over Indiana. This is classic disproportionality. As I mentioned briefly, the 2000 US Presidential election shone a bright light on this kind of complexity in human systems. The entire election was tossed, quite literally, into chaos all because of a single, small decision, made in a Florida electoral district long before that November, to use cheap paper ballots whose "chads" did not punch out fully. Within two years the entire world was feeling the results.[19]

Nonlinearity is also a product of the "nonadditive" qualities of chaotic systems. Synergies among the parts mean that the whole cannot be exactly the same as their sum. Another example from every day life: one may fumble for a keyhole in the dark, poking the key again and again at the door. When it finally eases into the lock, the easing is not made any smoother, nor is the unlocking made any more effective by the many failed attempts. The door unlocks because of the perfect fit, the synergy at that particular moment between shape of key and shape of lock. In essence, the successful opening turn of the key is not impacted by memories of the previous failed attempt at insertion.

Thirdly, a chaotic system is highly sensitive to "initial conditions," and even very small variations from one situation to another will lead to radically different results. This is what makes weather prediction so hard. A tiny variation in ocean temperature will make seemingly similar-sized storms veer off in very different directions. In fact, this sensitivity to initial conditions, applied to weather prediction, was the major reason that chaos theory moved out of the esoteric corners of scientific research and into public consciousness.

---

* The last chapter which centers on the interaction of memory and justice, mercy and truth, will bring up a fourth characteristic of chaotic systems, their irreversibility.

For years, weather forecasters had assumed that once they acquired enough computing power and once they finally fed enough data points into their computations, accurate long-term weather prediction would become possible. Instead, they discovered sensitivity to initial conditions. No matter how many weather balloons and computers they installed, they never could spot a storm at the very moment it first emerged as an updraft in the air. Nor could the forecasters get measurements for every single feature of a young weather system. Their truly accurate forecasts would forever be limited to very short time frames.

How do these images apply in ending a war? First, "Disproportionality." One troubling fact about war is that no one can tell for sure what impact any given action will have on the willingness to keep fighting. Why were outsiders moved to outrage and NATO into action after the deaths of 37 people in a Sarajevo marketplace, in February 1994, but not by the pictures of the bombed out buildings of Grozny a few months later? Why did the bombing in Omagh, the summer after the Irish signed their agreements, cement the peace while the death of the President of Rwanda reignited a war? These questions could be repeated ad infinitum. Why, for example, did George Bush the elder intervene in Kuwait and not in Bosnia? Those who blithely answer "oil" underestimate the many other factors at work including pre-existing war plans for a desert war in Iraq, and the impact of the European Union's claim that Bosnia was its turf. They ignore the discouraging Pentagon assessment that US ground troops might not operate very effectively in winter in mountainous Balkan terrain, and the difference a year made in the timing of the two wars in relation to the end of the Cold War. A truer characterization of Bush's decision is that all these events took place in turbulent times.

Disproportionality can just as easily mean that dramatic events have no

> Two shells slammed into the central Sarajevo market area today, killing at least 37 people and wounding 80 in the most devastating single attack on the Bosnian capital since a similar one 18 months ago led NATO to vow that the city would be protected.
>
> Limbs and flesh were splattered on storefronts, and bodies fell to pieces as they were lifted into cars. After 40 months of Serbian siege and bombardment, the scene was familiar, but the horrified frenzy among an exhausted population was still intense.
>
> Roger Cohen, *New York Times*, Aug. 29, 1995, p. A1

effect on peace-making. Mid-way through the IRA campaign for independence, the Republicans moved their violence from Ireland to England and attacked a London Underground station at the height of rush hour. The bombing disrupted transport, killed and wounded dozens of people, and forced a complete reevaluation of basic security in public places all over England. The dislocation and economic costs were orders of magnitude bigger than in any prior bombing, and yet there is no sign that the magnitude of the consequences stirred a flicker of interest in opportunities for cease-fire.[20] Further back in history, European memories of the carnage of World War I ought to have been strong enough to prevent the onset of another war, yet they could neither forestall World War II nor prevent another carnage.

"Nonadditive" relationships, next. This is the feature of chaotic systems that seems hardest to grasp intuitively. Surely, when the pressure grows great enough, the war will end? The first contrary example I offer is an illustration of nonadditive links between war and democracy or rather the lack of it. Legislative pressure groups even in peace-time yearn to have additive effects—whether in the form of petitions or campaign contributions, the assumption they make is that their effects should accumulate. In truth, even in peace democracy is inherently complex and all groups are destined to face surprise and disappointment. Wartime is even worse since it so quickly disconnects democracy from decision-making. In the winter of 2003, US activism gradually intensified against the Iraq war, beginning with letter writing campaigns to local Congressmen and culminating in vigils and demonstrations coordinated worldwide. But the war machine moved on unimpeded. Furthermore, Presidential decisions often seemed to carry no memory of decisions made just a short while before. Bush vacillated often about whether or not to seek UN approval for the war. The United States was already at war with Iraq and in the midst of an ongoing campaign; under such conditions the decisions really do change from week to week.

Another example of the non-additive in peace-making can be observed in comparisons of the different international mediators working in Bosnia. Cyrus Vance, with credentials as a mediator earned during the US hostage crisis in Iran, teamed up with David Owen, a smart and experienced British politician. Working away in Geneva, they prepared map after map and plan after plan, none of which contained the germ of peace, even though they accurately foreshadowed many aspects of the later geographical decisions. Jimmy Carter, equally experienced, could do no more than give people a winter's lull in 1994/95. Then Richard Holbrooke, brash and much less well known, did make progress—perhaps because he could make solid human contact with Milosevic. He personally reports being inspired to succeed in part because two of his team were killed in a car crash early on in the peace-making project.[21] His success at the end was barely connected at all to the groundwork laid by his predecessors.

As with my earlier hypothetical lists of dangers that threatened peace-making, any listing of all those factors in peace-making that manifest the different qualities of chaotic systems would be immense. I cannot possibly describe them all. Nor could one even know precisely which they were.[22] Still, it is important to emphasize that complexity does not suggest that attempts at peace-making are bound to be ineffective. In fact the opposite. Complexity means that almost anything might contribute to peace-making, even though those who make peace and the decisions they make must remain unpredictable. Complexity means it may never be too early to start searching for peace. It also means that no setback need be the final one.

Opting to work for peace or making a return to war is a matter of choice, a choice that the key leaders guard jealously. Leaders quickly learn that one of war's seductive qualities is that it allows them to act unilaterally more often and yet once peace-making starts, their ultimate power and thus their final responsibility for ongoing war becomes much harder to see. It is disguised by yet another form of complexity, a dramatic increase in the number and kinds of people who claim a part in the choices ahead, and on whose consent the success of peace-making almost seems to depend.

More decision-makers

Once peace actually becomes an option, ordinary citizens easily conclude that they too are entitled to a role in the decisions and they do make many private decisions whose consequences add yet another layer of complexity to the process. Thousands of refugees, deciding when and how to make their own travel plans to return home to their villages in Rwanda or in Bosnia, impacted the peace-making process much more broadly than any one family would have simply acting for itself. The people, en masse, spoke out for peace in the referenda in Ireland that sealed the Good Friday Agreements. This too added complexity. So did the thousands of Israeli mourners who took to the streets after Yitzhak Rabin's assassination, clearly advocates for peace. After Oslo, every Palestinian had valid reasons to believe that they also were entitled to a voice in the future politics and government of the region that had been denied them since 1948. Peace allows ordinary people out of their protective shells and back into the public discourse.

Peace also invites other groups into roles they claim, or they are offered, in deciding whether and how events are to unfold. In Bosnia, "peace-keepers," soldiers from many nations were deployed within weeks after Dayton, to help with the disentangling of the warring groups and the demilitarization of the region. Once there, these well armed US, Russian, British, Turkish and other forces held enforcement powers over the entire region. This turned into control over access to the broadcast media, control over the dates for elections, control over the particular people entitled to run for election, and even control over where the soldiers devoted their spare energies to humanitarian efforts. Their efforts were undoubtedly intended to sustain the peace, and yet they also increased its complexity.

Enforcement complexities in the Balkans increased yet again with the decision to establish an International War Crimes Tribunal at The Hague. In the Tribunal's first years, Slobodan Milosevic was kept beyond the purview of the prosecutors at the court; he was too important to creating the chance for peace. But by 1999, Chief Prosecutor Louise Arbor had become determined to make a case against him. On April 21, 2001, Milosevic was forced into surrendering himself to The Hague to await trial. How did this dramatic turn around occur? Milosevic himself had been driven from political power by his own people in an election the previous October. Then the "international community" stepped in and announced that no further economic aid would flow into Serbia until jurisdiction over Milosevic was transferred to the Tribunal.* Whether international intervention had furthered or hindered the peace it was too early to assess definitively. It is certain that peace-making brought many more parties into law enforcement and justice across the Balkan peninsula than had participated during the war years.

The international community often also intervened in the economic realm, either with incentives towards peace or with sanctions designed to hinder the war. In the mid 1980s, a grass-roots, worldwide effort for sanctions to bring down apartheid prevailed even in the United States. But what impact did sanctions have on making peace? South Africa's own advocates for black equality were convinced sanctions were essential and yet the US Congressional ban on trade was only passed nearly two years *after* the South African government and Mandela had begun their private talks. South Africa, which is the sole "success" in these stories, received far less economic assistance per capita than any of the other war zones apart from Chechnya. The biggest recipient by far was Israel, which received billions of dollars to spend just as it chose and yet the region remains mired in war to this day. Bosnia, too, received immense amounts of money. During and after the war, the biggest international agencies combined to spend more than $1 billion a year there, an enormous sum for a population of less than 3.1 million. In that region, at this moment, there seems to be some hope that troops, new schools and bridges and a decade of international intervention may have helped. But Bosnia is also proof that this kind of intervention need make no contributions to peace at all. UN peace-keepers doing enforcement, humanitarians bringing food and sanctions to punish the Serbs had all failed for

---

*The phrase "international community" is widely used to designate officials and organizations, which reserve the right to intervene in the domestic affairs of other countries. This community includes major international organizations, like the UN, NATO and the WTO. It also includes humanitarian and economic agencies, for example The Red Cross and Red Crescent, the World Bank, Médecins sans Frontièrs, OXFAM. It also includes the vast number of people who work in much smaller entities whose humanitarian purpose calls them into war zones. The most important one from my region of the United States is called Mercy Corps. Their organizational missions do at least as much as the requests of the parties to a war to determine where the humanitarians work and what they do.

many years to bring any kind of peace to Bosnia.

Furthermore, working towards peace forces all sides, participants and spectators equally, into a morally ambiguous world. During the war, the participants could turn to honor and patriotism to spur them on and then to revenge to keep the war fires burning. Spectators had equal clarity, that peace was bound to be better than war. But in fact, it is not. Early peace is a hard time. It presents choices by the hundred and none of them are either easy or simply good.

Many more decisions

At the end of the story of Iraq's long siege war, I speculated about a variety of actions and events any one of which might conceivably have persuaded the various decision-makers that the time to bring the war to an end had come. The list was grounded on events that had actually contributed to peace-making in the six other wars in this book.* Almost anything can inspire a peace-maker to take the first steps. But once the first approach has been made, the challenges all fall into similar categories, no matter where the war zone.

All peace-makers face choices about how to break down an active war machine, choices about the design of a new society with altered allocations of power and resources and choices about how to repair the residual damage and destruction left behind by the war. Furthermore, they face these choices in the company of the very people they once deemed ineligible to have a say. After all, that was why they were at war. We will return to moral ambiguities once more as the chapter ends. First a few examples of the choices in each of these major categories.

Breaking down the war machine—As one might expect, concerns about POWs and the remaining active soldiers in the field demand immediate and thoughtful handling. The evidence from the seven stories shows quite different responses to the shared problem. Release agreements were completed

*The earthquake example results from an observation of my own. Soviets and Americans bringing their 45 year long Cold War to an end, were helped greatly by the 1988 Armenian earthquake, which inspired President Reagan to offer generous amounts of US aid, and inspired President Gorbachev to accept the aid with a minimum of Soviet red tape and suspicion.

during initial talks over Ireland, Bosnia and Israel; prisoner releases though were delayed until well after the signing ceremonies. In South Africa, peace talks were unable even to begin until after the release of Nelson Mandela and the other ANC leaders.

On the front line, soldiers must be persuaded to stop attacking the enemy positions which just days before were their assigned targets. In theory, leaders have such effective control of armed combatants that at the hour a cease-fire goes into effect, the violence really does stop. In none of the seven cases did this occur. In South Africa Zulus, spurred on by resistant White Nationalists, took up arms against the ANC precisely because the government had laid theirs down. In Chechnya the fighting halted and then simply started all over again. In the North of Ireland and Israel, partisans continued armed attacks. In Bosnia, renegade military commanders tried hard to destroy the cease-fire. In the North of Ireland, the military settlements themselves turned into the single most important reason the peace process remained precarious for so many years. In Iraq, separating the soldiers on the ground was easy, but it never happened in the air. Though peace is supposed to replace violence, the military transition is rarely either instantaneous or easy to complete.

Policing and monitoring of disputed territories has the possibility of aiding trust-building. This too is likely to lead to patchy results. In the former Yugoslavia, Eastern Slavonia and Brcko were placed under absolute international jurisdiction for several years while, in the rest of the Balkans, international troops facilitated rather than governed. These foreigners were still deployed eight years after the peace was signed; the peace was still too fragile to place full enforcement authority in local hands. Israelis and Palestinians barely touched the most explosive policing question in their first talks, namely who would have control over Jerusalem. And yet among their first decisions was that the Palestinian governing authority would establish its own police force. For Palestinians, this was not simply a military settlement. It was the first sign of a new way to allocate powers and resources in the territories. Decisions about the Constabulary in the North of Ireland were equally significant.

Constructing the new world—In all seven wars, reaching agreements about the building of a new society and making new allocations of government and economic opportunities were pre-requisites for peace-making. History textbooks imply that such topics usually wait until a permanent treaty, as though solutions cannot be formulated until well after the end of the fighting. Nothing could be further from reality. Preliminary allocations are required before most will even consider peace. Neither South Africans crafting their non-racial constitution, nor the parties to the war in the North of Ireland, crafting an integrated form of government for the province, would have laid down their weapons without prior knowledge of the basic framework for a new political regime. In Dayton, the negotiators established jurisdictional boundaries and in Oslo they allocated actual lands to the PLO. Ledbed and Maskhadov reopened the autonomy question for Chechnya. Rwanda's government instituted power sharing at once. In all these regions, the complex realities of democratic process came up against the exigencies of peacemaking as well. In varying degrees popular consent became a factor once again. In the North of Ireland, the peace went so far as to give the people a say in the terms, by voting in a referendum. South Africa was the same. In Bosnia and in Israel/Palestine, ordinary people began working at the grass roots constructing intergroup collaborative programs on everything from health care delivery to shared stewardship of the environment.[23]

And yet, citizen commitments do not strip the leaders of their ultimate power over the situation. In South Africa, at the last moment, De Klerk and Mandela simply decided to turn their backs on concerns raised by other, less powerful parties to the Constitutional talks. In the North of Ireland over the long haul, David Trimble, Gerry Adams and their colleagues in the inner core of the leadership on both sides responded much more actively to each others' perceived slights and betrayals than the early pro-peace referendum results. In Israel, Ariel Sharon depended on support from the police, but his unilateral decision to invade the precincts of the Jerusalem mosque, known as the Dome of the Rock, in September 2000 represented his personal declaration of war, a body blow to the Oslo Accords. Yeltsin broke the peace in Chechnya. Mandela and De Klerk did not break the peace in South Africa, nor did any of their chosen successors, no matter how lukewarm the support given by the Whites to the new regime.

Of course, none of the early agreements provided comprehensive political or economic settlements. Each one left substantial issues to be clarified or implemented later. And yet, before the killing can stop, the opposing sides must put forward similar or closely related images of post-war political systems.[24] One of the signs of failure in the Iraqi cease-fire process was that the UN coalition had come together with a very limited mandate about government and economics in Iraq itself. After the intense fighting ended, the Security Council tried unilaterally to impose political and economic settlements on Iraq but rather than beginning a peace process, they re-energized hostilities instead. In their talks about government and politics, the parties to a war are usually, in some sense, re-engaging with the issues that prompted the fighting in the first place. Finding solutions is made all the harder because the damage and destruction wrought by the fighting place yet another set of difficult choices in front of everyone.

Repair of the old world—Reconstruction and recovery constitute yet another group of issues which can make or break the peace. I have come to think of these challenges as "the Re's"—and there are four that are particularly significant in anchoring or destroying the peace: "re"patriation, "re"pair, "re"parations and "re"conciliation. It is in the engagement with these issues that thirst for vengeance, that engine of war that keeps running when all else fades, can finally begin to recede.

Repatriation comes first. The combat in Rwanda, South Africa, Bosnia, Iraq, Chechnya and Israel/Palestine displaced untold numbers of people. Rwanda and Bosnia faced the socio-political consequences of "ethnic cleansing."[25] I have already discussed some of the dangers that result from repatriation. In Israel/Palestine and South Africa official government policies forced "displacement," condemning Palestinians and Blacks to crowded refugee camps and segregated townships, deprived of the ordinary basics of modern life— running water and sewage control, education and jobs. When peace came to South Africa, ordinary people regained the right to chose where they lived. One of the most dangerous parts of the war in Israel/Palestine centers on the Israeli government's destruction of Palestinian homes and the continued building of houses for Israelis on the West Bank side of the Jordan. Reopening access to safe housing would be a clear sign of peace.

Meanwhile, international agencies from the UN Refugee Organization to the Red Cross complicate repatriation by their internal decisions about whether and how to supply aid. Their criteria center on saving lives, rather than concerning themselves with securing the peace. The small number of aid workers in Chechnya left once they became the target of attacks themselves. In the aftermath of Rwanda, the problems inherent in larger operations that might encourage mass exodus have become much clearer to all humanitarian agencies, but since saving life remains the priority, saving the peace will continue to be at risk.

Repair costs for damaged buildings and economic infrastructure reach enormous proportions in almost all wars. This is particularly true in every US war, since Americans are so committed to destroying infrastructure, officially as an alternative to destroying human life. Even in the North of Ireland and England, where the targeting always intentionally aimed at people, rebuilding costs were not trivial. What is more, in the oppressed areas of war torn countries, decades of catastrophic economic isolation impose their toll on the people. By the end, most regions have become very poor, economically. So outsiders, moved by all of this suffering, intervened in the economics of every war zone. Neither positive economic incentives, like huge sums offered to Israel/Palestine and the North of Ireland nor negative economic sanctions, of the kind that were imposed on Iraq, Serbia and South Africa had a direct effect on bring people to the negotiating table. And yet there is clearly a connection between unfinished repairs and impatience with the peace process. Among Palestinians in the occupied territories, the slow rate of economic progress fueled the willingness to resort to violence once more. It is possible that in the Balkans, the reverse is becoming true, at least in Bosnia. The violence in neighboring Kosovo, outside the purview of this book, paints a much less encouraging view of the value of international intervention.

Demands for reparations, the next of the "Re's," are routinely mentioned in the rhetoric of war. Enemies threaten each other that they will have to pay for their actions, literally, once the war ends. In fact, in only one of the wars, the UN against the state of Iraq, were sizeable reparations ever mandated. The UN decided that Iraq owed Kuwait huge suns and that individuals and corporations could apply to the Compensation Commission as well. In its first five years, the Commission gave out over $15 billion, money taken straight off the top of Iraqi oil revenues, before repairs to Iraqi cities. Reparations on this scale can only be described as punitive. They are unique among the cases, and strongly suggestive of continued hostilities rather than peace-making.

The South Africans included token reparations payments in the design of their Truth and Reconciliation process, but as we will see in the next chapter, these payments were not very likely to re-enflame hostilities. Reparations concerns, though often part of the talks, are actually residual signs of combat, and not a part of the groundwork for peace.

Reconciliation, the last of the four "Re's" is impossible in the first stages of a peace-making process. Beginning serious negotiations is not in the least dependent on either forgiveness or reconciliation. If it were so, no war would ever end. The startling truth is that, for the first talks to have a chance of success, all that is necessary is that enemies become willing to work seriously together regardless of their differences.

Indeed, negotiators rarely make progress unless their talks are framed by fundamentally painful conditions.[26] The moral ambiguity of those first meetings between those who are still enemies creates all the pain they need. If their discussions are to succeed, offers and counter offers must build confidence on both sides that each stands to gain and lose in appropriate and equivalent ways. The offers need to entail costs and risks for the side that makes the offer. Also, offers need to be genuinely "path-breaking" and in some sense irrevocable.[27] Furthermore, negotiators must have enough authority both to grant concessions and to ensure that they are not overturned.

Certainty, ambiguity and the power of the loser

With hindsight, it is tempting to connect a series of events that contribute to making peace and thereby create the impression of an inevitable progress towards an enduring peace. But, this is only possible with hindsight. An honest description of peace agreements as they come into being must show that, right up until the last moment, each one risks total breakdown. No one can predict, until the last moment, often the very last day, whether the opportunity to make an enduring peace has really opened up. Leaders talking with their enemies about the right issues, and with the right amounts of popular and international will behind them, are the ingredients essential to resolve a turbulent war. In chaotic fashion one cannot predict exactly when the particular combination is truly in place, when the key will actually slide into place to unlock the door to peace.

The final stages in each of the seven episodes that occupy this book were replete with dangerous tension right to the very end. In Dayton Izebegavitch, President of Bosnia, nearly refused to attend the final meeting. The final talks to create the interim South African constitution almost broke down on the very last day. In the North of Ireland, the Good Friday Agreement looked doomed just a few short days before its terms fell into place. Whether the Irish and the British would finally cement this version of peace remained uncertain for years. In Rwanda, despite a clear "victory," peace instantly became entangled in two of the four "Re's"—repatriation and reconciliation. It also became entangled in the fates of other nations. It became clear well after the particular events that have been our focus, that peace-making would have to begin all over again in Israel/Palestine and in Chechnya.

And between the United States and Britain, and some newly constituted or older version of Iraq? Who knows? There were some in the Bush administration who argued that only an intense period of war, and its resultant regime change, could open up any opportunities for an enduring peace. I cannot quarrel with their focus on Saddam Hussein, though I would describe war as a terribly blunt tool to drive a single man from power.* Given the immensely destructive scale of the military campaign they planned, they were bound to encounter huge problems in repairing Iraq, even if they were successful in creating a a appropriate new system of government. In

---

* A US invasion did just that in Panama and Grenada, but the geographical conditions in these two places were dramatically easier. Still, the value the US placed on replacing that one man can be measured by their actions on the first day of the assault—35 cruise missiles and a 2000 pound bomb rained down on the underground bunker in which they believed the President of Iraq to be spending the night.

addition, there were considerable indications that even if the US officials managed to establish an occupation authority in the country, they would still be a long way from controlling Iraqis and any others who chose to attack the occupying forces or the United States itself. Many outside the United States feared that this war might destroy what equanimity there was in the entire Middle East. As I go to press with this manuscript, peace is so far beyond the horizon it is impossible to tell how it might come about.

All that remains therefore is to emphasize once again how much power over selecting a time to try to end a war rests in the hands of those on the losing side. Of course, often there is no clear loser. Saddam Hussein simply denied the interpretation almost everyone else applied to the dramatic Coalition military victory in 1991. In this denial he claimed a position from which to resist the resolutions and demands imposed by the UN. More to the point, he also managed to ensure his political leadership position remained secure—much more so than most of his leading opponents. Margaret Thatcher and George Bush were gone within two years. Gorbachev was forced out in less than a year. Mitterand retired, and was soon dead. Rabin was assassinated and Israel remains engulfed in dreadful combat. Saddam Hussein's refusal to accept defeat markedly improved at least some of his realities.

By contrast, Frederick De Klerk's insistence that the time had come to end the war in South Africa played an enormous role in bringing peace, even though in doing so, De Klerk assured the total defeat of his own side. Perhaps he never guessed how completely the Whites would lose government power. He did know that no change was possible if the defeated Whites were also at risk of unlimited recrimination for their part in apartheid. South Africa's path through the minefield of post-war justice makes the centerpiece of the last chapter of this book. The South Africans have a good deal to offer those who want to understand the transition from the first uncertain phases of peace-making to a durable peace.

危

JUSTICE, MERCY, MEMORY AND PEACE

Through patience, and a refusal to accept conflict as the ultimate reality,
a bridge has been built. Now to traverse it and move toward
a future based on cooperation.[1]

The bridge—a familiar and appropriate image of peace-making. William Ury, one of America's leading lights in the practice of complex negotiations, devotes a whole chapter in *Getting Past No* to building "a golden bridge."[2] Like many users of this image, he evokes two opponents facing off with a chasm dividing them. Ideally, when they decide to settle their conflict each party approaches from its own side and builds approximately half a bridge towards the other. If the parties can make their partial bridges meet, their conflict is most likely resolved.

The bridge I have in mind is quite different. It links a war-ridden past to a more peaceful future. All of its builders, one-time enemies, together must do the construction work on this variety of bridge, starting from the same, war-torn side. When finished, it can take them, in each other's company, across to a place where, despite recent hostilities, they can jointly establish a new form of peaceful coexistence. But the dangerous past remains very close. The bridge that delivered them to peace is so very easily traversed in the other direction as well, back into war. The risk remains nearby for quite a while.

For each of the seven war stories, I have already framed some of the geo-political issues impacting the chances of achieving peaceful coexistence. Chechens wished to coexist as sovereign equals with their enemies, the Russians, but the latter offered no better than semi-autonomy within Russia. Israelis and Palestinians were trying to divide territories, every square meter of which was strenuously contested. Iraq and the forces arrayed against that country by the United States and the United Kingdom were in conflict over the allocation of some of Iraq's most important sovereign powers, including the country's oil revenues, its military arsenals and the status of ethnic minorities.

Bosnians, Serbs and Croats spent the years after Dayton trying to work out yet another version of their centuries old, sovereign coexistence issues in the Balkans. In the North of Ireland, relations among the Irish government, the British government, the Northern Ireland Parliament and the European Union remained complex and fluctuating. Rwanda faced the reintegration of two hostile ethnic groups within one nation's geographic boundaries, groups which had earlier been flung apart by a genocidal centrifuge, ending up in camps all round the outside of Rwanda's frontiers. South Africans, too, were trying to merge populations, in their case resident populations previously segregated. The territorial scale of these problems varied enormously. South Africa, the United States, Iraq and Russia are huge; Israel/Palestine, the North of Ireland, Chechnya, the Balkans and Rwanda are all among the most compact regions of the world.

Those features of coexistence that can be furthered by economic and political choices for the future were the focus of the last chapter. It is now time to turn our attention to the other key ingredient of peace-making, finding an appropriate way to ease the suffering left behind by the war. This demands decisions about justice and remembrance. No matter how sound the constitution and the currency, neither will flourish in a society still riddled with pain, and pain is a haunting presence even after active violence ends. To leave the war behind them, survivors in the combatant communities must find a way to explain their suffering and to respond to it. Furthermore, understanding, healing and a morally sound response to the damage are dependent in large part on collective and public story telling about the war. Some stories come to light in the search for justice. Others come to light in acts of remembrance. Often enemies can make genuine peace with these parts of the past only when they construct at least some of their responses and explanatory stories together. Otherwise the past will reach out and drag them back into war.

Past grievances have caused just that in Israel/Palestine and Chechnya. Unresolved vengeance and unsatisfied loyalist urges reached out for years in Bosnia, Rwanda and the North of Ireland. Perhaps, with the 2003 renewal of intensive war in Iraq, the combatants will finally recognize the need for all sides to play a role in building a new bridge to peace in Iraq as well. Alone among the combatants I have described, the South Africans have built and walked across their bridge to a post-war world. They have truly left apartheid behind.

A variety of differing means were used after each of the wars to explain each one's pain and suffering, with differing consequences for helping the past become the past. This chapter looks first at the means used by criminal prosecutors to punish individual perpetrators, mechanisms that have been gaining powerful political momentum in the last five years, since the United Nations instituted a permanent International Criminal Court purposely to address war crimes. Rwanda and Bosnia are the key examples of prosecutorial justice, and as they experienced it, such justice has yet to show how it might in any way encourage former enemies to take on the shared work of building their "peace-bridge." Indeed the prospect of being subjected to a criminal trial seems most likely to prevent certain kinds of leaders ever even considering ending a war. Why would Saddam Hussein have wanted to negotiate a new political and economic regime for Iraq given that his personal withdrawal was most likely to lead to some kind of punitive action against him? Still, there is huge momentum for such a court, and thus the consequences of international justice among these seven cases demands exploration.

The chapter then takes up more varied and widespread peace-making practices aimed towards forgiveness and reconciliation. The central example here is South Africa's Truth and Reconciliation Commission (TRC). Its achievements will be described in some detail. Through the Commission, South Africa as a nation learned much more than it had ever publicly known about the horrors of its wars. Furthermore, hundreds of particular families learned the full truth about the deaths of the fathers, husbands and children they still mourned. Understanding and healing could finally begin.

However, the terms "truth and reconciliation" do not fully describe the kind of justice and the kind of remembrance South Africans actually achieved. The Commission also granted amnesty, mercy, to many of the perpetrators of the violence. In addition, its archives constitute, in effect, the first collective physical memorial to carry remembrances of all of the dead.

Dangerous peace-making becomes much less dangerous when those involved share the crafting of a far-reaching story to remember what matters most about the war. That is the path on which they can uncover the hope for peaceful coexistence for all, both those who lived with the pain and those who caused it.

Archbishop Desmond Tutu described his view of South Africa's hopeful prospects in the Foreword to the 1998 Final Report of the Truth and Reconciliation Commission:

> Ours is a remarkable country. Let us celebrate our diversity, our differences. God wants us as we are. South Africa wants and needs the Afrikaner, the English, the coloured, the Indian, the black. We are sisters and brothers in one family—God's family, the human family. Having looked the beast of the past in the eye, having asked and received forgiveness and having made amends, let us shut the door on the past—not in order to forget it but in order not to allow it to imprison us. Let us move into the glorious future of a new kind of society where people count, not because of biological irrelevancies or other extraneous attributes, but because they are persons of infinite worth created in the image of God. Let that society be a new society—more compassionate, more caring, more gentle, more given to sharing—because we have left "the past of a deeply divided society characterised by strife, conflict, untold suffering and injustice" and are moving to a future "founded on the recognition of human rights, democracy and peaceful coexistence and development opportunities for all South Africans, irrespective of colour, race, class, belief or sex."
>
> Like our Constitution, the [Truth] Commission has helped in laying the secure foundation for the people of South Africa to transcend the divisions and strife of the past, which generated gross violations of human rights, the transgression of humanitarian principles in violent conflicts and a legacy of hatred, fear, guilt and revenge.
>
> My appeal is ultimately directed to us all, black and white together, to close the chapter on our past and to strive together for this beautiful and blessed land as the rainbow people of God.
>
> The Commission has done its share to promote national unity and reconciliation. Their achievement is up to each one of us.[3]

South Africa, by 1998, had already begun to find answers to some very hard problems. What should they do about a past in which the government selected civilians on the basis of race, transported them to concentrated geographic regions and then deprived them of ordinary civil rights, education, health care and equal access to gainful employment? One answer was to change all the restrictive laws. Another answer was to restrict sharply the amount of money spent offering "reparations" to individuals. They spent the money instead on systemic improvements to the infrastructure in previously damaged areas. Another answer was to offer standardized reparations for those who were particular victims of violence, in the form of education and health care and other widely useful social benefits, instead of assessing compensation individually and assigning a private cash value to it. Another was to decide that the officials responsible for these civil policies were acting as agents of a state, and as such were not appropriately singled out as individuals to be held personally culpable.

But civil remedies and economic repairs such as these are solutions only for a small part of the problem confronting those who are trying to complete their crossing of the bridge to peace. The dreadful specter of war deaths still looms close behind. How can one account for and attend to each of the lives lost and families shattered by the fighting? Sometimes an individual death has disastrous consequences for an entire society. More often in war, uncountable numbers of people suffer dreadfully. Those who want peace must deal with questions of remembrance and questions of justice for that suffering.

What kind of justice can there be?

Can there be justice for the fact that someone assassinated a president by shooting down his plane, and thereby drove two million or more people to their deaths or into exile? What about three years of virtually daily shelling of civilians in a besieged city? What about suicide bombers killing themselves and a dozen people whose only crime is to be riding a bus to work? What about shutting down a regional elected assembly and then using the central government's armed forces to police that semi-autonomous region for 29 years? What about capturing a "traitor" and torturing him to death by encircling his head with a flaming car tire? What about killing, in a single massacre, 5,000 or more men and compelling the last to die to watch the killing of the others? What about designing a propaganda campaign to enable the conduct of a terror genocide that kills 800,000 people in six weeks?

Can one bring the United Nations to justice for designing and implementing a 100% embargo, enforced by military means, on all export and import trade with Iraq, thereby killing an average of 5,000 children a month for over five years? What about the entire South African police force, because it condoned the killing of a dissident and the burning of his body so as to hide all traces of his whereabouts from his family? Who is responsible for the Russian army's barrage of shells, which destroyed homes and apartments across blocks and blocks of Chechnya's capital city? Who is to be charged when thousands of men rape thousands of women as they did in both Bosnia and Rwanda, in their campaigns for "ethnic cleansing?" What about American loyalists, who sent clandestine shipments of guns and bullets to support a renegade Irish militia, even after a peace agreement had been signed? What about assassinating yet another president purely because he signed a peace agreement, thereby condemning a whole society to untold more years of war?

Every one of these acts occurred in one or more of the seven wars in this book. And there remain literally innumerable acts like them, many not noted in the public records but capable of leaving a burning scar behind in someone's heart and life. Such agonies inflict devastating consequences on real people who are still alive at the end of the war. Most will need some collective recognition of their suffering as much, if not more than merely private ways to work through the pain.

One option is selectively to prosecute and punish, through international courts, a very few of those whose conduct at war seems particularly outrageous. There is little evidence that this contributes either to justice or to remembrance. From recent history it is clear, though, that peace is made much stronger when combatants recognize all acts of war as causes of suffering, and see in each perpetrator the need for mercy and in each victim the need for remembrance. And therein lies yet another danger in peace-making. Who should decide how to remember the past? Should it be those whose future lives must be lived in the immediate shadow of the past, or some impartial and detached judge in a faraway place? Among other things, this chapter serves as a plea to keep the power over justice in the war-torn communities. They depend on control over their own past if they are to keep their present peace.

"Injuring is, in fact, the central activity of war…it is the goal to which all activity is directed and [also the] road to that goal."[4] Sheltered behind wartime rhetoric as it drums away at moral imperatives—honor and patriotism, and at strategic objectives—the capture of towns and the control of political power, lies the physical reality that, in war, all of these goals are achieved by means of injury. Those who stand in the way of an oncoming army face physical danger, unless they attempt to kill enough of the advancing forces to drive them into a retreat. Injury, bodily injury, is war's purpose. And the outcome of the war is made permanent in large part because the people who died are permanently dead. In that sense there is no way ever to return to the world as it was before. And yet those dead bodies, and the manner of each death, matter too much simply to be laid to rest, ignored like spent shell casings on the battlefield. In this they are quite different from a bombed out city.

Dead bodies are irreversibly dead. Their families are forever maimed and deadened too. Irreversibility is yet another attribute of chaotic systems and although justice, like remembrance, is seemingly a backward-looking process, neither justice nor remembrance can bring back to life those who have died. Justice and remembrance are critical, then, because they line important pathways forward across the bridge to peace.

Unlike dead bodies, towns and rivers, governments and art collections can be quite fully repaired. A visit to the battlefields of World War I testifies to the degree that material restoration is possible. Ypres, a medieval Belgian community, was literally pulverized during that war, and yet the city lives on today as a faithful replica of its medieval self. Hiroshima's appearance is even more dramatic. On August 6, 1945, the center of that city was vaporized, turned to dust and also made toxic in the very instant the atomic bomb exploded. Bodies by the thousand lay charred and disfigured on the ground and nearby were many thousands more who, although they had survived the blast and fires, were destined for slow and painful deaths, poisoned already by radiation. Today, Hiroshima is a thriving city with wide avenues lined by solid buildings. Every block is filled with commercial activity, housing and schools. The "bullet" trains to and from Tokyo pass through every 15 minutes.

Justice and remembrance for the dead are not so easily achieved. Leaders and combatants face troubling choices between punishment and mercy, between silence and remembrance, between crafting stories about their war collaboratively with erstwhile enemies or doing so in hostile confrontation with them. "Perhaps the most critical to…a sustainable peace is a reconsideration of violent offenses. Communalization—the act of sharing traumatic experiences, perceptions, resulting emotions, and responses with other people in a safe environment—together with a period of mourning over losses are essential beginnings of the healing process. Communalization, in addition, establishes a public record of historical events, an acknowledgement of circumstances and occurrences crucial for (re)establishing national identity."[5] When peace is just beginning, these issues are particularly salient; the grief is still fresh and the material repairs are far from complete.

Even those readers of this book living far outside a currently active war zone are involved in choices about war and justice. This world outside the war zone, the so-called "international community," has laid claim to substantial control over post-war justice by means of the United Nations and the International Criminal Court. Thus outsiders increasingly also control an important portion of the "history creation" to which those at war must in future submit. The trials conducted so far of Bosnians and Rwandans offer little indication that detached judges, miles from the war zone will support the reconciliation the combatants require. Indeed, the chances that UN justice will damage world peace seem rather high. These are dangerous times in peace-making, not just for combatants but for all of us.

Let me detour briefly here to sketch the history of international criminal justice in response to acts of war. The notion of collective, internationally mandated justice has its origins in international "conventions," the earliest of which are more than 100 years old. At gatherings in Geneva and in The Hague during the last part of the 19th century and in the first years of the 20th century, nation states placed limitations on the kinds of weapons and strategies they could use in war. International "law" has been hugely amplified ever since, most dramatically as a result of agreements among nations acting as members of the United Nations to limit many of war's worst cruelties, including torture, genocide and the use of children as combatants. International agreements also exist about thousands of matters that have no bearing on war at all. Until recently, nation-to-nation resolutions, conventions and agreements were binding only on states and governments, with no thought that individuals might be held accountable to an "international community."

The modern concept of international prosecution of individual people, as opposed to governments, as perpetrators of war crimes first occurred at the end of World War II.* In 1945, the leaders of the "Allied" nations chose to prosecute, as individuals, many of the key leaders of the Nazi war effort and a number of Japan's military and government leaders as well.[6] In fact, although the judges came from several nations, each one was there to represent one of the Allies, so although we call them "international," in truth their work is more accurately described as a modern version of "winners' justice."

Trials were conceived voluntarily by leaders in the key combatant countries, despite Churchill's plea that tradition entitled them to the victor's right summarily to execute any enemy official. When the trials were complete, many (though not all) among the central leadership in both countries were indeed executed. The trials had also offered an early forum in which to develop a collective understanding of the nature of the Holocaust and the Pacific/Asian war. Still, the War Crimes Tribunals in Tokyo and Nuremberg never attempted to account for more than a small part of the damage done in the Japanese and German wars. It took decades for significant joint progress towards harmony in Germany's relations with the countries against which she fought, and also with the terrorized groups—Jews, Communists, the mentally disabled and homosexuals—so many of whom were exterminated. The Japanese government, in relation to South Koreans and to the

---

* Although the United Nations is now a world body, it had its origins as an exclusive club for the Allied nations who had begun to call themselves the United Nations in the closing phases of the war. Neither Germany nor Japan were allowed to join in the early years, and despite years of behind the scenes negotiations, neither has made any progress towards what many see as their rightful place as permanent members of the UN Security Council.

Chinese in particular, is still not entirely over the bridge to peace. Too many apologies remain unsaid. Too little history has been accounted for fully.

And yet, despite the limited outcomes from those first trials at Nuremberg and Tokyo, and after a gap of nearly 40 years, the United Nations suddenly opted to institute Ad Hoc International War Crimes Tribunals for Bosnia (1993) and Rwanda (1994).[7] And then in 1998, at a meeting in Rome, delegates representing all UN member nations crafted a specific statute defining war crimes. By 2003, enough of the UN's members had ratified the statute that an International Criminal Court, based at The Hague in the Netherlands, was well on its way to being fully functioning.

International criminal justice, which targets particular individuals at the end of a war, is almost certainly here to stay. Whether such justice, which assumes and claims to define a universally applicable ethical stance, will foster peace-making or make it more dangerous remains in doubt.[8] Still justice remains critical and we now turn to an appraisal of its role in ending the wars that are the evidence on which the claims made in this book are based.

Justice—trials

Peace is dependent on a shared, collaborative approach to suffering in war. Trials and reconciliation commissions provide a response to violence and each creates a version of history. Their contributions to peace are very different.

Supporters of a legalistic/criminalizing approach to war believe that the social order can best be repaired by punishment and also that courts will act as a deterrent to anyone contemplating war in the future. Former UN Chief Prosecutor Louise Arbour described the International War Crimes Tribunals as an expression of outrage against "the culture of impunity" among war leaders.[9] Sadly, with that as a priority, neither the Bosnian nor the Rwandan trials have focused much on reconciliation or even geopolitical coexistence. Official international justice, as manifest in the United Nations Ad Hoc International Tribunals, bears little resemblance to a mechanism for the communalization of grief.

This is not the place for a detailed analysis of their practices, but some limitations of the Tribunals' approaches to justice and history-making are very obvious. The technicalities of prosecution in Arusha (Rwanda's court) and in The Hague, where the Bosnian Tribunal and the Appeals Court for both Tribunals were sitting, were so complex that between 1993 and March 1998 the only person to be sentenced (this one a Bosnian, Erdemovic) had confessed.[10] The courts cost an enormous amount of money, well over $1 billion in their first 10 years, almost all the money spent on buildings and on over 1200 lawyers, judges and court employees from 82 countries. Virtually none of the money was spent in the affected war zones. Despite these costs, in that same period only a handful of cases had progressed as far as sentencing—six cases for Bosnia and thirteen for Rwanda.[11] This would have to be described as a minimal response to the vast damage in both places. Indeed, judicial technicalities led, at least once, to the complete release of a key suspect.[12] Furthermore, United Nations justice refused to impose the death penalty, so key genocidiares (planners of the genocide) from Rwanda escaped execution while more than 200 of their underlings, tried in local criminal courts in Rwanda, were put to death. These Tribunals were barely able to meet their own punitive and deterrent objectives, let alone to offer substantial support for peace.

The trials shared many other fundamental problems when seen from the perspective of our other concern—as a means to create a history of events. Witnesses lived hundreds of miles away and often would testify only if compelled to do so. Out of fear for their lives, witness identities were also routinely kept secret. Thus, the legal history of each war was being produced out of coerced testimony from anonymous sources, hardly a persuasive recommendation by most standards for truth. Official reports of the testimonies were sometimes not published until years after they were spoken. Furthermore, the official languages of the Arusha court are French and English, so the records were not easily accessible to the local populations of the affected area. Lastly, most victims were never offered a chance to tell their stories, since the miniscule number of cases to be heard, and the tight evidentiary procedures that were followed, left almost all the injured people invisible to and uninteresting to the court.

Cooperation between the International Tribunals and local officials in both Bosnia and Rwanda was never easy. The UN's first Chief Prosecutor, Richard Goldstone, found he could not bring to trial two key Serb military leaders, Mladic and Karadic, being sheltered by loyalists in the Serb zone in Bosnia, in part because UN Peace-keepers threatened by physical risks to themselves refused to make the arrests. Rather later, in 2001, in a diametrically opposite situation, Serbia's Belgrade government, not originally a target of the court at all, was compelled to extradite Slobodan Milosevic to The Hague under threat of losing all economic aid from key UN member nations. Justice in The Hague was decidedly uneven.

Rwanda's government finally decided to sever links with the UN court in Arusha and turn inwards to solve its judicial problems itself. 1999 saw the government setting aside Western procedural models entirely for most of the 120,000 people it still held in prison, returning them to their home communities for justice using traditional Rwandan approaches. The government also established a Unity and Reconciliation Commission to discuss not only Hutu/Tutsi conflict, but also economic stress and the tensions between returning refugee Tutsi and the Tutsi living in Rwanda who survived the massacre. There was too much work to be done, and criminal prosecution for crimes in the past that had been committed with widespread official and popular sanction seemed to hinder rather than help progress towards peace.

Justice will be the central issue once again as we explore more fully the decision in South Africa to mete out no punishments at all to some people, in particular to those most committed to and central to the task of building a new post-war world. For now, though, it is time to focus on some of the other virtues of the shared effort to build stories after a war.

Memory and story-telling

The justice in The Hague and Arusha took the retributive approach—each offender must pay his own particular price for his crime. Many societies, Rwanda included, have a local tradition of a more restorative or "healing" justice that focuses first on the repair of damaged relationships, in part by recognizing the humanity of offender and victim alike. The restorative model is catching on in Western societies too. In the United States this has been spurred by the realization that many Vietnam War veterans have become that war's victims, suffering for years from traumatic and destructive emotional patterns. As psychiatrist Jonathan Shay describes the problem:

> The emergence of rage out of intense grief may be a biological universal; long-term obstruction of grief and failure to communalize grief can imprison a person in endless swinging between rage and emotional deadness as a permanent way of being in the world.[13]

Americans belatedly recognized the significance of healing such suffering, namely that the Vietnam War would finally come to an end only when the country took collective responsibility for healing each one of the traumatized veterans. When a whole society like Rwanda is traumatized, it is best advised to use its own traditional means for healing and repairing the social order.

Another restorative term, more common in Africa than in Northern countries, is "cleansing," explained here by anthropologist Carolyn Nordstrom describing the elder's words during a cleansing ritual:

> "Time will not erase the fact that you killed people. People we all care about. It is something…we cannot pretend you have not done. But you did these acts in a time of war so horrible none of us has been left unscathed. War makes terrible demands on people….We cannot condemn you for the war, you too were held in its grip….We have to go on now to create a better place for ourselves. Take what you have learned and turn it into good, into rebuilding." They then worked daily to help the soldier reintegrate into community life.[14]

To these two restorative strategies, many conflict specialists including genocide expert Ervin Staub would add a third: "understanding."

> What has seemed most galvanizing for participants, Staub says, has been learning in the workshops about the forces in society, in culture, and in the psychology of individuals that lead to genocide. When Rwandans realize that what happened in their society has happened to other people and that there are explainable forces that lead to these things, he says, it seems to give them back their humanity. "If there are understandable forces, even though they are so terrible and our fate was so terrible, then we are still part of the human family!" has been the response.[15]

Learning to live in a world shared with former enemies in Rwanda depended on all three: on healing, cleansing and understanding.

Vital restorative projects have long been under way in all of these conflict areas, instigated by local activists and international humanitarians. Through Health Bridge in the Balkans, medical professionals from conflicting ethnic communities collaborated to rebuild clinics and to provide the public health services essential in the post-war era. In Israel/Palestine, Oasis of Peace brought teenagers from the two communities together for days at a time to learn more about each others' way of life and thereby to begin to build trust. In the North of Ireland, aid workers from overseas delivered psychiatric care to children traumatized by the war years.[16] Sometimes the cleansing work was quite strenuous physically as well as emotionally. Mass graves in Bosnia and Rwanda required excavation so that the bodies could be more humanely buried, and so that survivors might definitively identify lost relatives. All of such work is vital and without it no peace can endure.

And yet these repairs are constructive only if the right kinds of justice are connected to them. A hidden grave for example, demands explanation—who are the dead, who killed them and how, why are they buried this way? What can we know and what action does the knowledge require of us? The Truth Commission in South Africa answered just these kinds of questions. It forced perpetrators to reveal the location of bodies long "missing" so that grieving families could finally say good bye as they learned the manner of their relatives' deaths as well. It was often a harrowing time, but at last, finally, there was a story instead of a mystery.

The Commission's final report tallied the enormous number of people who learned new truths about their own personal lives.

> "In identifying the principal organisations and individuals responsible for gross violations of human rights in its mandate period, the Truth and Reconciliation Commission had a vast range of information at its disposal. In addition to court records and press reports, it received over 21,000 statements from individuals alleging that they were victims of human rights abuses and 7,124 from people requesting amnesty for acts they committed, authorised or failed to prevent. In addition, the Commission received submissions from the former State President, Mr. P W Botha, political parties, a variety of civil institutions and organisations, the armed forces and other interested parties. All these submissions were seriously considered by the Commission."[17]

The Truth Commission's work spread well beyond those immediately implicated in and victimized by the violence as well. Every local hearing was broadcast fully, so South Africans together adapted to a whole new version of their history. The hearings were held across the country in all regions, so that ordinary people could gather and listen in person. Also, the hearings were conducted in local languages, often in quite ordinary meeting rooms, with Commissioners, audience, perpetrators and witnesses within easy physical reach of each other. Witnesses could request a hearing even before perpetrators had requested amnesty. When before the Commission, victims and accusers gave testimony without the demeaning and limiting constraints of adversarial court proceedings.

The Truth and Reconciliation Commission and all South Africans came to recognize that some of the "truth" and story-telling might damage rather than heal. Quite a few claimed the Commissioners re-opened wounds but did not stay long enough to make sure the injuries closed over once more. Still, the project represents a careful and truly comprehensive attempt to build a restorative story about past events, to enable South African society as a single whole to move forward into a new era. As South African Bishop David Beetge put it:

> [The Commission] has given the opportunity for people to tell their story, stories which [could] never be told before...There were so many unhealed wounds before the [Truth and Reconciliation Commission] began its work. The evidence of those who have given witness [is] that, by telling their story, they have shared a burden and found a new sense of peace. This is very obvious from the sheer look of some of them as they walk out of the meetings of the Commission...
>
> We tell our stories so that we shall remember the years that lie behind with all their struggles as the path to the new life ahead.[18]

All that remained, on the day the Commission's Report was presented to the public, was to decide finally on amnesty for about 2,000 of the cases. By then, 5,000 of the perpetrators already knew their fate. When the work was completed in 2001, amnesty had been granted to 849 people.* South Africa's Truth and

---

* Meeting amnesty provisions was strenuous. Alleged perpetrators first had to put their case into the Commission's hands, when there was still a chance that if they did nothing, they would completely evade prosecution and even scrutiny. Then, during the hearings, perpetrators had to listen to harrowing stories about what they had done and they too were forced to give full testimony to the events. To earn an amnesty they would have to convince the Commission both that they had been fully honest and that their actions were instigated by official policy and not by personal feelings towards their victims.

Reconciliation Commission provided inescapable proof that a dreadful war had happened, that it was well and truly over and that the racist Nationalist government would never recover enough credibility to govern again in South Africa.

Justice and mercy

The TRC gets its first two initials from "truth" and "reconciliation," attributes I have linked together by focusing on their capacity to create a shared, a communalized, narrative of events. Just as essential to the impact the Commission would have on South Africa's peace-making was the its power to grant amnesty. In the final event, the number of grants were sparing, about ten percent, but each one had a critical bearing on peace.

It is time for one last context-setting detour. The term "amnesty" has at best a mixed reputation. Associated too often with men like Chilean dictator Augusto Pinochet, who granted himself and his military staff lifetime amnesties the moment they resigned, amnesty is thought by many largely to serve to prevent the full expression of the desires for both justice or remembrance. No official in Chile who knew the dreadful facts of those long years needed to fear any demand that they tell the truth. There was no forum in which truth seekers could operate. Indeed, the word amnesty, whose meaning derives from the Latin word for forgetfulness, sounds as though it cannot possibly be useful for those in search of the truth.

In fact, amnesty is not useful when issued preemptively, as it was by Pinochet, to prohibit further investigation into an ugly past. But in combination with mechanisms for uncovering truth, South Africa discovered in amnesty a valuable resource. Amnesty allowed the country to learn that some of their dreadful violence came about because people on both sides were driven to action by their institutionalized status as policemen and soldiers, resistance fighters and innocent bystanders in a war zone. Furthermore, the amnesties in South Africa were part of a much broader acceptance that the time for punishment was over.

Much of the endurance in South Africa to keep working on peace-making was founded on a widely, though not universally, shared sense that on the bridge from war to peace they must pass through what I have come to visualize as a gate labeled "Mercy." Nelson Mandela and Frederick De Klerk had had to pass through that gate long before the Commission was even a dream in the South African Parliament's collective mind.

Mandela spent 27 years in jail. Though outsiders kept demanding his release, his was a life sentence. He was destined to die in jail. And yet, as we now know, he came out, was elected President of South Africa and awarded the Nobel Peace Prize. The man who released him, De Klerk, also became a Nobel Laureate. In what sense could the actions of a White supremacist President and a radical, military leader in the African National Congress be comparable? It was their reciprocal acts of mercy that made peace possible at all.

De Klerk was the first to move and he was under no pressing compulsion to act. South Africa had withstood inter-racial violence and economic sanctions for several years. Still, in 1990 De Klerk allowed Mandela to go free, unconditionally, in the knowledge that in some way he was opening the door to the defeat of his entire way of life. Mandela could not have come out of Pollsmore Prison any other way.

Nearly four years later, the ANC under Mandela agreed to an Interim Constitution for South Africa, which gave De Klerk and his Nationalist colleagues a role in the transition to a new permanent constitution and allowed their political freedom and personal dignity to remain intact.

At their best all acts of justice in wartime do so much more than punish and deter. They also cleanse, heal and create understanding. Still, even justice presents choices about means and outcomes. In 1990 when Mandela left jail, and once again in 1993 when together these two leaders forced unwilling others to accept their transitional constitution, South Africans at large were still a long way from experiencing any forgiveness towards each other. In the turbulent times just as the war was ending, each man had no choice but to depend on the mercy of the other. The other wars presented similar realities.

Milosevic had played an enormous role in inspiring Serbian ethnic cleansing projects in Bosnia, but America refused to press for a war crimes indictment against him in that war. He was too essential to peace. In Israel/ Palestine all of the key leaders on both sides have blood on their hands. Ariel Sharon, like his peace-oriented predecessor Rabin, ordered killings of civilians for which he surely could be prosecuted. And yet, it would be futile to hope he might even consider making peace were he to receive a credible threat of future prosecution for war crimes. Likewise Yassir Arafat, and also Vladimir Putin, should he be considering peace-making with Chechens. Most vivid to me at this moment is America's President George W. Bush, who has asserted a right to attack first in the war against Iraq, in the name of "preemption." Aggressive war is totally prohibited by the UN Charter, and yet Bush is most unlikely to face prosecution. One reason is America's global authority. The other is that in the interests of peace, many may be willing to grant him amnesty.

It could seem I am putting mercy on a par with a simple quid pro quo. The leaders in war zones get off free, because without them there is no chance for peace. The lesser perpetrators in South Africa receive amnesty because without it no one would tell the truth.

The equations are not that simple. Leaders in the war zone cannot be required to make peace. Each of them is free to continue fighting indefinitely. Ending a war is a matter of free choice. Mercy likewise is gratuitous. Mercy does not come because people deserve it. Mandela and De Klerk had both forfeited their right to mercy, at least in the eyes of their enemies. So, when these two men on opposite sides in a war met face to face amid the damage that both had done, neither could be called deserving. And yet both decided to act.

And that is where mercy differs most fully from forgiveness. Mandela could not simply *feel* compassion towards De Klerk; he had to make concrete decisions about whether and how the Nationalists fit into the next government. De Klerk could not simply forgive Mandela for his violence all those years ago. He had to decide whether and when to release him from prison. The Truth and Reconciliation Commission had to offer or deny amnesty. To end a future war, some leader will have to decide to call off a planned bombing raid. Another will have to decide to enter a room to negotiate with a man he deeply despises. Another will have to release prisoners he would much prefer to keep in jail. Yet another will have to hold back from capturing an enemy military unit in desperate retreat.

Mercy entails action, and merciful acts are possible even in the absence of forgiveness, before anyone has tendered an apology and well before reconciliation can even be contemplated. Indeed mercy may well be the only positive ethical stance that enemies still actively engaged in war can adopt towards one other. Without mercy, without the willingness to desist from the punitive and destructive acts that remain within their power, there is no way for leaders in a war to bring their fighting to an end.

Memory and memorials

In this analysis we have alternated between explorations of justice and of remembrance. They are inextricably linked and before closing with some final thoughts about suffering danger and peace, we must turn once last time to remembrance, this time in material rather than in narrative form.

On the day in September 2001 that those terrifying airplanes crashed into the World Trade Center, the notion of a formal memorial to the disaster was far from most people's minds. That day no one even knew how many had died, and certainly no one could name every one of them. Still, quite soon, informal memorials sprang up all over lower Manhattan—posters taped to walls, photos hung in storefront windows and flowers propped up against the chain link fences that stretched around block after block of the shattered neighborhood.

Those first personal memorials are long gone. Commerce has returned to the neighboring streets and the area inside the chain link fence is much smaller, just the region immediately adjacent to the fallen towers. In the months on either side of the first anniversary of the disaster, a bigger, more official memorial, two towering white lights piercing the sky from the site, brought the shared grief literally within view of everyone for miles around. Then design competitions to replace the two giant skyscrapers demanded proposals for a permanent physical memorial on the site.

In addition to the published narratives about each one of the dead, which appeared day after day in the *New York Times* and in addition to the endless reruns of video footage filmed on the fateful day, everyone in New York and around the country understood that the catastrophe warranted a permanent physical memorial. New York will not be the only site for memorials. There are war memorials all over the Mall in Washington DC and on the grounds of many state capitals as well. Americans have established National Cemeteries across the country in which row after row of identical, bright white gravestones mark the graves of veterans who served on a battlefield somewhere, buried there even if they finally died in their own beds at a ripe old age. Memorials are critical to allowing war dead to settle finally into the past.[19]

We are not alone in this, of course. In Hiroshima, the T-shaped, "ground-zero" bridge now marks the entrance to a huge memorial that expresses Japan's grief over their World War II dead, over the war itself, and over America's cold decision to use the bomb.* British armies bury their dead wherever they fall. At the height of the British Empire, this meant graveyards to be maintained all over the world, another way of laying sovereign claim to the land these men died fighting for. Once the facts of the Holocaust became clear, Germany could not in conscience build heroic memorials to its own military who died in World War II, but to this day Germans are constructing memorials to remind themselves never to repeat such a catastrophe again.

War memorials serve many purposes, but in the context of peace-making, one stands out. They keep the promise made at the beginning of the war, that not one death will be in vain. Each memorial's most essential feature is that particular deaths are recorded, carved into a stone wall, written in a book, repeated in community stories retold to commemorate the events. The dead are also evoked each time the community raises a flag, sings its anthem or revisits the graveyard for the annual Veteran's Day speech. While a given memorial still serves a specific ritual function, like the annual commemoration of Pearl Harbor in the United States, the war for which the dead gave their lives probably still has some power to instigate a new round of hostilities. Once the physical object becomes a mere backdrop, as Washington's Monument has become a backdrop for fireworks on July 4 in Washington DC, the war it commemorates is well and truly over. In the first instance though, physical war memorials serve as places where communities recovering from war can gather to reflect on their shared grief and acknowledge that the community's suffering has not yet eased.

Suffering, peace and safety

At the end of a war, leaders routinely suggest that easing the pain is the best

---

* Nearby a handful of trees are still living, trees which managed somehow to survive the blast and the radiation. These trees represent a powerful and moving testimony to the other side of irreversible death in war—an unimpaired survival instinct in organic life that makes existence possible even during war.

explanation for their decision to seek peace. In his speech at the White House during the signing of the Oslo Accords, Yitzhak Rabin began with suffering:

> We have come from an anguished and grieving land. We have come from a people, a home, a family that has not known a single year, not a single month in which mothers have not wept for their sons. We have come to try and put an end to the hostilities, so that our children and our children's children, will no longer experience the painful cost of war, violence and terror. We have come to secure their lives and to ease the sorrow and the painful memories of the past, to hope and pray for peace.[20]

Arafat echoed him in Oslo a year later, the day he, Rabin and Peres accepted their Nobel Peace Prizes:

> [T]hose who endured their wounds in the homeland and maintained their identity will be rewarded by return and freedom for their sacrifices. I have also been filled with faith that the arduous trek on the long path of pain will end in our home's yard.
>   As we celebrate together the first sight of the crescent of peace, I, at this podium stare into the open eyes of the martyrs within my conscience. They ask me about the national soil and their vacant seats there. I conceal my tears from them and tell them: How true you were; your generous blood has enabled us to see the holy land and to take our first steps in a difficult battle, the battle of peace, the peace of the brave.[21]

In America, on the first anniversary of September 11, 2001, every newspaper headlined pain. But on that day each one linked the pain with a commitment to act, to punish the perpetrators. Headlines with that dual message are emblematic that suffering can be used as easily to instigate renewed violence as to justify peace.

Ending a war will always be the epitome of paradox. Suffering spurs on the war. Danger is an important part of peace-making. If one thing is clear to me after all of this work on the challenges of ending a war, it is that the German theologian, Dietrich Bonhoeffer, was truly prescient when in 1934 he urged resistance to Hitler's ambitions. At a worldwide conference of church leaders, in a public speech so that the Nazis could hear him, Bonhoeffer spoke for the ages when he said peace must not be confused with safety:

> "Peace must be dared."[22]

危

LIST OF ILLUSTRATIONS

Page 29   Teach-in to end a war: University of Pennsylvania Gymnasium
            Vietnam War Moratorium Day, 1969

Page 31   Demonstrators trying to end a war at the US Capital
            Vietnam War Moratorium Day, 1969

Page 34   Desire for revenge—Die Osama
            New York City, October 2001

Page 38   Power of war to silence debate—General Grant and US Capital
            Washington DC, March 2003

Page 39   Demonstrators trying to forestall a war starting—US Capital
            Washington DC, March 2003

Page 41   Wartime perspective on civil liberties: soldiers in the streets
            New York City, October 2001

Page 45   Instilling honor in a soldier's heart: chapel at US Military
            Academy
            Westpoint, NY, July 2001

Page 48   Patriotic reflexes: flags fly nationwide after September 11, 2001
            New York City, October 2001

Page 54   Vengeance and justice merge after September 11, 2001
            New York City, October 2001

Page 58   An ideal world of international harmony
            Olympia, WA, October 2001

Page 61   Soldiers at the front, generals in the rear: Korean War Memorial
            Washington DC, March 2003

Page 64   "Peace is inevitable"—Every war must end
            Washington DC, March 2003

Page 161   Eisenhower—a President who never began a war, though he
            ended one
            Westpoint, NY, July 2001

危

ENDNOTES

PREFACE

[1] McKeown, (web page). Ironically, the Nobel Peace Prize money did huge damage to the solidarity of the leadership. Betty Williams left the Peace People and shortly after she emigrated to the United States.

[2] In a war-torn community, divided about whether or not to make peace, the "spoilers" who want to keep on fighting easily disrupt and confuse attempts to make peace. In Ireland, in the mid- 1970s, popular pressure both for the war and against the war was strong.

[3] Anon, (1977).

[4] Anon, (1977).

[5] Aarvik, (1977).

[6] Another vivid example of the powerlessness of ordinary people became visible in February 1996 when the IRA suspended their cease-fire. Despite demonstrations in 11 cities in the North of Ireland and an estimated turnout of 60,000, the bombings continued for several more months. It took two more years before the peace agreements were signed.

[7] After 1998, Hume retreated from public view in the peace process, while Adams remained constantly embroiled in both positive action and controversy.

[8] Miller, (1998).

[9] Pogathcnik, (1998).

[10] Hoge, (2001).

[11] In Israel/Palestine and Bosnia, and also in cases beyond the scope of this book —for example Cyprus and the Cold War—citizen dialogue and peace-making occurred among elite activists as well. The practice commonly called "multitrack diplomacy" included generals and political leaders, scientists and academics talking in informal and trust building meetings. Retired Ambassador John Macdonald first coined the phrase. Other US proponents and organizers of such talks include Hal Saunders of the Kettering Foundation and Joseph Montville, a retired U S diplomat. For a comprehensive description of multi-track diplomacy, see Saunders, (1997).

INTRODUCTION

[2] Clausewitz, (1976).

[2] Beyerchen, (1992/93) and Herbig, (1986). The day before this chapter went to press, *The Economist* cover consisted of a picture of a shadowy American soldier, lost in the midst of an Iraqi sandstorm. The headline read "The Fog of War." Mar 29-April 4, 2003.

[3] Strobe Talbott first brought the term into popular discourse (it had long been in use in strategic circles) in a book about negotiating nuclear arms control with the Soviet Union entitled *Endgame: the inside story of SALT II*, New York: Harper & Row, c1979. Similar titles focused on peace-making include McKittrick, David, *Endgame: The search for peace in Northern Ireland*, Belfast: (1994); Rohde, David, *Endgame: The betrayal and fall of Srebrenica, Europe's worst massacre since World War II*, (1997); Ritter, Scott, *Endgame: Solving the Iraq problem—once and for all*, (1999); Siegel, Jennifer (Jennifer L.), *Endgame: Britain, Russia and the final struggle for central Asia*, (2002); Mallie, Eamonn, *Endgame in Ireland*, (2001); Cohen, Robin, *Endgame in South Africa? The changing structures & ideology of apartheid*, (1988). Indeed, among books available in my college library which have "endgame" in the title, almost none refer to chess.

Once again, *The Economist* provided more evidence as we were going to press. It published an issue with the cover story: "Endgame Iraq." Mar. 1-7, 2003.

[4] This latter image is vital to the coherence of deterrence theory, because its predictive power is designed to help stop the onset of violence, or at very least to halt it before it "gets out of hand." Combatants in real wars frequently set aside this logic, replacing it with courage and a willingness to take astonishing risks.

[5] Milosevic was finally "defeated" in a local standoff in Belgrade shortly after he lost in a presidential election. He was actually defeated by Serb protestors prevailing against Serbian troops and police, not by the US military.

[6] William Zartman, (1989), argues that the fighting ends when it reaches what he calls a "hurting" stalemate which, when combined with good negotiations and with a change in the structures of the domestic power elite, makes a cease-fire possible. "Hurting" is induced by the prospect of additional military failures. His model and mine are similar, except that I challenge that "hurting" by itself can precipitate action. Many stalemates are painful by any definition, and yet most endure for months or years before a final cease-fire. See also Kriesberg, (1991).

One of the ironies of the failure to truly end the war with Iraq lay in the differential reception given those who fought 1990-1991 and those who served there in later years. The US soldiers who fought before the official cease-fire in 1991 were given victory marches and a heroes' welcome home, even though it was soon recognized that they had not achieved an absolute victory. After 1991, ground troops in Kurdistan and the US Navy forces running the MIF (embargo enforcement) and Air Force personnel covering the "no-fly" zone continued to face combat conditions, but no-one gave them a public "welcome home" once their tour of duty ended.

[7] For an extended discussion of the issue of rules and winning see Carse, (1986).

[8] Andrew Mack claims that such failures are "political" and not "military" defeats, and furthermore, that they are a modern phenomenon, never seen during the prime colonial period. For the British, one might date the onset of this "weakness." which I still would call military, to Gandhi's non-cooperation in India. Mack would probably say of the Israelis that their inability to "win" was a direct result of the fact that, militarily speaking, it is impossible for the Palestinians to defeat them. If the sides

were more equally vulnerable, Israelis might be more willing to destroy to win. Environmental interdependence is another possible explanation for Israeli "restraint." Mack, (1975).

[9] In January 2003, the U S military was proposing that 1,000 missiles and bombs be sent into Iraq in a matter of days to produce such "shock and awe" that Iraqi resistance was bound to crumble. West, (2003).

[10] Later, (Associated Press, 1994), an AP story, published nationwide described the events as they transpired in the Oval Office:

> On Feb 27, 1991, President Bush and his senior advisors assembled in the Oval Office to make what has turned out to be a pivotal decision of the Persian Gulf war to stop attacking Iraq's fleeing army.
>
> Seated at his customary white chair near the fireplace Mr. Bush was worried that the reports of carnage in Kuwait could turn a crushing military victory into a public relations defeat.
>
> But the President made clear that he would defer to the Pentagon's top general on the timing of the war's end.
>
> "What do you need?" he asked Gen. Colin L Powell [then the Chairman of the Joint Chiefs of Staff] according to previously undisclosed notes taken by a participant.
>
> General Powell was also concerned that the bombardment of the Iraqi forces would tarnish the image of the American military.

[11] Richardson, (1960); Levy, (1983); Levy, (1998).

[12] After World War II, assessments of the strategic bombing campaigns, which had been intended to speed the ending of the war by devastating German cities, determined that the bombing had had no appreciable effect either on the timing or on the outcome of the war. Bombing in North Vietnam seems to have strengthened not weakened resolve.

[13] A book about the work of U S diplomat Philip Habib, a tireless Middle East negotiator in the early 1980s, even carries the title "Cursed is the Peacemaker." Boykin, (2002).

[14] Nixon's acts could almost be said to align with the fundamental ethics of wartime: loyalty above all and winning through sacrifice. His error was to push each one beyond the confines of Presidential rights that pertain in wartime. That he lost sight of the boundary is hardly surprising. War so easily wanders across the boundary from heroic to corrupt. Joseph Heller's novel, *Catch 22* (1996) offers a satirical and entertaining view of the problem.

[15] An influential community of academics devotes itself to crafting watertight definitions of war, to enable the identification of the factors that correlate with a variety of manifestations of war. Any one of these definitional systems would have to stretch to include all seven of these cases inside it. See, for example, a definition focused towards civil wars, which nonetheless excludes South Africa. Roy Licklader (1995):

> "A civil war, by our definition, involves large-scale violence, killing people. I used the operational definitions of the Correlates of War project: (a) 1,000

battle deaths or more per year and (b) effective resistance, that is, at least two sides must have been organized for violent conflict before the war started or else the weaker side must have imposed casualties on its opponent equal to at least 5% of its own (to distinguish between civil wars and political massacres) (Small and Singer 1982, 214-15).

Several implications of this definition are worth noting explicitly. First, it includes both revolutions (a war for the control of the central state apparatus, regardless of the degree of social transformation sought) and wars of secession. Indeed, it may even include events often called coups (Argentina and Bolivia) if they meet the criteria. Second, international involvement is not included in the definition. While such involvement may indeed be critical in determining the course of the war, its presence or absence is irrelevant in determining its existence. If significant numbers of inhabitants of the area are combatants on both sides, the violence is classified as a civil war, regardless of the level of involvement of other actors.

Thus, the Palestinian uprising satisfies the first condition (since Arabs and Jews are likely to cohabit some states, regardless of the outcome) but is excluded because its death count is too low. The South African riots in 1976 met the first and third criteria but had insufficient central control to be classified as a civil war. Zimbabwe is included because the issue of the war was the nature of the government that would control the state in which most of the combatants expected to reside and because the combatants were primarily local on both sides. Indeed, this definition would include wars of conquest, where one group tries to incorporate another into the same state, but very few of them can be found after 1945."

[16] I examined only those conflicts that were listed in the tallies made by the Stockholm International Peace Research Institute, (SIPRI) which monitors state-related violence around the world. During the period 1990-2000, SIPRI's list averaged about 37 countries at war.

[17] Gilligan (1995).

[18] Clausewitz, (1976); Beyerchen, (1992/93).

ALTERED HEARTS AND MINDS

[1] Rose, (1997).

[2] This particular variety of choice was immortalized in a harrowing novel about the Nazi Commandant at Auschwitz compelling a mother to carry out the selection among her own children. Styron (1992).

[3] As I was completing the last revisions of this manuscript, the meaning of this last statement intensified dramatically at a personal level. Rachel Corrie, a young woman I had known since she was a child, died engaged in a non-violent, but direct confrontation with Israeli forces in the town of Rafah, in the Gaza region of Palestine. She died on the morning of March 16, 2003.

[4] Hedges (2002).

[5] Hedges, (2002) p. 10.

[6] Hedges, (2002) p. 35.

[7] Jane Fonda, who visited Vietnam without U S government permission in 1972, became the embodiment of treason to many Americans.

[8] To be given the Ten Commandments, Moses climbed Mt. Sinai. He descended with the actual words engraved in two stone tablets. The sixth commandment says, "Thou shalt not kill," although the rule had not applied to God, during the exodus of Moses and his followers from Egypt, when he commanded the slaughter of the first born sons of Egypt, and then saw to it that the Egyptian army drowned in the waters of the Red Sea. Moses returned to his followers carrying instructions for the construction of an ark and tabernacle to house the tablets. The Israelites, with their commandments secure in the ark, wandered in the wilderness until they reached the hills overlooking the "promised land." Having laid their battle plans, they marched down into the valley and surrounded Jericho. As the gospel song tells it: "Joshua fit the battle of Jericho, and the walls came tumbling down." The Israelites marched round and around the besieged city, blowing trumpets: "the armed men went before them and the rear guard came after the ark of the Lord." The Bible, (Joshua 6, v. 13).

[9] Clausewitz, (1976) p.90.

[10] Monbusho (Japanese Ministry of Education and Science), Moral education curriculum guidelines for 2000.

[11] Some peace-time endeavors mimic the intensity and the ethics of war, among them expeditions into wild and unexplored places. One of the first Americans to reach the summit of Everest, Tom Hornbein (1980) offers a vivid portrait of such groups' experiences. Climbers know, however, that they cannot possibly afford to engage in revenge against the object of their conquest. The mountain would not notice. Nonetheless, failures and difficulties on one expedition can easily become the spur for another trek into far off and high up places. A loss, if you will, in one contest, becomes the incentive to start another.

[12] Walzer (1994), offers a useful distinction for those making moral arguments across cultures: "thin" understandings are possible despite cultural difference. Moral terms, however, also have "thickness," a result of the actual implementation of mechanisms to enact "justice," for example, and comprehension of the thick dimensions is challenging across cultures. This has great significance in war, since communities at war genuinely find each other's strategies incomprehensible, often immoral. Consider America's attitudes to the honor accorded in Japan to Kamikaze pilots; the US attitude become comprehensible when viewed in light of the high value and honor accorded in the United States to strategies which do not "waste" a single human life.

A bibliographical search for "honor" linked with "culture" presented examples from the following regions, settings and times: Islamic women, Old Testament Law, modern France, Italy and Amsterdam, modern Micronesia, Mississippi, the Soviet Union, Czarist Russia, modern Himalayas, Shogun-era Japan, Renaissance Venice,

The US South, Andean Peru, Ancient Greece, modern Greece, Mexico, German Imperialism in Central America, the German atomic bomb, Nepal, Polish Jews, *The Odyssey* and *The Iliad,* Medieval Catalonia, Medieval Islam, Spain, US Western Movies, US Chicano Culture, African American song, and Palestine.

[13] These assertions about honor, protective/patriotic love and revenge are bald enough to suggest that I consider them universals, values found in all people across all time. While I follow Walzer, and thus I would never argue that moral codes are identical from place to place or time to time, I also consider that Wilson (1997) increases our understanding of ethics as moral "senses." He suggests that morality is integral to our biological capacity to form social communities. Wilson uses none of the language that I do, but he does conclude that animal communities are bound by a sense of "duty," which connects to my term "honor" by a sense of "fairness," which connects, via a sense of justice, to my term "revenge," and by a sense of "sympathy," which connects to my use of the word "patriotism."

[14] Rose (1997). Michael Rose also served in the North of Ireland and in the war against Iraq in 1991. He played a part in a third war covered by this book, heading the UN peace-keeping mission to Bosnia.

[15] Marshall, (1947) pp. 148 & 149.

[16] In bombing Iraq for the first time, Clinton seemed, at last, to have been presented with his first combat "medal" by the media, even though this was not his first resort to military force. Earlier, he had ordered military action in the Balkans, but somehow the direct confrontation with Saddam Hussein earned him much more credibility.
"For beleaguered President Clinton, the punitive air strike against Iraq represents a small but potentially important step down the long road toward gaining the public's confidence in him as a decisive and sure-handed leader...
Temporizing has often seemed to be the hallmark of Clinton's first months in office...[He] agonized at length and in public over whether to intervene in Bosnia-Herzegovina.
[Having bombed Iraq] "There could be kind of a residual effect from this in the sense of seeming presidential," said Vanderbilt University presidential scholar Erwin Hargrove. 'The nation's honor and prestige were at stake, and he made a measured response. He looked like he was in charge.'" Shogan, (1993).

[17] Humiliation is also critical in one-on-one violence among men in the United States:
"[M]ale gender codes reinforce the socialization of boys and men, teaching them to acquiesce in (and support, defend and cling to) their own set of social roles, and a code of honor that defines and obligates these rules. Boys and men are exposed thereby to substantially greater frequencies of physical injury, pain, mutilation, disability and premature death. This code of honor requires men to inflict these same violent injuries on others of both sexes, but most frequently and severely on themselves and other males, whether or not they want to be violent toward anyone of either sex." Gilligan, (1996) p. 238.

[18] Nisbett, (1996).

[19] I am grateful to Sophie Bryan, my research associate at the Bunting Institute, for her work on this project, which entailed conducting a content analysis linking the words "honor" and "humiliation" to media coverage of the war in Bosnia during the last three months of 1994.

[20] Sudetic, (1994).

[21] Ignatieff, (1998).

[22] Marshall, (1995).

[23] Ehrenreich, (1997) pp. 16-22, offers a detailed discussion of the ancient origins of these tendencies.

[24] This song, often translated as "God Bless Africa," was used as the ANC anthem throughout the struggle with apartheid. The permanent constitution for South Africa contains a new version of the song, now presented in combination with Die Stem, the Afrikaner anthem. Its four verses are each in a different language.

[25] Rose, (1997).

[26] Wood, (2000).

[27] Bray, (2000).

[28] One of the reasons many observers are particularly scared of guerrilla style warfare is that soldiers don't abide by this "domestic" discipline. This in turn implies that no command structure exists that can elicit loyalty or have any control of violence, cease-fire or peace-making.

[29] Glenn Gray, (1970) pp. 26-27.

[30] In 1992, 17,600,000 people are recorded as having become refugees and asylum seekers, according to one of the non-profit groups tracking their fate worldwide. The numbers were never lower than about 13,000,000 in this period. (Refugees.org)

[31] News Services, (1998).

[32] Dower, (1986) p.36.

[33] Gordon, (1996).

[34] Cullen, (1997).

[35] Philips, (1999).

[36] Specter, (1995).

[37] Susan Jacoby comments on "retribution," saying that it is used to cover "revenge" with a civilized veneer, though the two are virtually synonymous. Jacoby, (1983) p.9. See also Solomon, (1995).

[38] President Bush spoke of "hunting" the perpetrators of the September 11 attacks, language applied to animals and to criminals but never to honored people. Revenge had suddenly become a morally appropriate response.

[39] Jacobs, (1994). This is by no means the only work to analyze the paradoxes inherent in public policy decision-making, but it offers a particularly elegant summation of the contrasts between the warrior/protective state and other governing systems.

[40] MacArthur, (1992). During the second assault on Iraq, the control of the military over the journalists had become so intense that they were described as "embedded" in the military units. Independent journalism had completely disappeared, traded in return for the best access of all.

[41] All over Britain, people were searched entering museums and other public buildings. They also learned to adapt to sudden subway closures. Often they did not seem to mind:

> "It slows things down a bit, but I don't mind at all if it stops a bomb from getting through," said Ruskin as he worked on the clutch of his car in front of his apartment. "They can stop me every time I come through if they want." (Hubert, *Sacramento Bee,* Sacramento Dec. 1, 1996).

[42] Jacobs, (1994) p. 60.

[43] Death totals for 1994, the worst year in the 1990s, amounted to over 1 million "purposeful" deaths, plus an additional 750,000 deaths of people officially identified as noncombatant. These figures were calculated using the SIPRI (Sweden) yearbooks, and the Strategic Surveys produced by the International Institute for Strategic Studies (UK).

[44] By contrast, in the late 1960s, one of the signs that the Vietnam War was losing ethical legitimacy in the United States was that the country began to be riven by criticism of the class privileges which enabled well-educated and well connected men to avoid being drafted and sent to war.

[45] Sasson, (1999).

[46] UN data, provided during a public tour in June 2001.

[47] Douglas, (1986); Teger, (1980); Wildavsky, (1988).

[48] Douglas, (1986) p.123.

[49] The compensation system quickly became racked by complex debates and lawsuits. Finally, it was agreed that the civilian victims of the U S embassy bombings, thought to have the same perpetrators as September 11, 2001, would be included, but not the military personnel.

[50] Teger, (1980).

[51] Clausewitz, (1976) Book Three: Ch. 6 *Boldness* and Ch. 7, *Perseverance*. pp.190-193.

[52] Clausewitz, (1976) pp. 190 & 193.

[53] Young men, always the core of a fighting force, are particularly adept at crafting such a formulation. They often deliberately embark on risky quests as part of their transition to adulthood. In the United States such behaviors, for example joining a gang, are labeled "at risk." Thus it is easy to miss the fact that many violent young men are better classified as willing "risk takers." Military forces are using good sense when

they recruit first in this cohort of their population, which does not in fact have all that much to lose, and will willingly risk what they have.

DANGEROUS DYNAMICS

[1] Mandela, (1994) pp. 625-26.

[2] George Mitchell also gives special credit to the civil servants who drafted critical documents, but the lesser officials would never have had the standing to sign off on the accord. Suspending military operations must be ordered by the commanders of those operations. Mitchell, (1999)

[3] George Mitchell and Richard Holbrooke clearly contributed; their timing was just right. Later on, when Mitchell was sent to Palestine, his presence had no detectable effect on the ongoing Intifada and Israeli violence against Palestinians. The collapse of UN-mediated settlements which precipitated the 1994 Rwanda war are a reminder that even mediation can have fatal flaws.

[4] "It is precisely because there are not one but many possible settlements that a peace negotiation could produce, and because the probability of each depends on military conditions which are constantly in flux, that the timing of such an offer [to end a war] is critical." Pillar, (1983) p.49. Pillar has argued that the military situation sets the timing of peace. I have argued that direct negotiations are more significant than changes in military strength or weaknesses. In a government confronting unfamiliar risks, leaders must consider all of the complex interactions of the social, the cognitive, the individual and the cultural context in which their decisions are to be made.

[5] Responsiveness was drilled into Americans as children and as adults. The children spoke the pledge of allegiance daily, including a phrase "under God" newly added in the early years of the Cold War, which acted as a reminder of the godlessness of communists. Children also learned to "duck and cover" under their schoolroom desks, a rather primitive civil defense exercise against a Soviet atomic threat. The adults were subjected to a much more strenuous training for loyalty at the hands of Senator Joe McCarthy. His hunt for "Communist infiltrators," in the US State Department, the army and Hollywood, were intended to make all adult Americans fear that their most vital bridgeheads to the wider world had already been captured by enemy forces. The long traumatic experiences of the Congressional hearings reverberated via ongoing criminal prosecutions until well into the 1960s.

[6] The first book I encountered describing peace-making, Keckskemeti, (1958), contained a study of the crucial moments in peace-making during World War II, when the individual Allied nations surrendered to Hitler and also when the final allied victories over Germany and Japan were settled at last. Keckskemeti explains that if both sides maintained "cohesive residual forces…there did occur, as in most presurrender situations, a split within the political leadership of the losers, with 'defeatist,' prosurrender elements removing the war-committed leaders from their positions of

authority." (1958, p. 25) This applied even in Germany as the end loomed, although several key leaders in the pro-war faction committed suicide rather than surrender. Most wars in this book have no clear winners and losers, and in every one all sides still had cohesive forces.

    A doctoral study of peace-making in Zimbabwe, Stedman, (1988), confirms Keckskemeti's theory that changes among insiders in the parties to the war are more powerful as an explanation of the search for peace than the theory of the hurting stalemate. (Zartman (1989)). Another dissertation argues that these changes may well be inspired by the pressures of domestic politics. Holl, (1989).

[7] Mandela, (1994), Holbrooke, (1998) Mitchell, (1999) Beilin, (1999), et al.

[8] Mandela, (1994).

[9] Aronoff, (2001); Helvey, (1993). Helvey demonstrates that the core leadership intentionally designed television campaigns to garner support for these decisions to end wars.

[10] Wars are described as victories and surrenders, with clear purpose and costs, but not as chaotic and uncertain projects.

[11] Stedman, (1997) p7.

[12] Elijah Anderson's book explores the dilemma that "a few" violent people can both silence and make invisible the good solid citizens in urban America today. As he puts it: "The code of the street emerges where the influence of the police ends, and personal responsibility for one's safety begins." The war-zone analogy is that the "spoilers" believe the peace-makers cannot be trusted to ensure their protection in a new cooperative relationship with an erstwhile enemy. Anderson, (1999), p.10.

[13] A European 1998 Commission report described the Bosnian situation as follows:
    "(6) Out of a pre-war population of four million inhabitants 250 000 people were killed and one million displaced within the country, whilst a further 1.3 million fled to other countries. Generally speaking, the refugees originated in towns in Bosnia-Herzegovina, whereas the displaced persons were people who left their villages during the war in search of relative safety in the towns, in many cases occupying houses that had been abandoned when the inhabitants fled abroad. In order to enable the refugees to return, it was first necessary to help the displaced persons reoccupy their own homes in war-torn areas.

    (7) At the end of 1997 800 000 people were still displaced within Bosnia-Herzegovina, whilst only 200 000 refugees had returned; 612,000 refugees were still abroad, 263 000 of them in EU Member States, including 220 000 in Germany, without any lasting solution having been found." European Commission, (1998).

[14] Clausewitz, (1976), p.87.

[15] This image comes from Beyerchen, (1992/93). When I first began working on this issue, no-one was exploring the third of Clausewitz's axioms. Luckily, Beyerchen published

his article very soon thereafter and referred me to Herbig (1986). These two make an excellent resource on Clausewitz's connection to chaos and strategic theory. In recent years a considerable literature has been produced connecting chance to battlefield strategy. It has not yet expanded to the study of settlements to bring about the end of a war.

[16] Clausewitz (1976), p. 85

[17] Clausewitz (1976), p. 119.

[18] Echevarria II, (2000)

[19] This image was first suggested to me by Richard Danzig, former Secretary of the Us Navy. Richard also pointed out Jane Jacobs' book, *Systems of Survival*, for which I am very grateful.

[20] I would argue, in fact, that they were bigger than any subsequent bomb. The Kings Cross Station bombing changed so much about the way people lived from day to day. Clearly, when the bombing campaign moved to the City, the IRA were trying to ratchet up the costs one more level, by threatening London's function as a key node in the global financial network.

[21] Holbrooke, (1998).

[22] One can see in many events a confusing mixture of initial conditions that may never become ripe for resolution, disproportional responses to large and small events and nonadditive actions. The history of peace-making in Israel/Palestine is replete with such ambiguous moments, all direct contributors to the intractable nature of its conflicts. Louis Kriesberg, a specialist on the Middle East, once compiled a list of what he called "major Arab-Israeli de-escalation initiatives." (Kriesberg, 1992) The table covers six pages of single line entries. Even if one selects only those events which relate explicitly and exclusively to Palestinians, the West Bank and Gaza (the topics in the Oslo Accords), there are literally dozens of them between the first explosion of the conflict in 1948 and the Oslo attempt in 1993. Did the American envoy arrive for his tenth meeting on the wrong day?—Initial conditions. Were agreements made in the previous nine meetings no longer relevant?—Nonadditive. Did the nineteenth suicide bomb attack suddenly awaken world outrage?—Disproportionality. These factors also interact with each other, so the separations I am making are somewhat artificial.

[23] Yaakov Garb and several colleagues developed such a project in an Israeli/Palestinian environmental education program.

[24] Levy, (1997).

[25] Kaufmann, (1996), caused considerable controversy by suggesting that such wars would be much easier to settle if we, meaning the "international community," were less squeamish about ethnic partitions.

[26] Zartman, (1989) p.9.

[28] Mitchell, (1991).

JUSTICE & PEACE

[15] Editorial, (1998).

[2] Ury, (1993) pp. 105-129.

[3] Tutu, (1998).

[4] Scarry, (1985) p.80-81.

[5] Maynard, (1999) p.134.

[6] The Nuremberg trials are well known, and no one in an official position of power in Germany today continues to revere the Nazis. Indeed, Germans continued to prosecute and imprison lower level leaders for years after the war. Still, even in Germany, occupying Allied armies realized within weeks of the German surrender that, to re-establish civic order, the occupying forces would have to work collaboratively with those who had constituted local government and economic leadership during the Nazi era.

   The consequences of the war crimes trials in Japan were more ambiguous. At the International Tribunal in Tokyo, Japan's wartime leaders were prosecuted for their treatment of prisoners, their brutalities in China, their medical experiments and the fact that the Japanese waged a war of aggression across the whole Pacific region. The trials were tainted by the decision to exempt the Emperor Hirohito, despite his unquestioned role in fostering the war fervor in the country and indeed despite his role in specific strategic decisions. Furthermore, the convictions were not the last word on justice and remembrance, even for those who were executed. Yasukuni, a Tokyo shrine in which the Japanese memorialize their millions of war dead, placed the names of the men convicted on the rolls of the honored dead, for their heroic efforts on behalf of the Japanese people.

   Paradoxical interactions between postwar justice and remembrance continue to this day in Japan. The Japanese government has never apologized either to the Chinese or to the Korean people for their sufferings during the war, and a subtle but pervasive bitterness remains in their reciprocal relations. Furthermore, a building intended to house all the names of the people killed at Hiroshima will make no mention of those Koreans, brought to the city as forced laborers, who also died that dreadful day. In 2001, Japan's Prime Minister, Junichiro Koizumi, chose to visit the Yasukuni shrine to pay homage to the war dead. His decision to do so created a storm of international protest, which failed entirely to deflect him from his purpose. In early August, when all Japanese return home to honor their ancestors, the Prime Minister visited Yasakuni shrine.

[7] The UN has also been trying very hard to persuade Cambodian leaders to agree to international jurisdiction for trials to prosecute the perpetrators of the Cambodian horrors in the late 1970s, with little success.

[8] I have been particularly influenced by Elizabeth Kamarck Minnich, (1990) who proposes that universalizing claims such as these have a history as mechanisms to contain access to power within the group crafting the definitions. International war

crimes tribunals represent, in part, a mechanism whereby European and other nations challenge the United States for ethical and practical dominance.

[9] Knezevic, (2000).

[10] International War Crimes Tribunal for the Former Yugoslavia, (1998).

[11] The schedule for the prosecution of a Rwandan Mayor, Jean-Paul Akayesu, illustrates the problem. Akayesu was arrested on October 10, 1995 and held for 90 days in Zambia pending "completion of the investigation." Indicted, finally, on February 13, 1996, he had to wait to be transferred to the prison in Arusha until May 26, 1996. His first appearance before a judge occurred four days later. Then, in October 1996 he was declared indigent and thus entitled to publicly funded defense attorneys, so preparation of his case could at last get underway. There followed a series of motions about detaining witnesses in Rwanda and transporting them to Arusha. The trial finally began on in January 1997. Off and on, between then and the end of May 1997, the judges heard testimony:

"All Prosecutor and Defence (sic) eye-witnesses requiring protection benefited from measures guaranteeing the confidentiality of their testimony. No information, which could in any way identify the witnesses, was given. During the hearings, letters of the alphabet were used as pseudonyms to refer to protected witnesses and screens isolated the said witnesses from the public, but not from the Accused and his counsel. One Defence witness was heard in camera." *International Criminal Tribunal for Rwanda* (1998) para.18.

In the second phase of the trial, the defense, began October 23, 1997 with the defendant pleading not guilty to several new counts against him that were filed only after the prosecution phase had been completed. The trial finally adjourned, after a total of 60 days of sessions, on Mar 26, 1998. By then Akayesu had been in custody for over two years, and his case still remained unresolved. The court's findings, guilty on 10 out of 13 counts, were finally handed down on September 2, 1998, in a document containing over 700 paragraphs of findings of fact. After three and a half years, one man had finally been found guilty.

[12] Sellars, (1999). "But in Rwanda, where 100,000 peasants charged with genocide wait for years to go before a judge, the decision to set an educated, high-level politician free without a trial seems fundamentally unjust.

Relations have been historically poor between the Rwandan government and the UN tribunal, which is often considered too slow, too expensive, and too bogged down with complex legal procedures to render a meaningful justice to genocide survivors. Rwandan justice ministry officials say the $ 75 million the tribunal will spend this year could be better spent on Rwanda's overburdened courts."

See also Stockman, (2000).

[13] Shay, (1994) p. 39 ff.

[14] Lampman, (1999).

[15] Lampman, (1999).

[16] Two of these, the Balkan Health Bridge and the project to offer psychological repair,

were inspired by my sister-fellows at the Bunting Institute, Paula Gutlove and Judith Thompson. The third, Oasis of Peace, Neve Shalom/Wahat al-Salam, was founded by a man, Bruno Hussar. I learned about their work at a Peace Fellows' breakfast at the Bunting Institute in 1995. It is not a coincidence that women are to be found at the core of this kind of justice, committed to well being and sound relationships. Such work connects well into the "ethic of care" theories first propounded by another Bunting Fellow, Carol Gilligan.

[17] The Truth and Reconciliation Commission, (1998), Chapter 2, p. 1. Here, quoting directly from the Report, I am using the local South African form of spelling.

[18] Truth and Reconciliation Commission, (1998) Chapter 5, p. 1.

[19] America's efforts to create justice and remembrance after Vietnam offer an example of successful justice and remembrance, at least as far as the lives and memories of many young men were concerned. (A small number of women were killed in Vietnam, thus they are part of this story too, but the main struggle in the United States was centered on men, on the men who went to war and died and on the ones who refused to go.)

By 1975, when Saigon fell, thousands of young American men were living in exile, most of them in Canada and Sweden. They fled overseas rather than participate in the military draft. During the war years, "draft dodgers" swirled in a vortex of public debate. The official line was that they were in violation of the law and liable to lengthy jail terms, should they ever set foot on US soil. The populist pro-war sentiment despised them, cheering their departures with the slogan "America, love it or leave it." And yet, on the other side were hundreds of thousands of young men who, in secret, simply failed to register for the draft but still faced a future haunted by fear of discovery. Millions of Americans who opposed the war began to wonder whether, in exile for life, these young men would turn out to be the longest living casualties of the war.

The day after his inauguration, President Jimmy Carter issued a blanket and absolute pardon for all those young men. (His pardon did not apply to deserters, only to people who had never signed on for active service). Despite the criticisms that rained down on him from both sides—"a violation of due process," and "not broad enough"—the President's action made a significant and immediate contribution to healing American society which had been so divided by the war.

Imagine the alternative. Thousands of families agitating, using lawsuits and legislation, to obtain the right for their loved ones to come home—a visit to a dying mother must not lead to the risk of arrest. Suppose the hundreds of thousands of invisible resistors began to be visible. Should they face years of imprisonment even though the war was over? The pardon—it quickly became known as an amnesty— brought what some call "restorative" justice. For reasons that will soon become clear, I chose to call it "merciful" justice.

The draft evaders were not the only young men with troubled stories. Well over 50,000 soldiers were dead, and many thousands of veterans had come home to a nation which seemed to deny them any respect for their courage and suffering. It was going to take many Americans a long time to separate the war's policy-makers from the combatants on the ground, to recognize that most who served were in some way victims too, of ill-advised leadership entering into a doomed policy. Both the living and the dead received a whole new level of respect and concern through the Vietnam War memorial project in Washington DC.

It is hard to say which was more controversial, the Carter amnesty or the Veterans' quest for a memorial. The debates surrounding Maya Lin's memorial, a black granite wall sunk into the ground with every name inscribed on it in the order in which they died, make simply fascinating reading. The wall is emblematic of America's roles in Vietnam and manages to include both the realities of those who fought and died and those who remained behind, those who supported and those who opposed, those who want to forget and those who cannot forget.

Carter's pardon offered mercy and the Vietnam memorial offered a way to tell the story of the war, a way to remember. Any good system of justice offers both—a consequence and a narrative. We cannot turn away from the Vietnam War without commenting on the evidence which it offers that ending the war entailed people undertaking steps, quite literally, to make it possible to live together once more. Veterans needed to be seen. Draft evaders needed to come home.

Relations between the United States and the nation of Vietnam took two decades to reach the same situation, and the same understanding that the two countries were both part of the same world. In the immediate aftermath of the war, the fate of soldiers Missing in Action became the nexus for continuing confrontations and hostilities between the two. So, too, did refugees in flight from the new regime, hoping to make a home for themselves in the United States. Then, a few years later, the Vietnamese government, having observed the brutal genocide in Cambodia, invaded their neighbor. Under Reagan, the official US response to this action took little regard for ending a genocide, and instead described the invasion as proof that the fear of communist expansionism, the original justification for the war, had been proven correct. Neither Cambodia, nor the refugees, nor the MIA issue were a threat to peace that started combat once again. And yet, "normal relations," in the sense of open trade and the exchange of ambassadors took nearly 20 more years to come about. More evidence that peace-making takes a very long time.

[20] Rabin, Yitzhak, The White House Lawn, Sept. 13, 1993.

[21] Arafat, Yassir, Festival Hall, Oslo, Dec.10, 1994.

[22] Bonhoeffer, (1965) p.286.

危

REFERENCES AND ADDITIONAL READINGS

The following were directly useful in the creation of this manuscript. A bibliographical essay about the scholarly research into wartime peace endeavors is available from the author via e-mail: **meyerknh@evergreen.edu.**

A

Aarvik, Egil, "Peace Prize Presentation Speech," University Festival Hall, Oslo, Norway, Dec. 10, 1977.

Adams, David, "Why there are so few women warriors," *Behavior Science Research*, vol. 18, 1983, pp. 196-212.

Anderson, Elijah, *Code of the Street*, New York, Norton, 1999.

Anderson, Scott, *The Man who Tried to Save the World*, New York, Anchor Books, 2000.

Annan, Kofi, *Report of the Secretary General Pursuant to General Assembly Resolution 53/55, The Fall of Srebenica, (A/54/549)*, New York, United Nations, Nov. 15, 1999.
Anon, "Daily Press Briefing," *Office of the Secretary General*, New York, United Nations, Aug. 20, 1996.

Anon, "Don't Let the Endgame Be His," *Economist*, Oct. 4, 1999, p. 17.

Anon, "Mandela Affirms Guerilla Strategy," *St. Louis Post Dispatch*, Feb. 16, 1990, p. A1.

Anon, "Peace Prizes in Oslo," *New York Times*, Dec. 11, 1977, p. A6.

Anon, "Peacewatch: Iraq," *UN Chronicle*, New York, vol. 35, no.4, 1998, p. 54.

Anon, " Humanitarian Situation in Iraq," *Press Briefing*, New York, United Nations, Oct. 29, 1996.

Anon, "Security Council 6833 4120th Meeting (AM & PM)," *Press Release*, New York, United Nations, March 24, 2000.

Anon, "Secretary-General Discusses North Caucasus Situation with Prime Minister of Russian Federation," *Press Release SG/SM/7216*, New York, United Nations,

Anon, "The Fog of War," *Economist*, Mar 29-April 4, 2003.

Anon, "Ulster Peace Leaders Set Upon by Mob," *New York Times*, Oct. 11, 1976.

Apple, R.W., "Allies New Test: How to define victory," *New York Times*, April 6, 2003.

Appleby, R. Scott, *The Ambivalence of the Sacred: Religion, violence and reconciliation*, Lanham, MD, Rowman and Littlefield, 2000.

Aronoff, Yael, "When and Why Do Hardliners Become Soft? An Examination of Israeli Prime Ministers Shamir, Rabin, Peres and Netanyahu," in eds. Ofer Felman and Linda O. Valenti, *Profiling Political Leaders: Cross-cultural studies of personality and behavior*, Westport, Praeger, 2001.

Arnove, Anthony ed., *Iraq Under Siege: The deadly impact of sanctions and war*, South End Press, 2000.

Associated Press, "Thousands in Ireland Flock to Peace Rallies," *Seattle Post*

Intelligencer, Feb. 26, 1996, p. A2.

Associated Press, "Top Brass Reportedly Urged Halt to Gulf War," *Boston Globe*, Oct. 23, 1994, p.15, and *Seattle Times*, p. A.2 among other newspapers.

B

Battersby, John, "Massacre Shows how Crime Complicates S. Africa's Transition," *Christian Science Monitor,* Jan. 14, 1991, p. 4.

Beilin Yosi, *Touching Peace: From the Oslo Accord to a final agreement*, Weidenfeld and Nicolson, London, 1999.

Bennis, Phyllis, *From Stones to Statehood: The Palestinian uprising*, Zed Books, London, 1990.

The Bible, King James Version, World Publishing Company, 1945, Joshua, Ch. 6.

Biko, Steve, *I Write What I Like*, London, Bowerdean Press, 1996.

Bleck, Linda, "Tale of Two Africas," *Los Angeles Times*, May 8, 1994, p.1.

Blight, James G., *The Shattered Crystal Ball: Fear and learning in the Cuban missile crisis,* Lanham MD, Rowman and Littlefield, 1993.

Beyerchen, Alan, "Clausewitz, Nonlinearity and the Unpredictability of War," *International Security*, vol. 17, no. 38, 1992/93.

Blumenfeld, Laura, *Revenge: A story of hope*, New York, Simon and Schuster, 2002.

Bonhoeffer, D., *No Rusty Swords*, ed. Edwin H. Robinson, London, William Collins and Sons, 1965.

Boykin, John, *Cursed is the Peacemaker*, Applegate Press, Belmont, CA, 2002.

Bray, Stephen, "Mariners Seek Togetherness in Spring Training," *The Olympian,* Feb. 21, 2000, p. B1.

Brinkley, Joel, "Israel Fearing More Attacks, Talks of Retaliating," *New York Times*, Jan. 19, 1991, p.1.

C

Carlin, John, "Compromise Possible for the ANC says Mandela," *The Independent*, London, Feb. 15, 1990, p.12.

Carse, James, *Finite and Infinite Games*, New York, Free Press, 1986.

Clausewitz, Carl von, *On War,* ed. and trans. Michael Howard and Peter Paret, Princeton, Princeton University Press, 1976.

Cohen, Roger, "The Mirage of Peace," *New York Times*, Nov. 21, 1995, p. A4.

Conroy, John, *Unspeakable Acts, Ordinary People: The dynamics of torture*, New York, Knopf, 2000.

Cullen, Kevin, " Ulster Group Says Attack was Reprisal. Violence shakes peace hopes," *Boston Globe*, Dec. 29, 1997, p. A1.

D

Daly, Martin, and Margo Wilson, *Homicide,* New York, Aldine de Gruyter, 1988.

Dao, James and Steven Meyers, "US and British Jets Strike Air-Defense Centers in Iraq," *New York Times*, Feb. 17, 2001.

De Klerk F.W., *The Last Trek—A new beginning, The autobiography*, London, Pan Books, 2000.

Destexhi, Alain, *Rwanda and Genocide in the Twentieth Century*, Pluto Press, London, 1995.

Dower, John W., *War Without Mercy*, Pantheon, New York, 1986.

Douglas, Mary, *How Institutions Think*, Syracuse, Syracuse University Press, 1986.

E

Echevarria II, Antulio J. and Jacob D. Biever, "Warfighting's Moral Domain," *Military Review,* Fort Leavenworth, vol. 80, no.2, 2000, pp. 3-6.

Editorial, "Hope in N. Ireland," *Christian Science Monitor,* April 13, 1998, p.12.

Ehrenreich, Barbara, *Blood Rites: Origins and history of the passions of war*, New York, Metropolitan Books, 1997.

Ember, Carol R., and Melvin Ember, "Resource Unpredictability, Mistrust, and War: A cross-cultural study," *Journal of Conflict Resolution*, vol. 36, 1992, pp. 242-62.

Ember, Carol R., and Melvin Ember, "Warfare, Aggression, and Resource Problems: Cross-cultural codes," *Behavior Science Research,* vol. 26, 1992, pp. 169-226.

European Commission, "Special Report, No 5/98 on Reconstruction in the Former Yugoslavia (period 1996-1997)," *Official Journal C 241*, Brussels, July 31, 1998.

F

Falk, Richard A. and Samuel S. Kim eds., *The War System: An interdisciplinary approach*, Boulder, Westview, 1980.

Farley, Maggie, "2 Cite Iraq Sanctions in Resignations: Officials say they quit UN because the embargo is aiding regime and hurting ordinary citizens," *Los Angeles Times*, Feb 18, 2000, p. A6.

Federation of American Scientists, "Report on bombings in Iraq in 1991, fas.org/man/dod-101/ops/iraq_orbat.htm.

Friedman, Norman, "Carrier Forces Remain Free to Act," *Naval Institute Proceedings,* Annapolis, vol.124, no. 2, 1998, p.91.

G

Gabriel, Richard, *To Serve with Honor: A treatise on military ethics and the way of the soldier*, Westport, Greenwood Press, 1982.

Gallimore, Tim, "In Rwanda, Bodies Pile up as World Stands By," *USA Today,* May 23, 1994, p. 14A.

Gilligan, James, *Violence: Our deadly epidemic and its causes,* New York, Putnam, 1996.

Glenn Gray, John, *The Warriors,* New York, Harpers, 1970.

Gobodo-Madikizela, Pumla, *A Human Being Died that Night: A South African story of forgiveness*, New York, Houghton Mifflin, 2003.

Gordon, Meghan Cox, "Northern Ireland's Protestants Pine for Peace—and some ready for war," *Christian Science Monitor*, Mar. 14, 1996, p. 7.

Gordon, Michael R., "Pentagon Study Cites Problems with Gulf Effort," *New York Times*, Feb. 23, 1992, p. A1.

Grier, Peter and Scott Armstrong, "Bombing Campaign Hits Iraqi Society," *Christian Science Monitor*, Jan. 25, 1991, p.1.

Gourevitch, Philip, "The Return," *The New Yorker*, Jan 10, 1997.

Gourevitch, Philip, *We wish to inform you that tomorrow we will be killed with our families*, New York, Picador, 1998.

Gregor, Thomas, ed., *A Natural History of Peace*, Nashville, Vanderbilt University Press, 1996.

H

Heller, Joseph, *Catch 22*, New York, Scribner, 1996.

Hedges, Chris, *War is a Force that Gives us Meaning*, New York, Public Affairs, 2002.

Herbig, Katherine, "Chance and Uncertainty in War," *Journal of Strategic Studies*, vol. 9, no. 2/3, 1986.

Helvey, Laura, *Legitimizing Policy Shifts: Leadership television strategies in the cases of American withdrawal from Vietnam and Soviet withdrawal from Afghanistan*, Stanford University, Dissertation, 1993.

Hoge, Warren, "Prosecution in IRA Trial Will Focus on American," *New York Times*, April 15, 2001.

Holbrooke, Richard, *To End a War*, New York, Random House, 1998.

Holl, Jane E.K., *From the Streets of Washington to the Roofs of Saigon: Domestic Politics and the termination of the Vietnam War*, Dissertation, Stanford University, 1989.

Homer, *The Iliad*, trans. Stanley Lombardo, Indianapolis, Hackett Pub. Co., 1997.

Hornbein, Tom, *Everest, the West Ridge*, Seattle, Mountaineers Press, 1980.

Hubert, Cynthia, and Gary Delsohn, "As Fears Rise, Americans Ponder Their Own Security," *The Sacramento Bee*, Dec. 1, 1996, p. Al.

I

Ignatieff, Michael, *Warrior's Honor: Ethnic war and the modern conscience*, New York, Henry Holt, 1998.

Ingwerson, Marshall, "Peace With No Honor: Chechnya pact leaves Russian troops bitter," *The Christian Science Monitor*, Sept. 3, 1996, Pg. 1.

Institute for Strategic Studies, *Strategic Survey Annual*, London, ISSS, 1993-99.

International Committee of the Red Cross, World Disasters Report 1998, Oxford University Press, 1998.

International Criminal Tribunal for the Former Yugoslavia, "The Prosecutor v. Drazen Erdemovic," *Sentencing Judgement*, The Hague, March 5, 1998.

International Criminal Tribunal for Rwanda, "The Prosecutor v. Jean-Paul Akeyasu," *Decision, Case no. ICTR-96-4-T*, The Hague, Sept. 2, 1998.

Iraqi Government Military Spokesman, "Cease-fire Announcement," *New York Times*, Mar. 1 1991, p. A9.

J

Jacoby, Susan, *Wild Justice: The evolution of revenge*, New York, Harper and Row, 1983.

Jacobs, Jane, *Systems of Survival: A dialogue on the moral foundations of commerce and politics*, New York, Vintage Books, 1994.

K

Karahsan, Dzevad, *Sarajevo, Exodus of a city*, New York, Kodansha International, 1993.

Kaufmann, Chaim, "Possible and Impossible Solutions to Ethnic Civil Wars," *International Security,* vol. 20, no. 4, 1996, pp. 136-175.

Keane, Fergal, "Hutu Mass Murderer asks: Why Must I die?" London, *Sunday Telegraph*, April 26, 1998, p. 29.

Keckskemeti, Paul, *Strategic Surrender: The Politics of Victory and Defeat,* Stanford, Stanford University Press, 1958.

Knezevic, Gordana, "War-Crimes Prosecutor Quenches Thirst for Justice," *Seattle Times*, Feb 6, 2000, p. A 14.

Krammer, Jack, "Preserving Mission-Focused Command and Control," *Military Review*, Fort Leavenworth, vol. 77, no. 5, 1997, pp. 65-70.

Kriesberg, Louis, "Timing Conditions, Strategies and Errors," in eds. Louis Kriesberg and Stuart J. Thorson, *Timing and the De-escalation of Conflicts*, Syracuse, Syracuse University Press, 1991.

Kriesberg, Louis, *International Conflict Resolution: The US-USSR and Middle East Cases*, New Haven, Yale University Press, 1992.

Kumar, Krishna et al. "The International Response to Conflict and Genocide: Lessons from the Rwanda Experience, Study 4: Rebuilding Post-War Rwanda, Chapter 9, Promoting Human Rights and Building a Fair Judicial System," *Journal of Humanitarian Assistance,* 1996.

Kuperman, Alan J., *The Limits of Humanitarian Intervention: Genocide in Rwanda*, Brookings Institute Press, Washington DC, 2001.

L

Lampman, Jane, "Taming the Desire for Revenge," *Christian Science Monitor,* Nov. 4, 1999, p. 15.

Levy, Jack S., *War in the Modern Great Power System, 1495-1975*, Lexington, University Press of Kentucky, 1983.

Levy, Jack S., and Joseph R. Gocha, "The Causes of War and the Conditions of Peace," *Annual Review of Political Science,* no. 1, 1998, pp.139-65.

Levy Jack S., "Loss Aversion, Framing and Bargaining: The Implications of prospect theory for international conflict," in eds. Frank P. Harvey and Ben D. Mor, *Conflict in World Politics: Advances in the study of crisis, war and peace,* New York, St. Martins Press, 1997.

Licklader, Roy, *Stopping the Killing*, New York, New York University Press, 1992.

Licklader, Roy, "The Consequences of Negotiated Settlements in Civil Wars, 1945-1993," *The American Political Science Review*, vol. 89, no. 3, p. 681 ff., 1995.

Lieberfeld, Daniel, *Talking with the Enemy: Negotiation and threat perception in South Africa and Israel/Palestine*, Westport, Praeger, 1999.

M

MacArthur, John R., *Second Front: Censorship and propaganda in the Gulf War*, New York, Hill and Wang, 1992.

Mack, Andrew, "Why Big Nations Lose Small Wars: The politics of asymmetric conflict," *World Politics*, vol. 27, 1975, pp. 175 – 200.

Mandela, Nelson, *Long Walk to Freedom*, London, Abacus, 1994.

Marshall, S.L.A., *Men Against Fire*, William Morrow, New York, 1947.

Marshall, Tyler, "History Is Up Close and Personal—and Keeps Conflicts Alive; Warfare: The Balkans are but one region where ancient hatreds fuel present-day enmity. That's why some observers feel pessimistic about Bosnia," *Los Angeles Times*, Dec. 26, 1995, p. A12.

Maynard, Kim A., *Healing Communities in Conflict: International assistance in complex emergencies*, New York, Columbia University Press, 1999.

McCarthy, Colman, "Residue From the Rocket's Red Glare," *The Washington Post*, Aug. 20, 1996, p. D18.

McKeown, Ciaren, "History," *The Peace People*, Peacepeople.com.

Meyer-Knapp, H., "Siege War" in ed. Donald Wells, *Encyclopedia of Military Ethics*, Greenwood Press, 1994.

Meyer-Knapp, H., "Non-violent confrontation and Social Change: Vengeance, Gandhi and Martin Luther King," *International Society of Political Psychology Annual Meeting*, Amsterdam, July, 1999.

Miller, Marjorie, "'They Have the Power to Bomb and Kill Us;' N. Ireland: Protestants and Catholics had lived peacefully together in Omagh, where 28 died in blast," *Los Angeles Times*, Aug. 17, 1998, p.1.

Minnich, Elizabeth Kamarck, *Transforming Knowledge*, Philadelphia, Temple University Press, 1990.

Minow, Martha, *Between Vengeance and Forgiveness: Facing history after genocide and mass violence*, Boston, Beacon Press, 1998.

Mitchell, Christopher, "A Willingness to Talk: Conciliatory Gestures and De-escalation," *Negotiation Journal*, vol. 7, no. 4, 1991, pp.405-430.

Mitchell, George J., *Making Peace*, Knopf, New York, 1999.

Murphy, Jeffrie G. and Jean Hampton, *Forgiveness and Mercy*, Cambridge, Cambridge University Press, 1988.

N

News Services, "Outraged Israelis Call for End to Peace Talks: Jewish settlers are furious about slayings of pair who were patrolling settlement. Negotiations remain at a standstill," *St. Louis Post Dispatch*, Aug. 6, 1998, p. A10.

Nisbett, Richard, and Dov Cohen, *Culture of Honor: The psychology of violence in the South*, Boulder, Westview Press, 1996.

P

Peterson, Scott, "Thugs 'Cleanse' Sarajevo Suburb, So Serbs Won't Mix With Muslims," *Christian Science Monitor*, March 15, 1996, p. 9.

Peterson, Scott, *Me Against My Brother*, Routledge, New York, 2001.

Philips, Alan, "Saddam Vows to Avenge Deaths," *Daily Telegraph*, London, Jan. 27, 1999, p. 12.

Pillar, Paul, *Negotiating Peace: War termination as a bargaining process*, Princeton, Princeton University Press, 1983.

Pogathcnik, Shawn, "Another Group Declares Truce in N. Ireland: Thousands join in grieving in town where blast killed 28," *Seattle Times*, Aug. 23, 1998, p. A3.

Politkovskaya, Anna, *A Dirty War, A Russian reporter in Chechnya*, Harvill Press, London, 2001.

R

Rehnquist, William, *All the Laws But One: Civil liberties in wartime*, New York, Knopf, 1998.

Richardson, Lewis, *Statistics of Deadly Quarrels*, Pittsburgh, Boxwood Press, 1960.

Robertson, Geoffrey, *Crimes Against Humanity: The struggle for global justice*, New York, New Press, 2000.

Rose, Michael, "How Soon Could Our Army Lose a War?" London, *Daily Telegraph*, Dec. 16, 1997, p. 20.

Rotberg, Robert, I., and Dennis Thompson eds., *Truth v. Justice: The Morality of Truth Commissions*, Princeton, Princeton University Press, 2000.

S

Sampson, Anthony, "The Evil Must be God-given, not Forgotten," London, *The Observer*, May 1, 1994, p. 23.

Sarkin, Jeremy, "The Necessity and Challenges of Establishing a Truth and Reconciliation Commission in Rwanda," *Human Rights Quarterly*, vol. 21, no. 3, 1999, pp. 767-823.

Sasson, Saskia, *Losing Control?* New York, Columbia University Press, 1999.

Saunders, Harold H., *A Public Peace Process*, New York, St. Martins Press, 1997.

Scarry, Elaine, *The Body in Pain*, Oxford, Oxford University Press, 1985.

Scarry, Elaine, "The Declaration of Wars: Constitutional and Unconstitutional Violence," in eds. Austin Sarat and Thomas R. Kearns, *Law's Violence*, Ann Arbor, University of Michigan Press, 1995.

Sciolino, Elaine, Roger Cohen and Stephen Engelberg, "Balkan Accord: The play by play, 21 days in Dayton," *New York Times*, Nov. 23, 1995, p.1.

Sellars, Kirsten, "Rights Tribunal Falters Amid Legal Wrongs; Rwanda: Procedural delays result in order to release prime genocide suspect," *Los Angeles Times*, Dec.

23, 1999, p. 11.

Sharrock, David and Mark Devenport, *Man of War, Man of Peace: The unauthorized biography of Gerry Adams*, London, Pan Books, 1997.

Shawcross, William, *Deliver us from Evil: Peacekeepers, warlords and world of endless conflict*, New York, Simon and Schuster, 2000.

Shay, Jonathan, *Achilles In Vietnam: Combat trauma and the undoing of character*, New York, Atheneum, 1994.

Shea, Dorothy, C, *The South African Truth Commission: The politics of reconciliation*, Washington DC, United States Institute of Peace, 2000.

Shogan, Robert; "For the President, a Chance to Act Presidential," *Los Angeles Times*, Jun. 28, 1993, p. A1.

Shriver, Donald, W. Jr., *An Ethic for Enemies: Forgiveness in Politics*, Oxford, Oxford University Press, 1995.

Simpson, Brooks D., *Let Us Have Peace: Ulysses S. Grant and the politics of war and reconstruction, 1861-1868*, Chapel Hill, University of North Carolina Press, 1991.

Singer, J. David and Melvin Small, *Resort to Arms: International and civil wars, 1816-1980*, Beverley Hills, Sage, 1982.

Sipes, Richard G., "War, Sports, and Aggression: An empirical test of two rival theories," *American Anthropologist*, vol. 75, 1973, pp. 64-86.

Smallwood, William L. *The Westpoint Candidate Book: How to prepare, how to get in, how to survive*, Sun Valley, ID, Beacon Books, 2000.

Smith, Sebastian, *Allah's Mountains: The battle for Chechnya*, London, I.B. Tauris, 2001.

Solomon, Robert, *A Passion for Justice: Emotions and the origins of the social contract*, Lanham, MD, Rowman & Littlefield, Publishers, 1995.

Sparks, Allister, "The Secret Revolution," *The New Yorker*, April 11, 1994, pp. 56-78.

Specter, Michael, "For Chechens in Mountains, Fighting is Winning," *The New York Times*, May 13, 1995, p. A1.

Stanley, Alessandra, "Russian War Dead Lie in Filth, Awaiting Claim by their Kin." *New York Times*, Aug. 25, 1996, p. A1.

Stedman, Stephen John, *Peacemaking in Revolutionary Situations*, UMI, PhD Stanford University, 1988.

Stedman, Stephen John, "Spoiler Problems in Peace Processes," *International Security*, vol. 22. no. 2, 1997.

Stewart, Frank Henderson, *Honor*, Chicago, University of Chicago Press, 1994.

Stockholm International Peace Research Institute, *Year Book of World Armaments and Disarmament*, New York, Humanities Press, 1993 - 1999.

Stockman, Farah, "At Stake: Credibility of War Crimes Tribunal" *The Christian Science Monitor*, Feb. 24, 2000, p. 7.

Styron, William, *Sophie's Choice*, New York, Vintage Books, 1992.

Sudetic, Chuck, "No Shift Seen in Serb Policy in Bosnia," *New York Times*, Dec. 16, 1994, p. A3.

Sudetic, Chuck, *Blood and Vengeance: One family's story of the war in Bosnia*, New York, Norton, 1998.

T

Talbott, Strobe, *Endgame: The inside story of SALT II*, New York, Harper & Row, 1979.

Taylor, Phil, "The International Tribunal on Rwanda: 'Western Justice' Comes to Africa," *Africa Direct Conference*, London, July 27, 1997.

Teger, Allan I, with Mark Cary, Aaron Katcher, Jay Hillis, *Too Much Invested to Quit*, New York, Pergamon Press, 1980.

The Truth and Reconciliation Commission, *Final Report*, Johannesberg, Dec. 1998.

Turnbull, Stephen R., *The Book of the Samurai: The warrior class of Japan*, New York, Gallery Books, 1982.

Tutu, Rev. Desmond, "Foreword by the Chairperson," *Final Report, The Truth and Reconciliation Commission*, Ch. 1, vol. 1, Johannesberg, Dec. 1998.

Tutu, Rev. Desmond, *No Future without Forgiveness*, New York, Doubleday, 1999.

U

UNESCO, "Males and Masculinities in a Culture of Peace," *Expert Group Meeting, Section 8*, Oslo, Sept. 24-28, 1997.

Ury, William, *Getting Past No: Negotiating your way from confrontation to cooperation*, New York, Bantam Books, 1993.

V

Vertzberger Yaacov, *Risk Taking and Decision-making: Foreign military intervention decisions*, Stanford, Stanford University Press, 1998.

W

Walzer, Michael, *Thick and Thin: Moral argument at home and abroad*, South Bend, Notre Dame University Press, 1994.

Webster, Donovan, *Aftermath: The remnants of war*, New York, Vintage Books, 1998.

West, Andrew and agencies, "800 missiles to hit Iraq in first 48 hours," *The Sun-Herald*, Sydney, Australia, Jan. 26, 2003.

Wildavsky, Aaron, *Searching for Safety*, New Brunswick, Transaction Books, 1988.

Wilson, James Q., *The Moral Sense*, New York, Free Press, 1997.

Wood, Gail, "Baumgartel Swims with Fast Crowd," *The Olympian*, Feb. 21, 2000, B1.

Y

Yamamoto, Tsunetomo, *The Hagakure: A code to the way of Samurai*, Trans. Takao Mukoh, Toyko, Hokuseido Press, 1980.

Z

Zartman, William, *Ripe For Resolution: Conflict and intervention in Africa*, Oxford, Oxford University Press, 1989.

Zartman, William, "Prenegotiation: Phases and Functions," in ed. Janice Gross Stein, *Getting to the Table*, Baltimore, Johns Hopkins Press, 1989.